# Change Your Life's Direction

# Change Your Life's Direction

## Break Free from Your Past Inertia and Chart a Better Future

Jim Taylor, PhD

*Rowman & Littlefield*
Lanham • Boulder • New York • London

Published by Rowman & Littlefield
An imprint of The Rowman & Littlefield Publishing Group, Inc.
4501 Forbes Boulevard, Suite 200, Lanham, Maryland 20706
www.rowman.com

6 Tinworth Street, London SE11 5AL, United Kingdom

British Library Cataloguing in Publication Information Available

**Library of Congress Cataloging-in-Publication Data**

Names: Taylor, Jim, 1958– author.
Title: Change your life's direction : break free from your past inertia and
 chart a better future / Jim Taylor.
Description: Lanham : Rowman & Littlefield, [2021] | Includes
 bibliographical references and index. | Summary: "Jim Taylor illustrates
 how our lives are like asteroids hurtling uncontrollably through space,
 but he instructs on the ways in which we can convert those asteroids
 into starships for which we provide the guidance system, pilot, engine,
 and fuel that can propel our lives in the direction of our own choosing
 toward happiness, success, and connection"— Provided by publisher.
Identifiers: LCCN 2020046479 (print) | LCCN 2020046480 (ebook) | ISBN
 9781538146699 (cloth) | ISBN 9781538146705 (epub)
Subjects: LCSH: Change (Psychology) | Self-actualization (Psychology) |
 Self-realization. | Happiness. | Success.
Classification: LCC BF637.C4 T39 2021  (print) | LCC BF637.C4  (ebook) |
 DDC 158.1—dc23
LC record available at https://lccn.loc.gov/2020046479
LC ebook record available at https://lccn.loc.gov/2020046480

# CONTENTS

# ACKNOWLEDGMENTS

I first would like to express my deepest gratitude to Dr. Samantha Sandersen-Brown for her role as my presubmission editor. Let me tell you her backstory: Samantha originally volunteered to act as a chapter assistant for my previous book, *How to Survive and Thrive When Bad Things Happen*. The role of the chapter assistant was to find useful research and provide quotes that supported my ideas in the assigned chapter. As Samantha embraced this role, it quickly became clear that she could offer so much more. As she reviewed the chapter to which she was assigned, Samantha not only fulfilled her basic responsibilities but also edited my writing in a way that clearly improved the chapter. Given my publishing track record, I consider myself a very capable writer. At the same time, I've always valued the ability of my editors to make my writing even better, and I saw such an opportunity with Samantha. I reached out to her and, for only a small stipend and my undying appreciation, she agreed to edit the entirety of that book (and it was much better written thanks to her efforts). When I signed my contract with Rowman & Littlefield for *Change Your Life's Direction*, Samantha immediately came to mind, and, with only a slight raise in her stipend and even more undying gratitude from me, she graciously agreed to act as my editor again. In addition to her usual editing responsibilities, Samantha

ACKNOWLEDGMENTS

took it upon herself to be my "constructive critic," providing me with honest and direct feedback about the value and clarity of my ideas and letting me know when what I was writing wasn't working. Not surprisingly, *Change Your Life's Direction* is much better for her contributions. So, Samantha, thank you, thank you, thank you for your generosity of spirit and time, your exceptional editing capabilities, and your keen and critical eye for cogent thinking and writing. *Change Your Life's Direction* couldn't be what it is today without you.

I also would like to thank Dr. Austin "Wade" Wilson for his willingness to join my writing team in support of *Change Your Life's Direction* as the research and quote expert. In this role, I usually look for a graduate student who is looking for experience with book writing and the chance for some mentoring from me. When Wade first reached out to me, I told him that, as an already established professional, he was overqualified. But Wade persisted, and I accepted his offer to contribute. Boy, am I glad I did. Within days, I saw the time, thought, and energy he devoted to his responsibilities, finding research and quotes that were lying well below the surface. Wade also read my manuscript with a critical eye and offered valuable insights about my ideas. Wade, I so appreciate your engagement, professionalism, and passion for the role you took on in helping to make *Change Your Life's Direction* the best it could be.

Last, but decidedly not least, I want to express my love and gratitude to my wife, Sarah, and my daughters, Catie and Gracie, for their love and support of the time and energy I devote to my career and to my writing, both of which I am so passionate about.

# INTRODUCTION
## Hurtling Uncontrollably through Life

*In·er·tia (ĭ-nûr'shə):* The tendency of a body at rest to remain at rest or of a body in motion to stay in motion unless acted on by an outside force; resistance or disinclination to motion, action, or change.

I n 1687, Sir Isaac Newton had an epiphany that led to his three famous and influential laws of motion:

1. Law of inertia: Every object persists in its state of rest or uniform motion in a straight line unless it is compelled to change that state by forces impressed on it.

2. Law of momentum: Force is equal to the change in momentum per change in time. For a constant mass, force equals mass times acceleration.

3. Law of action-reaction: For every action, there is an equal and opposite reaction.

Three hundred and thirty years later, I experienced my own eureka moment—human beings are subject to similar laws of motion, what I call Taylor's laws of human motion:

1

1. Law of life inertia: Every life persists on its established trajectory unless it is compelled to change course by internal or external forces.

2. Law of life momentum: The force that propels a life trajectory is determined by the individual's investment in and amount of time already spent on that course. The intensity and point in time when a force is applied determine the extent of the change in direction of the life path.

3. Law of life action-reaction: For every action taken by a person in his or her life, there is an equal and opposite reaction that maintains a life's current trajectory.

My observation turned out to be more than an interesting metaphor. As I looked more closely at human behavior, the similarities became more startling. Like an asteroid when it first breaks away from a larger celestial body, people are set on a path by early forces including genes, parenting, and society. As defined by Taylor's laws of human motion, we continue on that path, for better or worse, throughout our lives unless other forces compel us to change course. Our life inertia can carry us on a trajectory that is as arbitrary as that of the asteroid because as children we have no more influence over the direction of our life inertia than an asteroid over its course. Neither asteroids nor people choose their initial path. And, like the asteroid, we are often unaware of the course we are on or what is propelling us down that path.

The parallels explain why it's so difficult for people to make changes in their lives.

Many people think of inertia as an object at rest staying at rest, like a large boulder in a field. Although this concept applies to objects, our lives are never at rest, unlike a rock or any other inanimate object. In fact, we are moving swiftly and inexorably along a path driven by powerful forces. Seeing people from this dynamic perspective is the foundation for understanding what it takes to bring change to our lives. We aren't "stuck" in one place, as so many express when they are dissatisfied with their lives.

In reality, our lives are in constant motion and are being propelled by multiple forces along our life path (law of life inertia) that is highly resistant to a change in direction (law of life momentum). As a result, small forces, such as a modest insight, a brief "aha!" moment, or a nudge from a friend, are simply actions that produce equal and opposite reactions that nullify the original action and leave us where we started (law of action-reaction). Minor forces don't adequately compel us to counteract the forces that drive us along our inertial path. In fact, significant change can occur only when forces are applied that are greater than the forces that are already controlling our lives.

## Origins of Life Inertia

Life inertia propels us along a particular course indefinitely, much as an asteroid hurtles through space continuing on its inexorable course for eternity. Unfortunately, as I noted earlier, we are unable to consciously choose the initial path on which our inertia takes us. Rather, our life inertia is shaped at an early age by our genes, upbringing, and environment.

Despite how we may feel about our life inertia now, it came into being as a means of serving our best interests when we were children. When we are young, we lack the self-awareness, experience, and sophistication of thinking to be able to reason through what is best for us. Instead, two forces direct our life inertia.

First, we rely on our primitive instincts to protect ourselves at a time when we are most vulnerable. Because we live in a developed society where threats to our physical life are rare, those instincts to survive are now directed at emotional survival. In the best-case scenario, this involves feeling safe, secure, loved, and valued. In a less-than-good scenario, it means avoiding sadness, anger, and loneliness. And in a truly worst-case scenario, it is simply anesthetizing ourselves from the pain of an abusive parent or otherwise hostile environment. For example, as children, we expressed anger when we felt rejected because this kept us from feeling hurt and ashamed. Another situation may demand the need to be "perfect" to ensure we receive the love of our perfectionistic father. We can also develop a need for order in an attempt to gain control and reduce anxiety in a chaotic situation. Unhealthy forces like these that were established in childhood continue to propel us today, even though they drive us along a life trajectory that may not be healthy in adulthood.

Our life inertia is influenced significantly by external forces outside of our control, including our parents and family, peers, schools, community, popular culture, and society at large. As with our primitive instincts, we were not aware of, capable of discriminating among, or able to control these forces when they first began to drive our life inertia as children.

As such, the first important consideration when beginning to understand life inertia is that the trajectory that was established early in our lives was not of our own choosing; yet it became the path that has shaped our lives ever since, for better or for worse. Our life inertia shows itself through the lens with which we view the world, the emotional reactions that we have, the actions that we take, and the relationships that we create. Not only is our life inertia, which was set in motion at a young age, already powerful, as Sir Isaac Newton would attest, but we also create external and social forces as we get older that act as further "propulsion" to our life inertia. The jobs we hold, the people with whom we surround ourselves, the activities in which we participate, and the routines that we follow all serve as additional forces on our life inertia that create a more powerful momentum, which makes changing the trajectory of our inertia even more difficult.

When you don't investigate what's going on with your words, thoughts, and beliefs, you risk stumbling through life on autopilot.

—Jen Sincero, author of *You're a Badass at Making Money*[1]

## Expressions of Our Life Inertia

Ideally, life inertia propels us toward our healthiest goals of growth, success, happiness, and love. When we're on this path, we have the ability to feel joy and to be inspired. We're hopeful and optimistic about the experiences and opportunities that present themselves to us. We are able to participate in thriving relationships. A healthy path shows itself in our happiness at work, warm and loving family and friends, and fun in meaningful hobbies and recreation.

Yet, for many of us, the path we are on is one that is much less meaningful, fulfilling, or enjoyable than we would like. We know we're on this trajectory when we frequently feel angry or sad. Our thinking tends to have a pessimistic or fatalistic cast and our behavior often undermines what we're trying to accomplish. Our work is unsatisfying, we often feel lonely, and we really don't have many ways to enjoy life.

The unfortunate result of life inertia developing at such a young age and without conscious thought or consideration is that the current trajectory may not be in our best interests as adults. If we look closely at our lives, we may find that we react to certain situations much as we did when we were children and those same reactions now hinder our life. For example, that anger that we expressed as children to protect us from feeling rejected now alienates us from family, friends, and coworkers. Or our need for control causes us to be rigid and unforgiving with others. Despite these negative outcomes, our life inertia continues to exert its influence, and changing our life trajectory seems impossible. I call this sort of person an "Inertial," whom I define as a person whose life inertia is stuck on a trajectory not of their choosing and is not meaningful, satisfying, or joyful. Inertials' lives are on a fixed trajectory (law of life inertia), have considerable momentum propelling them forward (law of life momentum), and are resistant to a change in direction (law of action-reaction).

> Progress and growth are impossible if you always do things the way you've always done things.
>
> —Dr. Wayne Dyer, author of *Pulling Your Own Strings*[2]

## Changing Course

Many of us feel helpless to change the trajectory of our lives. No matter how much we may want to change the path of our life, we just haven't found a force powerful enough to alter its course. This situation can lead us to develop the belief that we simply don't have the ability to change its course and we quietly hope that other people or life circumstances will alter the trajectory for us. Many of us may feel that we have become victims of our life inertia. Following a life path that was not of our creation and that has caused us struggles can lead us to feel like those proverbial asteroids hurtling uncontrollably through space.

> Hell is to drift; heaven is to steer.
>
> —Don Juan, in *Man and Superman*[3]

Fortunately, we are not asteroids hurtling through space, lifeless pieces of rock over which we have no control. Unlike the Inertials I just introduced you to, your goal is to become the Captain of Starship You, which I define as being in control of the forces that propel your life and having the capabilities to guide your life trajectory in a direction of your own choosing. In *Change Your Life's Direction*, you can take command of Starship You and—as the creator of *Star Trek*, Gene Roddenberry, wrote—be free to "explore strange new worlds, to seek out new life and new civilizations, to boldly go where no one has gone before."

When you become Captain of Starship You and choose to change the course of your life, you need to generate a force that can overcome your inertia's current momentum. That course correction requires a change in the forces impacting your life inertia that surpasses the forces that currently propel it. The forces that you must generate can be applied either in a series of small, unrelenting strikes or in one massive blow. Small strikes might include gradually changing unhealthy thinking patterns, modifying deeply ingrained emotional habits, or altering long-standing life routines. This approach is a process of slowly forcing your life inertia to veer off its present course. It demands patience, persistence, and a literal minute-to-minute commitment to awareness and control over the forces that will enable you to make the changes to your life that you want.

Applying one colossal singular force to your life inertia involves making one major change in your life—making an internal change "cold turkey" or altering your external and social environment dramatically—that may be keeping you from making the necessary changes to your life's direction. Examples of a major force include ending an unhappy marriage, leaving an unsatisfying job, or moving to a new city. In all of these cases, changing your life inertia is a conscious and deliberate process of self-understanding, of marshalling of your resources, courage, and determination.

> You've got to make a conscious choice every day to shed the old—whatever the old means for you.
>
> —Sarah Ban Breathnach, author of *Something More*[4]

## Four Life Forces

Many of us wonder what forces propel us down the paths of our lives, why we go in the directions we do. To help you with this, I have identified the four major life forces that govern our life trajectory: values, self-esteem, ownership, and emotions. The good news is that being aware of and understanding these four life forces helps you take control of them and enable you to take the helm of the Starship You.

## Values: The Guidance System That Directs You

Values lie at the heart of our life inertia. What we believe is important should be the guiding force in our lives. Our values should direct us in every aspect of our lives, including the educational and professional choices we make, the people with whom we surround ourselves, and the activities in which we participate.

Unfortunately, because our life inertia is established long before we have an awareness or understanding of our values, it is first propelled by more simplistic forces that include the satisfaction of basic needs such as safety, security, and comfort. In less fortunate circumstances, forces can include compulsions that are aimed at protecting our psychological and physical well-being against real or perceived threats.

Identifying the needs and compulsions that are driving your life inertia is a necessary first step. Once these forces have been identified, you must critically examine them against your values. Consciously choosing values that are consistent with who you are now and what you want in the future is necessary for you to alter your life inertia. Once you have a better idea of your values, you can critically examine the needs and compulsions that have been fueling your life inertia against your values. As a result, you can remove or mitigate these problematic forces, thus freeing you to guide Starship You in a healthier direction.

## Self-esteem: The Pilot That Steers You

Self-esteem has been misunderstood and misused for the last forty years. Unfortunately, you may have been a victim of the "self-esteem movement" of the 1970s and 1980s. In misguided attempts to ensure that their children would be successful and happy, parents connected self-esteem to level of achievement. The foundation of this idea was that if success is connected to how we feel about ourselves, then we would make darned sure to be successful. In this way, we would maintain a positive self-image.

This approach worked—sort of. Although you may have become successful, achievements became so connected to your self-esteem that no amount of success was ever enough. This result likely left you living in a constant state of fear of failure. Instead of experiencing the exhilaration of success, your achievements provided only temporary relief from your trepidation of failure. Additionally, you may have been told that your goal was to "get there," which was supposed to be happiness and contentment. But when you did arrive "there," it wasn't what you expected. In other words, your life inertia didn't take you where you expected to go. This left you wondering, "Now what?"

An essential part of changing your life inertia involves "rewiring" the connections to your self-esteem. You need to reduce the connections between your self-esteem and your achievements and increase the connections between your self-esteem and who you are as a person, your values, the relationships you have, and the way you want to live your life. This rewiring will relieve the immense and unrelenting pressure you feel to become more successful. It will liberate you to seek a trajectory of your own choosing for your life based on what you value.

> Low self-esteem is the result of deficient learning. You're not bound forever by what happened to you in your childhood. You can overcome it.
>
> —Dr. Dan Kiley, author of *Living Together, Feeling Alone*[5]

## Ownership: The Engine That Drives You

Since we didn't know any better when we were children, many of us bought into the narrow and confining messages that our parents and society communicated to us about the kind of life we should lead. We came to define ourselves based on what others believed we should be rather than who we were and what we wanted to be. Since we unknowingly accepted these definitions from the outside world, we never developed the sense of connectedness and responsibility for our lives. We weren't able to say, "This is mine" or "I did this because I love it and I really wanted to." Without truly owning the reasons for the lives we led, we could never fully gain ownership of many aspects of our lives. This lack of ownership limits our ability to find true meaning, satisfaction, and joy in our lives.

A necessary part of changing your life inertia is gaining ownership of your life, which means that you engage in your life because of the deep connection you feel with its many aspects, an enduring love for it, and an internally derived determination to fully experience it. This ownership also provides you with an immense source of fulfillment from your efforts that brings you happiness regardless of your success, though acting with ownership will often lead to success.

> Until you take ownership for your life, you will always be chasing happiness.
>
> —Sean Stephenson, author of *Get Off Your "But"*[6]

## Emotions: The Fuel That Propels You

Emotions are perhaps the most neglected force that impacts the path our lives take. For many of us, our emotional lives were shaped by our families in one of two ways. Some parents believed that feeling negative emotions would hurt our self-esteem and scar us for life. These parents protected us from feeling and expressing negative emotions, such as frustration, anger, and sadness. They rationalized failure, distracted us from unpleasant emotions, placated our negative emotions, and artificially created positive emotions. So our parents shielded us from feeling bad, which robbed us of the opportunity to become familiar with and master these emotional experiences.

In contrast, some of us were raised in a family in which negative or difficult emotions may have been ever present, intense, and out of control. This "emotional overload" of frustration, anger, hurt, guilt, and shame required us to shut these emotions away or express them inappropriately. They also kept us from feeling many positive emotions and interfered with the opportunity to learn how to experience and express all emotions in a healthy way.

If one of these two scenarios fits you, then you likely will have paid a high price through the development of a life inertia that has continued this emotional turmoil. Emotional mastery and positive feelings are two of the most basic elements of the healthy life inertia that you crave but may be alien to you. Your early experiences with emotions created a life inertia that may have limited your emotional growth, sabotaged your professional life, wreaked havoc on your personal life, and hurtled you down an unhealthy path. The only way to mitigate the toxic emotional fuel that has propelled you through your life is to allow yourself to grow emotionally, experience the full spectrum of emotions, and use them to propel you in a new direction in your life.

Like that asteroid plunging through space, our current life inertia is highly resistant to change because of the great forces that put us on our path in the first place. A little effort here or there is unlikely to change the direction of our lives because the momentum that has built up and the potent forces that have been in place for a long time are resistant to counterforces. *Change Your Life's Direction* is devoted to showing that you *can* take control of Starship You, you can harness these four life forces, and you can take your life in a new and healthy direction. Once you can see clearly what launched your initial trajectory and understand the lasting power of those initial forces, you can recognize what it will take to channel those forces and change the direction of your life.

> I don't want to be at the mercy of my emotions. I want to use them, to enjoy them, and to dominate them.
>
> —Oscar Wilde, author of *The Picture of Dorian Gray*[7]

## Explore Your Inner World

Perhaps the most difficult part of changing your life inertia involves the need to explore your inner world. True change does not occur on the surface or outside of you. It doesn't just occur with your behavior or your interactions with others. On the contrary, altering your life inertia requires making fundamental changes in your thinking, your feelings about yourself and your world, and your actions on and reactions to the world around you. Change means understanding not only who you are but also why you are—that is, seeing the different forces that propel your life inertia. It involves making connections between your experiences as a child and how you respond to your world as an adult. Only by understanding these connections are you able to recognize the forces that have guided your life trajectory to this point and gain control of those forces that are exerted based on who you are now rather than who you once were.

> The man who views the world at fifty the same as he did at twenty has wasted thirty years of his life.
>
> —boxing legend Muhammad Ali

The thought of exploring our inner world can be scary. We may fear what we find. We think, "Life is not so great now, but at least it's familiar to me and I have learned how to deal with it. What if what I find out about myself is much worse?" Rarely are the skeletons in our closets that terrifying. More often than not, they are the same skeletons that most other people have: insecurity, hurt, sadness. It's uncommon that we find anything new or shocking. Rather, these issues are what have always been present in our lives and have unfortunately propelled us along a life trajectory of unhappiness without us knowing the forces behind it.

Bringing these skeletons out of the closet demystifies them, removes their ferocity, and allows you to let go of them. This exploration provides a sense of understanding and relief. "Now I know why I have always acted that way" is a common statement I hear from my clients. Bringing these issues into the light also likely will act as a great cathartic. You finally will have proof that there is nothing really wrong with you and that the challenges you have are actually quite common and manageable. It's more likely that your skeletons are not monsters but a normal part of the human condition.

I also will bet that, if you're reading this book, you actually will enjoy this exploration process. Yes, you probably feel a bit of trepidation about what you might find, but you're also curious about what is going on deep inside of you. And more than anything, you want to figure out whatever is going on inside of you so that you can let it go and redirect the trajectory of your life.

Having come to learn who you are and why you are, you will be in a position of strength and readiness to decide who you want to be and what you want to do. In other words, you'll be ready to reengage those forces and change your life inertia. These explorations of your inner world will liberate you to move away from the path on which your life inertia has been carrying you and finally put the past behind you where it belongs instead of in front of you where it has been. You will be able to actively shift your life's path in the direction of the future person you want to be and the future life you want to live.

## Your Goal: Complete Freedom

What is the point of harnessing your four life forces, creating a new life inertia, and changing the trajectory of your life in a new and healthier direction? The point is to experience *complete freedom* in your life, which involves knowing what you don't want and liberating yourself from the forces that have propelled your life inertia down its current unsatisfying path. Freedom from:

- Fear

- Pain

- Anxiety

- Doubt
- Worry
- Frustration
- Anger
- Despair
- Unhealthy needs
- Passivity
- Victimhood
- Dependence

Complete freedom also means knowing what you want and propelling yourself along a new, fulfilling course. Freedom to:

- Feel all emotions
- Be vulnerable
- Have hope
- Take risks
- Give
- Love
- Choose
- Believe
- Realize your dreams and goals
- Fully engage in life
- Be an active and intentional participant in your life
- Live consistently with your values

- Be happy

- Be at peace

With this complete freedom, you can achieve several essential goals in your life. You can know that you did everything in your power to live the life that you wanted most, the life that would bring you the greatest meaning and satisfaction. Also, at the end of the day, you can be sure that you will not have to experience the most frustrating of all emotions—regret. And you won't have to answer what is perhaps the saddest question of all: "I wonder what could have been?"

> In the truest sense, freedom cannot be bestowed; it must be achieved.
>
> —Franklin D. Roosevelt, thirty-second president
> of the United States of America[8]

## The Payoff

When you change your life inertia, you liberate yourself from the forces that have, until now, propelled you in a direction you would not have chosen and that is lacking in meaning, satisfaction, and joy. Instead of being an asteroid hurtling uncontrollably through life with no ability to alter its course, you are the Captain of Starship You, over which you have control to determine its direction. When you are in command of Starship You, you are on track to live the life of which you have always dreamed.

What does it feel like when you gain control of your life inertia? Not long ago, I was working with an accomplished businesswoman, Tricia. She came to me because she felt she was living a life of profound emptiness. Her job had created a toxic lifestyle of too much travel, too little sleep, and poor eating. She had little time to exercise, had put on considerable weight, and just felt lousy about herself. Plus, the long hours prevented her from maintaining meaningful friendships or exploring romantic relationships. After several months of working to understand and control the four life forces that were propelling her life inertia, Tricia had been able to free herself from the seemingly intractable trajectory of her old life. One day, Tricia came to my office and told me that she had an exciting and healing epiphany the previous night. With tears in her eyes and a smile on her face, she said, "I realized that I would never have to go back to the way I used to live my life. And I have never felt such joy and peace!"

## What Lies Ahead

The purpose of *Change Your Life's Direction* is to guide you in changing the trajectory of your life for the better. This process includes understanding who you were, who you are, and who you want to be. It involves identifying the path on which your life inertia has taken you and appreciating how that inertia has led you to lead a life that is neither fulfilling nor nourishing. Taking these steps will help you understand what course you want to take and ultimately how you can use the four essential life forces to alter the course of your life trajectory.

The process of change that I describe in *Change Your Life's Direction* begins with identifying your current life inertia, what is unhealthy about it, and, most important, what forces are keeping you from the life path you want to be on. Next, you must clarify your new life inertia. What course do you want your life to be on? What internal changes—thoughts, emotions—do you need to make? What behavioral, social, lifestyle, and environmental changes are necessary to create enough force to alter your life inertia? Most important, you must make an unwavering commitment to those changes. Only with relentless determination to change will you be able to muster enough force to alter your life inertia and shift the path of your life. Finally, you must act! You must build the momentum of new forces until they are powerful enough to move your life inertia in the direction that you consciously and deliberately choose—to let go of the past and achieve what you want in the present and in the future.

> We must be willing to get rid of the life we've planned, so as to have the life that is waiting for us.
>
> —Joseph Campbell, author of *The Hero of a Thousand Faces*[9]

## Part I

# VALUES: THE GUIDANCE SYSTEM THAT DIRECTS YOU

A t an early age, our most basic needs initially provide the direction for our life inertia. Yet, despite their obvious importance, the most confounding questions I ask my clients are "What needs drive you?" and "What do you need to be fulfilled and happy?" Some look at me as if I have asked them to explain the theory of relativity. Others come up with the obvious needs: to be happy and successful, to have good relationships, and so forth. However, most people can't articulate their deepest personal needs or why and how those needs have impacted their life trajectory.

Often, needs that became dominant in childhood continue to exert influence over our adult lives even when the satisfaction of those needs is no longer healthy or actually makes us unhappy. It is crucial to be able to identify the needs that drove your life inertia when you were young and, if they are unhealthy, to let go of them and replace them with healthier needs in order to change your life inertia.

Values are what we hold to be important in our lives. They should be the foundation of who we are and how we live our lives. They are also the starting point for changing our life inertia. Values act as the road map that guides our lives. Values tell us where to devote our energy, time, and resources in all aspects of our lives, including career, family, social life, and physical, cultural, and spiritual activities. Values should act as the guidance system for our life inertia, providing a new direction of our own choosing. Do the values you live by enrich your life and bring you happiness, or do they corrupt your life and cause you discontentment? Understanding what you hold most dear in your life and asking yourself whether those values are life affirming or life negating is an essential first step in redirecting your life inertia. Chapters 1 and 2 provide an in-depth exploration your needs and values as a means of ensuring that you have control of your guidance system for the life course you really want.

> Clarifying your values is the essential first step toward a richer, fuller, more productive life.
>
> —Carl Rogers, founder of Person-First Psychotherapy[1]

# CHAPTER ONE
# DARK MATTER
## From *NEEDS!* to Needs

**Need** /nēd/: A condition requiring relief; a physiological or psychological requirement for the well-being of an organism.

Just as your basic physical needs (e.g., food, water, shelter) must be met to ensure your physical survival, there are psychological and emotional needs that must also be satisfied for your survival and healthy development. These needs include feeling:

- Loved ("Others care for me")
- Valued ("I'm worthwhile")
- Secure ("I'm safe")
- Competent ("I'm capable")
- In control ("I'm in charge")
- Positive emotions ("I'm comfortable")
- Connected ("I'm attached")

Every human being has these needs. In and of themselves, these needs are neither healthy nor unhealthy, functional nor dysfunctional; they are simply a part of what makes us human. We don't have the capabilities at a young age to satisfy these needs ourselves, so they must be taken care of by parents, caregivers, teachers, and other adults. The degree to which these needs are satisfied determines which are beneficial or harmful to us. Importantly, these needs inform whether our life inertia begins on a positive trajectory.

Unfortunately, our inability to satisfy these needs on our own leaves us vulnerable to the neuroses, pathologies, and just plain whims of our parents and childhood environment. The vagaries of childhood can mean that the prominence of certain needs and how we satisfy those needs don't necessarily turn out to be healthy or functional in the long run. Yet these fundamental personal needs are the first impetus behind our life inertia: our values, thoughts, emotions, and actions. Our reactions to people and how we respond to different situations are also initially formed to satisfy those most basic needs.

## Needs or *NEEDS!*

For needs to exert a functional force over the initial creation of our life inertia, they must be met sufficiently and in a timely and appropriate manner by loving parents and a supportive environment. Our needs must be satisfied unconditionally by our parents without needing us children to make a special—and often, in the long term, dysfunctional—effort to have our needs met. When this happens, we develop a healthy and balanced place for these needs that creates the initial force propelling our life inertia. Needs that have been satisfied in a positive way start out functional and continue to exert a healthy influence over us into adulthood. Most basically, these types of needs encourage rather than interfere with your healthy psychological, emotional, and interpersonal development. As a result, these needs tend to act in your own best interests.

In contrast, needs that were not readily or adequately met in childhood often gain a disproportionate prominence as we get older. This is similar to a child who grows up in a poor environment being vulnerable to developing an obsession with making money because of his or her early financial deprivation. I distinguish the needs that disproportionally impact our life inertia by capitalizing and italicizing them and following them by an exclamation point: *NEEDS!* These *NEEDS!* are characterized by their influence over us in ways that are neither healthy nor functional and that often run counter to our best interests.

*NEEDS!* are those that can be satisfied in only dysfunctional ways (i.e., only if we conform to our parents' or environment's unhealthy demands). We don't choose whether we have needs met in functional or dysfunctional ways. As children, we lack the cognitive capabilities and experience to understand why our parents treat us as they do. We also don't have the wherewithal when we're young to choose what needs take precedence or how they get satisfied. In other words, we are at the mercy of our parents and the environment in which we were raised.

Young children are not conscious of these dynamics; yet their survival instincts intuit what they must do to have their needs met. As a result, we assume roles and behaviors that ensure we have our needs met—even if they ultimately prove to be dysfunctional. These *NEEDS!* become a central and powerful force that initiates and propels our life inertia to satisfy those *NEEDS!* in any way possible. If these *NEEDS!* continue to be unmet despite increasing efforts to have them fulfilled, we often resort to impulsive measures. These *NEEDS!* create a desperation to be satisfied at all costs, even at the expense of our overall well-being. This dominance of *NEEDS!* in our life inertia results in the weakening or exclusion of other needs, much like a starving person will do anything to obtain food even if it means breaking the law. This urgency to fulfill those *NEEDS!* drives our life inertia on a trajectory in that is neither healthy nor functional.

The poorer we are inwardly, the more we try to enrich ourselves outwardly.

—Bruce Lee, legendary martial artist and movie star[1]

## From Needs to *NEEDS!*

The real litmus test of whether needs are functional or dysfunctional is how those needs are satisfied and whether they help or impede your psychological and emotional health and well-being. At a basic level we can ask, "Do my needs and the way I satisfy them enable me to find happiness, meaning, connection, and success in my life?" Needs and need satisfaction become *NEEDS!* when they detract from the quality of our lives; interfere with our happiness, relationships, or work efforts; or prevent us from achieving our goals. Unfortunately, what can begin as functional (though not necessarily healthy) behavior early in our lives can become dysfunctional behavior if they place us on a life course that ultimately prevents us from meeting the healthy needs I described at the beginning of chapter 1.

For example, Matthew felt out of control, unsafe, and afraid as a child in a family with an alcoholic and sometimes violent father. To satisfy his needs for security and control, he attempted to reduce the chances that his volatile and unpredictable father would become angry with him by becoming a "pleaser" and being compulsively neat and organized. The behaviors that he developed to reduce his fear and instill a superficial sense of safety and control included being avoidant of and submissive to his father, having a preoccupation with cleanliness and order, and adhering to strict routines. Though these behaviors helped Matthew to minimize the chances of being the recipient of his father's alcohol-driven wrath and satisfy his needs to feel safe and in control as a child—and, as a result, were functional at that time—they became *NEEDS!* in adulthood. Fast-forward twenty years, Matthew continues to satisfy those security and control *NEEDS!* in the same way he did as a child. He is submissive and acquiescent toward people of authority in his life (e.g., teachers, bosses), maintains excessive control and order in his life, and distances himself from others. Moreover, the thoughts, emotions, and behaviors related to satisfying those *NEEDS!* now cause him to feel inadequate, unfulfilled, anxious, and unhappy. They prevent him from getting his fundamental needs met in a healthy way. These *NEEDS!* are a barrier to developing healthy connections with others; Matthew has been unwilling to enter into emotional relationships (platonic or romantic) or let go of control so as not to risk the hurt he felt as a child. Unfortunately, this vulnerability is essential to trusting in and feeling deeply for others.

You might be wondering, "Why would someone continue to satisfy their *NEEDS!* in ways that are no longer functional?" The reason is that we continue to respond to the world in the same way we did as children unless we intentionally change it. That is, we have the same life inertia that developed in our childhood, guided and propelled by our most powerful *NEEDS!* that are being met in the same way as when we were young, even when they are no longer functional in adulthood. Here's a metaphor that may help you understand why we maintain our life inertia despite a desire to change course: Athletes who practice bad technique for many years become really skilled at bad technique and can't readily change these techniques because they are so ingrained. Similarly, you may have "practiced" certain ways of thinking, feeling, and behaving to meet your *NEEDS!* for years. They become entrenched as habitual parts of you that no longer contribute to your psychological, emotional, or interpersonal health and well-being. Moreover, the immense force of our life inertia that is established in childhood gains momentum over time and prevents us from understanding, confronting, or resolving those *NEEDS!*, reducing them to needs, or finding healthier ways of meeting them. An additional obstacle is that we are often not fully aware of the self-sabotaging influence that our life inertia has on us. We can see that our lives are not working out the way we had wanted (e.g., failed relationships, career setbacks), but we are at a loss to understand why. In sum, our life inertia is driven by our

*NEEDS!* that propel us down a path unchanged since childhood. We continue to interact with the world based on who we were rather than who we are now. The ultimate outcome of continuing in this way is a life trajectory that is neither of your choosing nor in your best interests.

This notion is powerfully illustrated in a 2007 documentary titled *Protagonist*, in which four men with dysfunctional life inertias are profiled. *New York Times* film critic Stephen Holden observed that these men created life inertias "as ways of transcending painful, oppressive childhoods that left them with feelings of inadequacy and shame." For all four of these men, *NEEDS!* that arose due to traumatic early life experiences (suicide of a mother, beatings from a father, being the "school punching bag," and awareness of homosexuality in a religious family) led to severe and obsessive means of satisfying their *NEEDS!* through terrorism, crime, martial arts, and missionary Christianity, respectively. Only later in life did they experience crises that caused them to question and confront their life paths and exert change over their life inertias. Although these are extreme cases in both the strength of the *NEEDS!* and the severity of how those *NEEDS!* were met, we all have varying types and degrees of *NEEDS!* from our childhoods and dysfunctional ways of satisfying them.

> Nothing is more desirable than to be released from an affliction, but nothing is more frightening than to be divested of a crutch.
>
> —James Baldwin, author and activist[2]

## It's Not Your Fault

One of the most painful aspects of *NEEDS!* is that we often blame ourselves for not getting our needs sufficiently met as children. We come to believe that we didn't deserve to have our needs met by our parents in a healthy way. This perception creates in us a profound sense of inadequacy that propels us to prove our worth and demonstrate that we do, in fact, deserve to have our needs met. Unfortunately, the only way we know to get our needs met is how we got them met as children, thus turning them into *NEEDS!*

So let me say something as emphatically as I can to you that I hope will lighten the load that you have carried for so many years: *It's not your fault!* Why your needs as a child became *NEEDS!* had nothing to do with you. Do you know whose fault it really was? Your parents! It was their *NEEDS!* that caused them to not meet your needs and that led your needs to become *NEEDS!* My gosh, you were just a helpless child who only wanted to be loved and didn't do anything to deserve such treatment. So I encourage you to blame your parents for what they did to you. "Whoa!" you might think, "that doesn't sound like a very mature way of handling this epiphany. We are adults now. Isn't it childish to blame our parents for things that happened so many years ago?" My response to that: no and yes.

I stand by my statement that you should blame your parents. Because you have carried around an immense burden of self-blame—and shame!—for years, you can't just take it off of your shoulders. Instead, you have to pass that burden onto those who rightly deserve it: your parents. The simple reality is that they treated you in a way that you didn't deserve and you suffered for it.

The sins of the father are to be laid upon the children.

—William Shakespeare (1564–1616), playwright[3]

But it is not that simple. I don't make this accusation to be mean to your parents or suggest that they are bad people. They didn't intentionally treat you as they did. They treated you poorly because of who they were, not who you were. One thing that people often forget is that parents are human beings too, and they were victims of their own parents. Reality becomes a lot more complicated when we recognize that many of our parents had *NEEDS!* of their own and passed them on to us, just as previous generations transmitted them to future generations without awareness or understanding.

An unpredictable parent is a fearsome god in the eyes of a child.

—Susan Forward, author of *Toxic Parents*[4]

So blame your parents for the *NEEDS!* that propelled your life inertia toward who you became; it is their fault. But then—and I'm sending this message as loudly and clearly as I can—forgive them! The complicated reality is that your parents loved you and wanted what was best for you, despite how it may have appeared. Remember, just as you were at the mercy of your parents and upbringing, they, too, were victims of their parents and their upbringing. In theory, could they have done better by you? To be sure. But they did the best they could with what they had. Unfortunately, it wasn't good enough, and it put your life inertia on an unhealthy trajectory. But that was then, and this is now. So, yes, blame them for who you became, but don't hold them responsible for who you want to become. You are an adult and continuing to hold them accountable for your life is not only childish but also counterproductive. It doesn't change your *NEEDS!* back to needs, and it doesn't help you change your life inertia. In fact, on the contrary, it keeps you on your current life path by continuing to give your parents the power to determine the direction that your life inertia carries you. After blaming your parents and freeing yourself from the shame that you felt because you believed how you were treated was your fault, it's now time to seize control of your life.

We didn't deserve to be treated the way we were, and we don't deserve it now. But it's not our parents who are treating us badly now; it's us! It is our life inertia—our thoughts, emotions, habits, baggage, and actions—that continues to propel us down a bad path. So blaming our parents now isn't going to help us; in fact, continuing to do so will only be hurtful. We have to take control of our lives and actively change our life inertia; no one else can or will. And that's what *Change Your Life's Direction* is all about.

Children begin by loving their parents; as they grow older they judge them; sometimes they forgive them.

—Oscar Wilde, author of *The Picture of Dorian Gray*[5]

## Identify Your Needs

Understanding your needs—and your *NEEDS!*—is not an activity that is encouraged in our society. When I begin working with people with dysfunctional life trajectories, I ask them what their needs are. Most often, they are unable to describe their needs or how they satisfy them. They usually rattle off the typical needs most people think of—for example, to feel loved and happy—without really knowing what *their* needs are. Particularly for men, exploring needs is considered a sign of weakness and dependence—having needs of any sort can be seen as a chink in their armor. Among women, many are raised to have little concern for their own needs and are told that the needs of others, particularly men's, should take priority. Many women believe that they don't deserve to have their own needs satisfied and that it is selfish and would create conflict with others. The end result is that many people, men and women alike, never truly understand their needs, healthy or otherwise, or how to fulfill them.

Your first goal is to identify your deepest and most powerful needs in childhood, why they assumed a place of prominence in your life, and what measures you took—however extreme—to satisfy those needs. Then identify what needs you now have as an adult and how you currently meet them. Are your needs the same now as when you were a child? Do you satisfy them in the same way? Are those needs and means of fulfilling them enhancing or impeding your life? Do you have needs or *NEEDS!?*

Learning what your needs are and how they developed have many benefits. It makes your needs more tangible and real. In this more concrete form, *NEEDS!* seem less mysterious and fearsome because you understand what they are and where they came from, and needs seem clearer and more reachable because you actually know what your needs are. Understanding your needs and *NEEDS!* often brings some sense of relief because you have greater clarity in your life—you finally see your life inertia for what it is and why you have thought, felt, and acted as you have all of these years. You also feel empowered to address your *NEEDS!* because these insights—and the hope that they bring—offer you greater commitment and resolve to change the course of your life. This relief offers positive new emotional energy to fuel your quest to shift your life inertia.

> Your mind and body will not recover until you identify and treat the underlying deficiencies.
>
> —Steven Magee, author of *Toxic Health*[6]

## Identify Your NEEDS!

Identifying your *NEEDS!* is both a difficult and an easy process. It's difficult because you must look at aspects of yourself that you may have always tried to avoid because they are scary and painful. Yet it is easy because, without realizing it, you have been staring them in the face your entire life; you live with those *NEEDS!* and their consequences every day.

The process of identifying your *NEEDS!* involves acting as a detective to uncover clues about what those *NEEDS!* are. Begin by examining what lies on the surface of your life: how you behave. What precise actions do you take that sabotage your life? For example, Eric, a former client of mine, was passed up for a promotion that he really wanted. He belittled his promoted colleague to other coworkers and told them that their boss didn't know anything. This behavior made Eric feel better, but it hurt his relationships with his colleagues and his chances for a promotion. Nobody likes people who speak badly about others, and he began to be viewed as a complainer. As a result, he lost out on several higher positions in his company.

With the self-defeating expression of your *NEEDS!* identified, continue to play detective and see what emotions underlie that behavior and those thoughts. Eric was consumed with anger at how badly he had been treated and at the unfairness of his life. Anger is an especially useful clue in discovering your *NEEDS!* Whenever you feel anger, don't assume that it is the real emotion you are feeling. Rather, anger is often a defensive emotion aimed at protecting you from facing the intolerable emotions (e.g., sadness, fear, or hurt) related to them that were not adequately met as a child. If anger is your dominant emotion, uncover the primary emotions related to your reaction. Through our explorations, Eric learned that his life inertia had been propelled since childhood by shame and fear. The shame came from feeling that he never lived up to the expectations of his perfectionistic mother. And he feared that he wasn't worthy of her love. These two emotions acted as the fuel that propelled his life down a path of insecurity, self-sabotage, and disappointment (more on the impact of emotions on life inertia in part IV). What emotions emanate from your life inertia and what emotions lie at the heart of your emotional reactions to your *NEEDS!*?

> Our feelings are not there to be cast out or conquered. They're there to be engaged and expressed with imagination and intelligence.
>
> —T. K. Coleman, educator[7]

You are now one step closer to identifying your *NEEDS!* Now reveal the thoughts that powered your painful emotions and self-defeating actions. And be aware of whether your thoughts are focused on you (i.e., I, me, my) or on others (i.e., him, her, they). Eric's thoughts were directed inward initially and filled with negativity toward himself ("Why wasn't I complimented for my hard work?"), a sense of unfairness ("I deserve to be promoted"), and feelings of inadequacy ("Maybe I'm not cut out for this line of work"). He then would shift his gaze onto other people and demean and blame them.

He would think, "She doesn't deserve that. I am so much better than she is." But these thoughts don't get to the heart of Eric's *NEEDS!*

Here's a clue for you: If your thoughts focus on someone or something outside of you, then you haven't yet arrived at the underlying thoughts connected to your *NEEDS!* Just as anger is a protective emotion, these "externalizing" thoughts safeguard you from painful thoughts that are closest to your *NEEDS!* You have to ask yourself what you think about *you*, not others. Eric started by beating himself up with self-critical "I" statements. But that became too painful very quickly. In order to protect himself, he unconsciously directed his criticism outward onto others. In a subsequent session with Eric, I had him return his focus back to himself, and he soon discovered that "I'm incompetent and worthless" was the most powerful reflection of his *NEEDS!* and had been the driving force in his life inertia for years. Once you identify these thoughts, your *NEEDS!* are within reach.

> Remember, you have been criticizing yourself for years and it hasn't worked. Try approving of yourself and see what happens.
>
> —Louise L. Hay, author and founder of Hay House[8]

The next step is to specify which *NEEDS!* lie at the heart of your self-defeating life inertia. Refer back to my list of needs at the beginning of this chapter and choose the needs that are most connected with the thoughts, emotions, and behaviors that you have just identified. In addition to processing those needs intellectually, or "thinking" about them, I encourage you to close your eyes, quiet your mind, and allow each need to pass through your "emotional filter" and see which triggers strong emotions. My experience with my clients has been that emotional warning bells start ringing loudly when you connect to a need that became a *NEED!*

The final step in this detective work is to understand how these *NEEDS!* developed. This requires you to return to your childhood and confront the sometimes painful demons that originally propelled your life inertia. Looking at yourself so closely likely will provoke trepidation and avoidance. However, this step is essential to changing your life inertia because it brings to light the connection between who you were and who you now are: it reveals the source of your life inertia. I would encourage you, if you have the opportunity, to engage in this exploration with a trained mental health professional who can provide guidance and support in your journey of changing your life trajectory. At the same time, take comfort in the fact that you have vastly more capabilities and resources as an adult than when you were a child, so this uncovering will not be nearly as painful as you might think. Finally understanding why you are who you are—perhaps for the first time—and seeing hope in changing your life inertia can ease the pain of facing your demons. It can even inject some positive feelings such as pride and inspiration into your "fuel system."

> It takes courage . . . to endure the sharp pains of self-discovery rather than choose to take the dull pain of unconsciousness that would last the rest of our lives.
>
> —Marianne Williamson, self-help author[9]

Eric described how, as a child, he had felt stupid and incompetent compared to his older sister, who always did better in school. Their parents seemed to give her more attention, causing Eric to feel neglected and worthless. In response, Eric became an overachiever, maniacally driven to succeed in order to feel capable and to get his parents' attention. He also became hard-edged and unforgiving with people. When people he studied or worked with didn't perform up to his expectations, he became furious. Through high school and college, Eric hated when others did better than he did. He always reacted the same way: by demeaning their efforts and trumpeting his own accomplishments. He simply couldn't stop himself even though he knew his behavior caused him to feel worse about himself and alienated him from others.

Eric's unmet needs to feel competent and loved became *NEEDS!* that were the dominant force propelling his life inertia. Its purpose was to cover up his sense of inadequacy and worthlessness, as well as the feelings of hurt and fear that accompanied them. Eric channeled his feelings of sadness and pain into righteous anger. In devaluing others, Eric built himself up in his own mind, thus countering his feelings of inadequacy.

From the first step of identifying your unhealthy behavior through engaging in detective work, you now have found a deeper understanding of your *NEEDS!* that have propelled your misguided life inertia for so many years. You may feel some relief simply because you finally understand why you are who you are and why you have been thinking, feeling, and acting in ways that have been self-destructive. You will likely feel that, because you know why you are, there is hope to change your life inertia. But knowing your *NEEDS!* isn't enough to leave them in your past. *Change Your Life's Direction* is about letting go of those *NEEDS!* that have guided your life trajectory to this point and charting a new life course based on your needs and values that will bring you the meaning, fulfillment, happiness, connection, and peace that you have long sought.

And you? When will you begin that long journey into yourself?

—Rumi (1207–1273), Persian scholar and poet[10]

## Identify Your Needs

Identifying your needs can be more difficult than recognizing your *NEEDS!* because you haven't experienced them since childhood so you may have completely lost touch with them. Yet unearthing and acknowledging your needs is a profound step toward changing your life inertia because it enables you to shift your focus from the unhealthy past, which has been at the heart of your current life trajectory, to how to change your life inertia to work toward a healthy future. Instead of a life inertia that has been aimed at meeting *NEEDS!* that have brought you unhappiness, you will now be propelled by a life inertia that satisfies your needs and brings you happiness.

Your needs as a grown-up should differ greatly from your *NEEDS!* as a child. When you are young, you have little ability to meet your own needs and are at the mercy of your parents and others to satisfy them. As an adult, your acquired experience, knowledge, skills, and resources make you, at a very basic level, less needy and more able to satisfy the needs that you do have.

There is a paradox here. Even though we are very different people as adults, those of us with unhealthy life inertias still respond to the world based on the same *NEEDS!* as when we were children. By the same token, even though we are very different people, we have many of the same needs as when were young. Take another look at the list of needs at the beginning of the chapter, and you'll see that we still have those needs; in fact, they are a normal part of being human. Ideally, our *NEEDS!* should be different, but our needs should be the same.

How, then, do you figure out your needs at this point in your life? You can use much the same process of detective work that you used to identify your *NEEDS!* Think about something you do that brings you a sense of meaning, satisfaction, and joy. It may be something at work, a hobby, or an interaction with another person. Eric enjoyed renovating the house he had just bought, doing his own carpentry, plumbing, and electrical work. He spent hours in the evenings and on weekends on various projects to make the house his home. He became immersed in these efforts and felt an ease and peace that was unheard of in other aspects of his life.

Then ask yourself what emotions those experiences generate in you. Feeling these emotions is an essential step in this discovery process because it allows you to connect these experiences with positive and life-affirming emotions. The healthy satisfaction of needs comes in many forms. You may feel excitement, joy, fulfillment, or contentment. You may experience pride, inspiration, a sense of competence and confidence, or an inner stability and comfort. Eric experienced a tremendous sense of satisfaction at committing himself to a home project and completing it with great care and quality. He also had a strange sense of calm that was largely alien to him.

Having reconnected with the positive emotional impact of meeting essential needs, take a look at the thoughts that emerge when you are immersed in this activity. What perceptions, thoughts, impressions, ideas, images, or memories come to mind? As you gather these cognitions associated with satisfying these healthy needs, connect them to the emotions you are feeling and the experiences that are driving them. The more you can connect these positive experiences with the related behavior, emotions, and thoughts, the more you can tap into them to guide and fuel a change in your life inertia. Eric would have flashbacks to when he was a child playing with his toy toolset. These memories conjured up thoughts and feelings of competence, accomplishment, completion, and pride in the long-past tasks that he recalled.

Next, what need does the experience and the related emotions satisfy in you, such as a need to help others, to create, to challenge yourself, or to feel an adrenaline rush. Then, connect those specific needs that you identify with the overarching needs that I describe at the start of this chapter. Making these connections will reveal your needs to you. You may have different activities that produce different emotions and thoughts, each of which tap into a different healthy need. The more needs you can identify and bring to the fore, the more readily you'll be able to allow those needs to reassert themselves, reduce the influence of your *NEEDS!*, and generate sufficient new force to shift your life inertia propelled by your healthy needs.

Importantly, notice the overall tone of your inner life when you're connected to your needs compared to when you are driven by your *NEEDS!* You should sense a vast difference, from doubt, angst, and distress to safety, self-worth, and peace. In doing so, you will get your first experience of what it will be like to exert a healthy force on your life inertia and propel your life in a new and positive direction. By making the connection between the past and present,

*NEEDS!* and needs, and unhealthy and healthy life inertia, Eric was able to bring those memories into the present and use them to strengthen the power of his healthy needs and diminish the force of his *NEEDS!* In doing so, he began to exert a force to change his life inertia. You will be able to do this too!

Know thyself.

—Socrates, ancient Greek philosopher[11]

## What Do You Wish For?

A client I worked with, Gloria, is thirty-eight years old, successful professionally, a committed athlete, and struggling with her romantic relationships. Gloria always was focused on her past and perceived failures. It was a major epiphany for her when she realized the need to redirect her focus onto the future, her talents, and her successes rather than dwelling on the painful upbringing she had. So I asked her what she wished for her future. With this question, Gloria became teary-eyed and quiet. She told me that she never believed in wishes because, as a child, her wishes never came true. I responded by telling her that may be true, but children's wishes are often fantasies that are either unattainable or dependent on others to see them realized. I told Gloria that she is an adult now and she can make her own wishes come true. This notion brought a hopeful smile to her face. Over the subsequent months, Gloria worked hard to understand her *NEEDS!* and needs, let go of her *NEEDS!*, and use her needs to guide her life in a new and affirming direction.

This idea of wishes has become important for me recently. At some very basic level, I think wishes describe our most fundamental needs. Perhaps it is because I associate wishes with children, and there is a purity to the needs of children. Their wishes are simple: They wish to feel loved and safe. Children wish to feel capable and in control. They wish to feel happy. Of all people, children know what they need. Unfortunately, parents and our culture at large often corrupt those wishes and transform them into *NEEDS!* Reconnecting with your childhood wishes—your needs—will enable you to make that shift from *NEEDS!* to needs and allow your present needs, based on who you are now, to take precedence over those past *NEEDS!* and propel your life inertia in a healthy direction in the future.

> What you can do, or dream you can, begin it. Boldness has genius, power, and magic in it.
>
> —Johann Wolfgang von Goethe, German writer and statesman[12]

# CHAPTER TWO

# STARSHINE IN A BOTTLE
## From Needs to Values

Val·ues /val-yüz/: Assumptions, convictions, or beliefs about the manner in which people should behave; priorities that individuals hold that govern their choices and decisions; values evolve from circumstances with the external world and can change over time.

When you take back control of your life from your *NEEDS!* and hand the helm over to your needs, you've taken an important first step toward changing your life inertia. But you aren't done yet. Although needs are healthy and important contributors to your life inertia, you don't want them to be what ultimately determines your life trajectory. I see needs as just the beginning of guiding the course of your life. When healthy needs guide your life path, you can be assured that your life is heading in a generally good direction in which all of your basic needs are being met: you feel loved, valued, secure, and so forth. However, there are limitations in simply living to meet your basic needs because they put you in a state of perpetual survival, and we all know that a fulfilling life is more than just getting by. Fulfillment involves growing, thriving, and living a life that is intentional and purposeful, one that maximizes the meaning, satisfaction, and joy you experience.

Our values are what enable us to live that rich life by acting as the guidance system for the direction that our lives take. Similar to our *NEEDS!*, we rarely choose our values. Mostly, we simply adopt the values of our parents and the dominant values of the culture in which we live. In general, the values that we internalized as children remain with us through adulthood and are often shaped by the *NEEDS!* that I described in chapter 1. Unfortunately, those *NEEDS!*-based values can often lead to an unfulfilling and unhappy life.

Here are some important questions to ask yourself about your values:

1. What values are you presently living in accordance with?

2. What were the values you were raised with?

3. Are they the same or different?

4. Do your values enable you to live a healthy life of your choosing?

These are essential questions that you must ask if you are to gain control of your life's guidance system and propel your life inertia in a healthy direction of your choosing. Yet answering these questions can be a challenge, not to mention the greater challenge of using your answers to shift your life inertia.

The only impossible journey is the one you never begin.

—Tony Robbins, author and motivational speaker[1]

## Deconstructing Your Values

The most difficult aspect of answering the first question involves avoiding describing values that have high social desirability. I could, for example, list some common values—hard work, generosity, consideration, discipline, responsibility, commitment, faith, health—and almost everyone would say that they believe in and live by those values. Yet if most of us looked at how we actually live our lives, another set of vastly different values would likely present itself.

To truly understand what values guide your life inertia, you must deconstruct your values until you are able to clearly see what exactly you value and why you hold those values. Looking openly and honestly at the way you were raised is the first step in identifying the values with which you were instilled growing up. What were your parents' values that were impressed upon you—achievement, wealth, education, religion, status, independence, appearance? Think back to your childhood and ask yourself several questions:

1. What values were emphasized in the way your parents lived their lives?

2. What values were stressed in your family's day-to-day life?

3. What values were reflected in the way you were rewarded or punished?

You might even ask your parents to reflect back on your childhood to see what they perceived their values to be and what values they wanted to emphasize in your upbringing. Your next step in the deconstruction process involves looking at your present life and the values your life reflects. In responding to these questions, you should ask yourself what values underlie your answers. What do you do for a living—are you a corporate employee, business owner, teacher, salesperson, caterer, or social worker? This is a common question asked in social gatherings. Periodically people may become rather defensive in response to this question. They might say, "Who cares what I do? What I do is not who I am." I would suggest otherwise, at least to some degree. Assuming people have choices in their career paths, the one they choose reflects who they are and what they value. For example, though a bit of a generalization, it is probably safe to say that someone who becomes an investment banker has different values than someone who becomes an elementary schoolteacher. What those underlying values might be may vary, but one might assume that the investment banker values money, whereas the teacher values education and helping children.

Where you live—whether in a high-rise apartment in a city, in the suburbs, or in the country—is partially informed by your values. What values led you to where you live? The activities you engage in most—cultural, physical, religious, political, social—also reflect your values. Even what you talk about with others. Do you mostly talk about politics, religion, the economy, or other people? What does this tell you about your values?

Finally, perhaps the most telling question reflecting what you value is: what do you spend your money on—a home, cars, travel, clothing, education, art, charity? Because money is a limited resource for most of us, we will use it in ways that we value most. Over and above what we say and other indicators in our lives, where we spend our hard-earned money says the most about our values.

> Happiness is that state of consciousness which proceeds from the achievement of one's values.
>
> —Ayn Rand, Russian American writer and philosopher[2]

Once you've identified the values of your parents and the values you have now, you can then ask yourself whether your current values are the same as those you grew up with. Have you gone through a period of examination and reconsideration? Have you consciously chosen to discard some values from your upbringing and adopt new ones? My experience with people whose values aren't the guidance system of their life inertia is that their present values haven't changed since childhood. They never questioned the values they accepted early in their lives, even when those values guided their life inertia on an unhealthy trajectory. In contrast, those who intentionally choose their values and allow those values to direct their life inertia lead more meaningful, fulfilling, and happy lives.

Now that you have deconstructed your values and, perhaps for the first time, have a clear idea of what you value, you have more insight into what has been propelling your life inertia. You can see whether those values contribute to your dissatisfaction or bring you happiness. Look at which aspects of your life contribute to where you are right now—your career, relationships, lifestyle—and ask yourself what values underlie those parts of your life. For example, if your career in the business world makes you unhappy—no judgment intended, but many of my clients happen to come from corporate life—you need to ask yourself what values have led you to a career in business and examine how those values are presently guiding your life inertia in an unhealthy direction.

> If you . . . check in with yourself, to ask yourself, "What's really important?" you may find that some of the choices you are making are in conflict with your own stated goals.
>
> —Dr. Richard Carlson, author of *Don't Sweat the Small Stuff*

## The Influence of Societal Values on Life Inertia

A recurring theme throughout *Change Your Life's Direction* is that inadvertently buying into the values that predominate modern culture—"winning," wealth, power, appearance, and conspicuous consumption—is a leading cause of an unsatisfying life trajectory. The popular culture in America today no longer has the time, attention span, or energy to devote to weighty and deep issues such as values. It is much easier to focus on the superficial things in our culture. As such, the pursuit and accumulation of wealth and material goods has become a dominant value in much of our society. The underlying mistaken belief is that these values will guide us along a healthy life path.

Don't buy things you can't afford with money you don't have to impress people you don't like.

—Dave Ramsey, author, radio host, and businessman[4]

One of the most powerful ways in which these values are impressed on us is in how we define success and failure. Our parents and popular culture may have defined success and failure in a way that led us to develop values that are narrow and limiting, which ultimately guide us toward an unsatisfying life path. For example, much of American society defines success simplistically in terms of winning. Growing up, the message was that only one winner is possible and everyone else is automatically a loser. Society placed great emphasis on wealth, social status, physical appearance, and popularity as indicators of success—the more money and power you have and the more attractive and popular you are, the more successful you will be. Growing up with these definitions of success rendered it largely unattainable for the majority of us. At the same time, society made losing even more intolerable to contemplate—being poor, powerless, unattractive, and unpopular is simply unacceptable. With these restrictive definitions, many of us are left feeling caught in the untenable situation of having little opportunity for success and a great chance of failure, yet receiving the message that we should still be successful.

As children, many of us were sold a "pig in a poke." We were told that success was in that bag, but we weren't experienced enough to know to actually open the bag and look to see what was really inside—if we had, we would have seen an unhappy life inertia. Nonetheless, we may have believed our parents and society. Why shouldn't we? If we can't trust our parents, who can we trust? As for society, if so many people say that is the best life trajectory to take, can they be wrong? Many of us bought into those values and goals and worked mightily to achieve them. What are we left with now? Sure, we may have succeeded, but the achievement is likely empty and the direction our lives are headed is not where we really want to go.

Blindly accepting society's narrow definitions of success and failure took away control of our life's guidance system. Rather than choosing definitions based on our own values, we bought into these limiting definitions that forced us along a life course not of our choosing nor in our best interests. Although we may have become successful in the eyes of society, we often really don't feel like a success. And this trajectory in our lives has certainly not brought us happiness.

Make yourselves sheep and the wolves will eat you.

—Benjamin Franklin, a founding father of the
United States of America[5]

## Reconstructing Your Values

It is one thing to finally recognize what values have guided you along an unhappy life trajectory. It is an entirely different thing to understand what values actually will direct you to a new and healthy life inertia. This process requires reconstruction of your values so that they actively guide you onto a more positive life path.

There are several questions you can ask yourself to help you figure out what values will make you happy. First, what do you *choose* to do in your life? Assuming that you choose activities in your life freely, specifying what they are is a first step in identifying the values that bring you happiness. Even if you can't choose all of your activities, select a few that you can control, such as cultural, spiritual, or athletic activities. Second, what activities do you find you have great passion for and bring you true joy? There is no better clue to what you deeply value than activities such as these.

Having answered these questions, you can now dig beneath the surface of those activities and identify the values that underlie them. One client, a business consultant, had enjoyed photography since childhood, but his parents had discouraged him from pursuing it in greater depth. Upon recognizing that he wasn't happy in his current life and being asked to answer these two questions, he realized that his love of photography was the only thing in his life that had kept him sane. Through careful consideration of his values, he learned that the inspiration of creating, the physical expression of his ideas, and the challenge of pushing himself to the limits of his creativity were fundamental values that he was never able to express in his career in consulting. With this insight—this epiphany, as he said—he was able to more actively pursue this passion with greater clarity and purpose. For the first time in his life, he found a sense of purpose, balance, and contentment.

An important part of this reconstruction process is to reframe success and failure in a way that is consistent with your true values. Success can be redefined as setting and achieving goals that express and affirm your values. Conversely, failure can be seen as either not achieving those self-affirming goals or achieving goals that are not consistent with your values, even if achieving those goals makes you successful in other people's eyes. With these new definitions, you can now succeed without winning and fail without losing.

> I am the master of my fate: I am the captain of my soul.
>
> —William Ernest Henley, English poet[6]

## Living Your Values

You may be thinking, "This whole reconstruction thing is pretty easy." But recognizing the values you were raised with and coming to understand the values that make you happy are the easy parts. The real challenge is using your values as your life's guidance system and allowing them to redirect your life inertia. Your life up to the present may be causing you dissatisfaction and unhappiness, but it is nonetheless familiar, predictable, and, in a perverse sort of way, comfortable because you've gotten used to it. You have lived this way for many years, your life habits are deeply ingrained, and your life inertia is powerful and difficult to change.

Living your life in accordance with these newly identified values that make you happy means discarding values, beliefs, habits, and ways of living that you have identified with for most of your adult life. However unhappy you may feel now, the prospect of altering your life inertia and the uncertainty and instability that accompanies it can be intimidating, if not downright terrifying. At some point, you must come to believe that the direction your life is heading now is no longer acceptable. You just need to decide that enough is enough and that it is time for a change. Once you make that commitment, you will have exerted the first great force on your life inertia and begun the process of changing its course. From then on, learning to live your new values will be a bit easier. It will also be easier because living your values is self-rewarding and self-perpetuating; participating in activities and experiences that are consistent with your life-affirming values will bring you freedom, fulfillment, and happiness. In other words, you just plain feel good.

> Change might not be fast and it isn't always easy. But with time and effort, almost any habit can be reshaped.
>
> —Charles Duhigg, Pulitzer Prize–winning journalist[7]

Once you make the commitment to allow your most deeply held values to act as the guidance system of your life, you need to decide how much of a change you want to make in your life. A part of you would probably like to throw your entire life away and start fresh, perhaps on a tropical island in the South Pacific or in a mountain cabin in Idaho. But living your newly realized values does not necessarily mean a radical shift in your life trajectory (i.e., discarding your old life entirely) and choosing a new life path that is 90 degrees or more from its current direction. The reality is that few people can dramatically alter their basic life course; they are just too invested in it in too many ways. Few people can afford to quit their jobs and become starving artists or some such equivalent. But that does not mean that you can't make meaningful change in your life and alter its course just enough for it to be heading in a healthy new direction. You also have to recognize that a small change in direction now can lead to exponential change the farther you travel in your life. So it might very well be that a seemingly minor shift in the direction of your life trajectory may result in additional forces being applied to your life down the road that may lead to an accumulative greater change in direction as time goes by.

Living your values means placing greater emphasis on and making a greater commitment to activities, experiences, and people that express those values. It also involves creating balance in your life. I use the metaphor of scales to help illustrate this idea of balance. For years, your "life scales" have been weighted heavily toward the values that you adopted from your parents and our popular culture. This imbalance may have brought you some benefits, such as material success, but it has also guided you along a life path that is not fulfilling your most basic needs or allowing you to live a life in accordance with your most deeply held values. Living your values means reducing the weight of the values you grew up with and those you may have accepted from our culture and placing greater weight on the side of the scale that holds your new, life-affirming values. By doing so, you take your life's guidance system out of the hands of the unhealthy values and place it in the control of values that will lead you along a much healthier and happier life path.

> You have the capacity to believe and have faith in your own abilities. It is your responsibility, however, to develop that faith by making a commitment.
>
> —Dr. Robert Nideffer, sports psychologist[8]

A friend of mine, Andy, has always had a fascination with physics. As a child and teenager, he read about the great physicists and explored theories of physics. But Andy's father discouraged him from pursuing the study of physics by saying that the only way to make a decent living as a physicist was to be Stephen Hawking. In college, Andy majored in prelaw and then graduated from a prestigious law school, all the while wishing he could study to become a high school physics teacher. In the ensuing twenty years, Andy established a successful law practice but was profoundly unfulfilled and unhappy. Recently, while maintaining my role as his friend, I shared with him my views about life inertia and the importance of basing one's life trajectory on our most fundamental values. Andy realized that what he loved most about physics was the challenge of understanding the theories and making them understandable to others. He also recognized that he has always wanted to help young people but had been doing so only by donating money to educational programs.

Andy knew it was time to regain control of his life's guidance system and allow it to be directed by his deepest values. At the same time, he realized that he couldn't just quit his job and become a high school physics teacher. Andy had a family to support and a somewhat lavish lifestyle that he enjoyed—the proverbial "golden handcuffs." So he found a way to balance his family and career with activities that fit his newly realized values. Andy enrolled in a physics class in an adult-learning program at a nearby university. He also volunteered to tutor high school students one night a week. Finally, he signed up for a one-week stint as a counselor at a summer science camp. I saw Andy recently. I have never seen him so happy and at peace!

People rarely succeed unless they have fun in what they are doing.

—Dale Carnegie, author and lecturer[9]

# Part II

# SELF-ESTEEM:
# THE PILOT THAT STEERS YOU

Needs act as the foundation of our self-esteem. Think back to the list of needs at the beginning of part I. The way in which those needs are satisfied determines the quality of our self-esteem. If our needs were met in a healthy and timely way, we feel loved, worthwhile, safe, capable, and in control, all of which are key contributors to healthy self-esteem. From this foundation of self-esteem, our emotional life is grounded in positive and manageable emotions that further encourage and buttress a strong sense of self-esteem.

In contrast, if our needs weren't met in a healthy way and those needs coalesced into *NEEDS!*, then we likely will feel unloved, unworthy, insecure, incompetent, and out of control, which are all detrimental to self-esteem. These feelings also create an emotional life that is grounded in negativity and experienced as chaotic and unwieldy. This impact on self-esteem is where the real harm of *NEEDS!* occurs. Our *NEEDS!* produce deep-seated and harmful perceptions and feelings about ourselves and the world. Their impact is long lasting and injurious from that moment forward.

> Accept yourself, love yourself, and keep moving forward. If you want to fly, you have to give up what weighs you down.
>
> —Roy T. Bennett, author of *The Light in the Heart*[1]

## What Is Self-esteem?

When people are asked to define self-esteem, most say something like "It's how you feel about yourself." Do you like yourself? Do you feel like you are a good person? Do you feel valued by others and worthy of love and respect? Those with healthy self-esteem feel worthwhile, loved, and appreciated by others. These supportive self-perceptions enable us to:

- Establish and be guided by deeply held values

- Make and commit to sound decisions

- Live in the present without regretting the past or worrying about the future

- View ourselves as competent people

- Embrace the entirety of our emotional lives (both supportive and detrimental feelings)

- Gain pleasure and enjoyment out of life pursuits

- Empathize with others

In contrast, those of us with low self-esteem don't believe we are worthwhile and don't feel loved or valued by others. These damaging self-perceptions produce diametrically opposed reactions as we become:

- Highly self-critical

- Overly sensitive to critical feedback from others

- Indecisive

- People pleasers

- Overwhelmed with guilt and shame

- Generally pessimistic in our view of life

- Poorly reactive to obstacles, setbacks, and failures

Self-esteem is made up of two essential components. The first part of self-esteem is our perception that we are loved, valued, and appreciated by parents or other significant people in our lives. The sense of security and the "I'm okay no matter what I do" attitude that comes from these feelings serve as the foundation for a healthy self-esteem. People who grew up with this sense of security know that, regardless of what they do or what happens, they will still be loved and valued. As a result, they can express love and value toward themselves.

We also know that there are people to whom we can turn to protect us when we are at risk or feeling vulnerable. This "anchor" encourages those of us with healthy self-esteem to confidently explore our world, take risks, and test our limits. Knowing that we are loved and valued by others, no matter the outcome, and that others will protect us from harm acts as the foundation for our self-esteem. However, this sense of love and security alone is not sufficient to build strong and resilient self-esteem.

The second essential part of self-esteem involves the development of a sense of competence and mastery over our lives. Masten and Coatsworth (1998) found that competence can be defined in broad or narrow ways. Broadly speaking, competence refers to a person successfully achieving expected developmental milestones (e.g., toilet training, language acquisition, and social skills). From a narrower perspective, competence addresses attainment in terms of specific areas of achievement, such as education or career. This latter sense of competence is based on several aspects of the person. In its most basic form, competence is derived from our belief that our actions matter. In other words, when we act, we expect certain outcomes will result (e.g., when we do good things, then good things happen, or when we do bad things, then bad things happen). We also know that when we do nothing, nothing happens. A sense of competence develops when we believe that we have the capabilities necessary to have control over ourselves and our world.

> I am my own experiment. I am my own work of art.
>
> —Madonna, queen of pop music[2]

Having a foundation of genuine, deeply rooted self-esteem gives us the confidence to challenge ourselves, to find satisfaction and validation in our efforts, and to push the limits of our capabilities. This combination of the grounding in feeling loved and secure with the desire to explore one's abilities, which comes from a strong sense of competence, acts as the true source of self-esteem.

> Positive self-esteem is important because when people experience it, they feel good and look good, they are effective and productive, and they respond to other people and themselves in healthy, positive, growing ways. People who have positive self-esteem know that they are lovable and capable, and they care about themselves and other people.
>
> —Jean Illsley Clarke, author of *Self-Esteem: A Family Affair*[3]

## Self-esteem and Life Inertia

Unfortunately, those of us with low self-esteem often steer our lives toward an unhealthy life trajectory. Moreover, the direction that our lives take is piloted by insecurity. We have the need to protect the little self-worth we have and prove to ourselves and others that we are worthwhile people.

Paradoxically, we can be successful despite the challenges of having low self-esteem. Unfortunately, this result is most often accomplished through power, control, manipulation, ingratiation, intimidation, and denigration. We usually become successful by the sheer force of our need to show ourselves and others that we aren't worthless or incompetent people. Sadly, whatever level of success we achieve is rarely accompanied by meaning, fulfillment, happiness, or connection, thus making our achievements Pyrrhic victories.

In contrast, when we have healthy self-esteem, we pilot our lives based on a strong sense of self-worth, faith in our abilities, confidence in the quality of our efforts, satisfaction gained from those efforts, the healthy relationships we nurture, and the support we provide to others.

> Successful people have fear, successful people have doubts, and successful people have worries. They just don't let those feelings stop them.
>
> —T. Harv Eker, author, businessman, and motivational speaker[4]

## CHAPTER THREE
# BRIGHTEST STAR IN THE GALAXY
## From False Self to True Self

*True self /troō selfl:* The part of a person's psyche that consists of his or her fundamental virtues, values, attitudes, and capabilities, which supports a meaningful, healthy, and happy life.

As we grow up, all of us experience the discovery of our identities, development of our personalities, and growth of who we are and what we will become. This developmental process is similar to building a house. In this case, the brick and mortar of our *self* includes genetic predispositions and the influences of different levels of society—parents and family, peers and immediate social world, schools and communities, and the larger culture of society as communicated through its many forms of media.

Given the importance of the self in our lives, it's unfortunate that we have little or no influence over what self is created. Instead, we internalize and grow toward becoming the messages we are exposed to most often when we are young and not yet "conscious" or deliberate beings. In fact, we are at the mercy of whatever forces are most dominant in our lives. Those forces dictate what pilots our lives and steers the trajectory that our lives take. If those forces are positive and healthy, a *true self* develops that cultivates growth, maturity, and strength. If those forces are negative and defeating, a *false self* emerges that restricts development and fosters stagnation, immaturity, and weakness.

> Until you make the unconscious conscious, it will direct your life and you will call it fate.
>
> —Carl Jung, founder of analytical psychology[1]

## Construction of the False Self

As we all know, there are often barriers or setbacks in the construction of a house, such as the use of substandard materials or poor construction methods. As a result, the house either may not be completed or is shaky, unstable, and offers little protection from inclement weather. Similarly, poor construction of a person's self is a danger and often results for children who are raised in an environment of insecurity, fear, and emotional isolation.

> From the moment of birth you are programmed to become a human being, but always as defined by your culture and your parents and your educators.
>
> —R. D. Laing, psychiatrist[2]

This usurping of the self occurs when the construction of the true self is halted and the creation of a false self begins. In their well-intended, though misguided, attempts to ensure that their children are successful, parents can neglect children's most fundamental needs (leading to the emergence of *NEEDS!*) and instill values, attitudes, and beliefs that oppose and suppress the true self. All of a sudden, these parents change the construction plans and use different materials to complete the house. This radical change causes the internalization of unhealthy values, defeating attitudes, contradictory beliefs—unattainable expectations, valuing results, and a need to be perfect—and self-esteem becomes attached to these unhealthy views. This shift in the foundation of self-esteem results in a false self that is in direct conflict with the true self.

When the false self becomes the pilot of our lives, it steers us away from the direction of our true self. Over time, we slowly and inexorably lose touch with parts of ourselves that are essential for a meaningful, fulfilling, and happy life. Dr. Barbara De Angelis, the author of *Real Moments*,[3] identifies where these pieces go: "Some of them were taken away by our parents or caretakers, in an attempt to turn us into what they thought we should be. Some of them we've given away to others in an attempt to be accepted or loved. Some of them we've hidden away, frightened of what others might think if they knew our secret selves. And some of them we've simply forgotten about, because we've been trying so hard to be something other than who we really are."

> And then the horror of it all is that we become hooked on this learning, and we begin to equate the learning with us. Here we are, ourselves, and then onto that self we pile thousands and thousands of things that may not indeed be ourselves, but rather belong to our families, our cultures, our friends and so on and so forth. We take them with us, and then they become us.
>
> —Dr. Leo Buscaglia, author of *Living, Loving, and Learning*[4]

As previously mentioned, parents play a central role in the emergence of the self in their children. At the same time, the impact of society and culture on the development of the self has grown exponentially with the proliferation of the internet. It has become a constant and intense presence in our lives.

The messages that society communicates to children can conflict with their true self and further strengthen the false self that is fostered by the unhealthy attitudes taught by parents. Whether it's the importance of wealth and power, being handsome or beautiful, or being thin, children are often unable to avoid internalizing these powerful negative messages. Children can be overwhelmed with the construction of this unhealthy false self, particularly if these internalizations are consistent with their parents' messages. The need to gain love from their parents *and* to be accepted by society causes the true self to be pushed far into the background of children's psyches. As a result, the false self comes to the fore and asserts control.

> There is a Faustian drama all about us in this world of role playing. Everywhere we see people have sold their souls (or their real selves).
>
> —Dr. Sidney Jourard, author of *The Transparent Self* [5]

Due to external pressures, children repress their true self with its positive values, attitudes, beliefs, and healthy needs, which allows their false self with its faulty judgments, rigid rules, and dangerous prohibitions to gain dominance. Doing anything but surrendering to their false self would cause them to have to face the painful realization that their parents may not love them for who they are and that their society does not accept or value them. Ironically, a child accepts the preeminence of the false self to relieve this fundamental pain; yet this "choice that really isn't a choice" leads to a life filled with other unceasing pain.

The false self puts children in a position of weakness and deficit. They live in a constant state of vulnerability and are driven by a strong need to relieve that feeling of helplessness. In a sense, these children are always playing catch-up. The primary goal becomes to simply maintain a tolerable level of self-worth and respect from others. All of their efforts are devoted to pushing away their feelings of inadequacy to replace it with a minimally acceptable feeling about themselves.

Once parents have completed construction of their children's false selves, they no longer need to dangle the carrot of love and acceptance. Instead, that conditional love and acceptance become the child's own, and the false self offers its own unreachable carrot to the child. Having established supremacy over the true self, the false self creates a life inertia that meets its most basic *NEEDS!* at an early age. The false self strives to avoid failure, feel competent, and gain love and acceptance from others and of themselves. As these children transition to adulthood, the life inertia that is created by the false self leads children down a path that will certainly lack meaning, satisfaction, happiness, and connectedness.

> The reward for conformity is that everyone likes you but yourself.
>
> —Rita Mae Brown, America author[6]

## Who Is the False Self?

The false self is composed of a set of qualities, rules, and a belief system that were imposed on Inertials by their parents and the broader culture when they were young. By understanding the components of the false self, we are better able to wrap our arms around the impact on our life inertias, break it down into more manageable pieces, and slowly remove its ability to pilot our lives in a direction we don't wish to go.

### Qualities of the False Self

Though a false self is created in every person based on their unique circumstances, experiences, and interactions, there are some shared characteristics common to all of them. Most notable of these qualities is an overinvestment in everything they do because their self-esteem is excessively linked their life's activities. As a result, almost all of their activities—from the mundane to the outlandish—are imbued with the word *too*: they care *too* much, it is *too* important to them, or they try *too* hard. To those of us observing these individuals, this overinvestment often borders on the absurd. One client was so invested in everything she did that if she didn't brush her teeth that well or get the dishes as clean as she could, she felt bad about herself.

Though this is an extreme example, those with a false self look for any opportunity to validate their value as people.

The false self is insatiably hungry for competence and love. Inertials can never stop trying to gain competence and love because ceasing their efforts would admit that they are, in fact, as worthless and undeserving as their false self keeps telling them. So every moment of their waking lives (and often in their dreams while they sleep) is devoted to satisfying a hunger that the false self will never allow to be sated. What makes it trickier is that there are momentary periods of satisfaction and relief when an Inertial meets the internalized expectations. This relief is fleeting because the false self always needs more, more, more! Good effort and excellence by most people's standards are never good enough. Only off-the-charts determination and perfection are sufficient to provide even the briefest moments of self-validation for Inertials.

The false self is also driven maniacally to satisfy its most basic *NEED!*—to gain self-affirmation. This drive is boundless and extends well beyond reason, goals, or purpose. A common example are the people who are workaholics. They work far beyond the point of productivity or efficiency and are certain that the only way they will be successful is by devoting more and more time to their work. They simply *must* succeed to feel any sense of self-worth, and they are driven to do anything in order to be successful.

Ironically, the false self is not driven to succeed. Rather, people with a false self are fundamentally driven to avoid failure. More basic than feeling successful, their every effort is directed toward not feeling that they are failures. All of their achievements are attempts at gaining constant validation that they are not what they fear the most: failures unworthy of love, respect, and value from themselves or others.

The false self is emotionally disabled. Those with a false self attempt to avoid their emotions at all costs as a way of anesthetizing their emotional pain. They come to fear their emotions because of the discomfort they have caused in their lives. People with a false self have little awareness or understanding of their emotional lives. They deny, repress, or displace their emotions in order to maintain their psychological equilibrium. Unfortunately, avoiding their negative emotions also precludes them from experiencing positive emotions such as joy, happiness, and contentment.

The false self is needy. Since it cannot give love to itself, it must reach out to others and gain their love. People with a false self become dependent on others and can need others the way drug addicts need their fix. This need can be so great that they will go to any length to gain the love that they crave. They can become desperate and indiscriminate regarding those from whom they get their love and in what form that love is given.

The false self is a miser; it must defend and protect what it has because the false self feels inadequate. Its goal is to minimize its deficit and ensure that it doesn't grow larger. It has little to give to others. The false self is unable to open up to others and can only take in a relationship.

The false self is rigid and dichotomous in its approach to life. Because the false self is fundamentally insecure, it must create a predictable and controllable world in which to live. To protect itself, the false self constructs an uncomplicated world that can be neither confusing nor overwhelming. By seeing the world as black and white, the false self simplifies life while simultaneously limiting the freedom to choose, experience, and grow.

The false self is extreme in every way. It has no boundaries that allow for balance or moderation. It has no understanding of appropriate limits in how people think, feel, or behave. Its most powerful need is to protect self-esteem, and it will take any steps to fulfill that need, no matter how excessive or unreasonable. This is why people with a false self often exhibit inflexible and dogmatic thinking, express strong and unsuitable emotions, and behave in ways that may be seen as socially inappropriate.

People guided by a false self are often reluctant to cut their losses and get out of bad situations. They may stay in a marriage well beyond the point of there being any redeeming value in it. They may remain in a job that is no longer challenging or rewarding. To them, it is far better to stay in something that is unhealthy than to admit failure. By having to admit failure by leaving, they would be admitting that *they* are failures. The admission of failure is much more painful than the discomfort they may feel by staying in a bad relationship or an unsatisfying job because failure is equivalent to being unworthy of love.

People with a false self are often "constellation" people. They surround themselves with many people and are often part of a large social group. Since they are unable to gain quality love—a deep and lasting love from themselves or those with whom they are close— they seek out a larger quantity of love as a substitute. These people rely on the multiplicative principle, which means that a lot of small amounts add up to one big amount. Because they perceive themselves as being unable to get the love of important people in their lives (themselves and their parents), they get a little love from many people in an effort to fill that void. Unfortunately, the multiplicative principle doesn't work with love. These small and superficial doses of love from many cannot replace the rich and affirming love from an important few.

Those with a false self are either givers or takers. The primary role for givers in their relationships is to please people in their lives. In a way, they surrender to the fact that they are not worthy of love and must earn love. People with false selves don't believe that they are worthy of love simply for who they are. By pleasing others, givers believe that others will feel obligated to love them for all that they are being given. Unfortunately, trying to please so many people in order to receive the love that they need often results in givers over-extending themselves. They don't end up pleasing anyone, including themselves.

Takers are the opposite of givers. They are often angry people who feel entitled to love and will take whatever love they feel they deserve. If people won't give them the love they deserve, takers will get respect through intimidation, fear, or control. Takers often express scorn at others to prove that the takers don't need them, despite the fact that takers are actually angry at the others for not giving them the love that they so crave. What takers don't realize is that their attempts to co-opt love from others through force actually undermines any possibility that they will gain the love that they yearn for and deserve. They don't understand that love can't be taken—it can only be given freely. They also don't realize that no one wants to give love to someone who is angry and spiteful.

The worst loneliness is to not be comfortable with yourself.

—Mark Twain, author of *The Adventures of Huckleberry Finn*[7]

### Belief System of the False Self

People with false selves have beliefs that weaken their true selves, perpetuate their false selves, and hinder their ability to find meaning, fulfillment, happiness, and connection in their lives. Most common among these beliefs is that they are unworthy and unhappy because they lack something fundamental that makes them worthy of love. They believe that they are inherently flawed in some way and this deficiency ensures that they will never be good enough to be loved.

Because the standards they set for themselves are unreachable, the false selves cause people to view themselves as failures who are not deserving of love. In fact, those with false selves not only don't think that they are worthy of love but also believe they are incapable of love because they didn't receive genuine and unconditional love from their parents. Because it has not experienced true love, the false self can't show, give, or receive love for itself.

The false self believes the person is a *human doing* who is only worthy of love if he or she is successful (more about a human doing in chapter 4). The human doing never finds peace because he or she must constantly be working, achieving, and accomplishing in order to feel self-love or the love of others.

The false self believes people are unacceptably imperfect and will constantly fail to live up to the internalized expectations of parents and society. In order to receive love—from society, from their parents, and from themselves—people controlled by their false self must meet the impossibly high standards that have become their own. This becomes a self-perpetuating cycle. They keep trying to succeed despite falling short of these unrealistic expectations because they can't admit failure without acknowledging their most fundamental fears.

Because of these perceived flaws, people with a false self believe that they are the cause of their difficulties. They feel wholly—and unreasonably—responsible for anything that befalls them. If a relationship turns bad, it is something that they have done and the other person has no culpability in the problems that have arisen. Difficulties at work are due to their incompetence. This perception leads them to take blame for any problems without consideration of other people or circumstances that may have contributed. Every problem that arises is further evidence demonstrating what they (and everyone else) have known all along—they are useless and unlovable people. They have thoughts like "This just proves how worthless I am."

Because of their fundamental perceived inadequacy, they feel they deserve the bad things that happen to them. When bad things happen, they accept them as their lot in life. After a time of frustration and perhaps rage against their life, they despair of it getting better and surrender to what they see as the inevitable—a life of dissatisfaction and unhappiness.

Despite the belief that they are the cause of their problems, the false self also believes that people have little control over their lives and little ability to change their lives. The only control the false self believes it has is the ability to act on its belief and maintain a basic equilibrium in which the person is able to function and meet the false self's most immediate needs. The false self is helpless to alter this unfortunate fate or to make a significant change toward happiness and contentment.

These beliefs cause people with a false self to view the world in a pessimistic light. They think, "Well, nothing has ever worked out before. Why should things change?" This defeatist attitude creates a self-fulfilling prophecy in which they actively or passively ensure that things don't work out, even when—with just a modicum of hope and determination—good things could happen. So their life inertia is perpetuated by the very beliefs, emotions, and actions that will keep them on that continuing trajectory of unhappiness.

> Low self-esteem is like driving through life with your hand-brake on.
>
> —Maxwell Maltz, best-selling author of *Psycho-cybernetics*[8]

## Rules of the False Self

People with a false self follow a set of unconscious rules that govern how they think, what they feel, and how they behave and interact with others in order to meet the needs of the false self—to feel competent, to gain love from others, to minimize emotional pain, and to protect self-esteem. Unfortunately, this creates a sort of "autopilot" state that maintains their life inertia. Those with a false self are largely unaware of these rules and become victims of their life inertia.

These rules are directed toward satisfying each false self's *NEEDS!* in the context of their own unique upbringing and life circumstances. At the same time, my work with many people with a false self suggests that there are some rules that appear to be shared.

*Rule 1: I must succeed in order to be worthy of love.* This rule drives people to incessantly avoid failure and achieve success. This allows them to feel valued and loved by themselves and others. It also serves as a constant reminder of their fundamental worthlessness and their need to achieve. To quote a client, "If I hadn't accomplished everything I needed to at the end of the day, I felt terrible about myself."

*Rule 2: Nothing is ever good enough.* This rule also pushes those with a false self to relentlessly reach for a level of success—and distance further from failure—that will make them feel worthy of love. This rule never allows for a moment of respite from the drive to achieve. They have set impossible standards, yet can never acknowledge that their expectations are unreasonable. Remember, to do so would be to admit that they are, in fact, worthless. Another client told me, "No matter what I achieved, my father made me feel like it wasn't good enough. My life was devoted to proving to him that I was good enough and I did deserve his love."

*Rule 3: I have to be better than anyone else.* People with a false self think they are special but in a perverse way. Unlike many people who think they are special and deserve preferential treatment, those with a false self feel they are below others and don't deserve even normal treatment. Thus, all of their efforts are directed toward earning the right to be treated by others with even a minimal level of respect. "I felt like everyone was smarter, more talented, fitter, or more attractive than me. I was always feeling like I had to play catch-up," a third client stated.

*Rule 4: To love myself, I must be loved by others.* Because people with a false self are incapable of loving themselves, they seek love from others. When they do receive love from someone else, this "booster shot" allows for the briefest of moments in which they can love themselves. Inevitably, the temporary self-love passes and they must again seek out love from others in a never-ending cycle.

*Rule 5: I can show no emotions.* Many people with a false self grew up in families in which healthy expression of emotion was neither acceptable nor present. They learned that emotions were a sign of weakness. Expressing emotions caused them to feel vulnerable and insecure. Because one of our fundamental needs is to protect our self-esteem, those with a false self could not allow themselves to risk exposure to this pain through emotional expression. To remember this rule, one client kept a brick on her desk to represent how she had to be and would say "I am a brick" whenever she felt threatened.

*Rule 6: I can change the rules to ensure that I can't win.* People with a false self are so set in the trajectory of their life inertia that they will do anything to satisfy their *NEEDS!* and maintain that course. Even when opportunities present themselves that would enable them to "win," those with a false self alter their rules so that they ensure that they lose. Yet another client said, "No matter how much I thought I wanted to change my life, I would always work things out so I kept making the same stupid mistakes."

> The real difficulty is to overcome how you think about yourself.
>
> —Maya Angelou, best-selling author, poet, and
> civil rights activist[9]

## Consequences of Letting the False Self Pilot Your Life

The belief system of the false self has a direct impact on how people interact with the world around them. Although the false self is without bounds in its demands, it provides people with a very limited view of themselves, the world, and their future. These limitations are meant to protect them from the enormous potential for harm that they believe they might suffer. By keeping themselves in a circumscribed environment, people with a false self can maintain control of their lives and reduce their chances of further hurt and threat to self-esteem.

People who are guided by the false self live in a perpetual state of threat. All of their thoughts, emotions, and actions are directed toward protecting themselves from experiencing failure and not feeling loved or valued. Because ill feelings are just a step behind them, those with a false self must be ever vigilant to the ongoing perceived threat. This "on alert" state eliminates any opportunity for experiencing lasting peace and contentment.

The weight that those with a false self carry on their shoulders takes a toll on their physical life. This burdensome stress acts to wear the body down in several ways. First, people with a false self often suffer from a lack of rest caused by poor sleep habits. In addition, the liability of the false self can impact one's level of physical activity, such that the person either becomes sedentary (often in response to depression) or develops exercise addictions (in an attempt to validate their fragile self-esteem). Either way, there are physical risks. For those who are inactive, there is higher risk of developing hypertension and coronary disease. For those who are excessively active, injuries are common. Often, the stress associated with having a false self can lead to the development of an unhealthy relationship with food in which they overeat (to placate themselves) or undereat (to gain control of themselves). In this sense, the immediate and long-term implications of the stress of having a false self in terms of obesity and eating disorders, respectively, cannot be overstated.

Trust is a big issue for people with a false self. If they are givers, they tend to be too trusting of people because they need regular doses of love from others to maintain a minimal level of good feeling about themselves. Givers have few boundaries with others and are willing to give well beyond what is appropriate and healthy. This situation often results in an over-reliance on others and leaves givers vulnerable to being taken advantage of by those who misuse that trust.

By contrast, people with a false self who are takers have little or no trust in others and assume that other people will only hurt them. Takers have very rigid boundaries that attempt to protect them from harm. Unfortunately, those boundaries also act to keep people away from them and stop others from fully trusting them. As a result, takers are often unable to develop close and affirming relationships.

In either case, the fundamental problem is that people with a false self don't trust themselves. Since they don't truly believe that they are competent and lovable people, they question themselves and others. They never have faith in their own decisions or the intentions of others. The end result is that they keep others out and become trapped in a life created by their false self.

Though people with a false self sometimes achieve a high level of success, they feel that they have no real ownership of what they do—almost as if they are "on the outside looking in" on their own lives. Often, these individuals feel that they didn't really choose their career path; rather, it was thrust upon them by their family or culture, they fell into it because they showed some competence in the area, or it satisfied some need of their false self (e.g., wealth or social status). Those with a false self often don't feel invested and engaged in their work. As one client described it, "I feel like I am just going through the motions." They are often good at what they do; yet they don't believe it and gain little satisfaction or joy out of their efforts or accomplishments. It is as if they are observers who watch themselves achieve success rather than being fully active participants in their lives.

Because of this lack of connection with their work, people with a false self feel an ongoing dissatisfaction and frustration with their lives. A common indication of this lack of ownership and persistent angst is the presence of "escapist" fantasies in which they frequently fantasize about leaving their job, selling everything, and moving somewhere peaceful and stress free. Though escapist fantasies are normal and healthy diversions from the pressures of everyday life, they can cause greater unhappiness if they become frequent. When those with a false self experience "escapist" fantasies, they are confronted with the painful juxtaposition of their current life reality versus their ultimate desire.

People with a false self recapitulate their past relationships and conflicts in their present ones, thereby maintaining their life inertia. Many with a false self come to recognize that they are unhappy and something unhealthy is piloting their life. They may take steps to uncover the source of their unhappiness, whether through introspection, self-discovery seminars, self-help reading, psychotherapy, or religious exploration. They may even make attempts to alter their life inertia and break free of self-defeating patterns that have plagued them in the past. In these attempts, they construct and try to correct past conflicted relationships, such as those with their parents, through current relationships. More often than not, however, people with a false self are unable to break the inertial pull of their life trajectory since they do not understand the forces that have propelled their life inertia—their false self and its rules that guide them.

Perhaps the most profound aspect of having a false self is the inescapable feelings of loneliness and emptiness. People with a false self may surround themselves with friends and acquaintances; yet they often feel disconnected and isolated, even in a crowd, because they do not feel fully invested in or connected to their lives. This lack of engagement causes a vague yet gnawing feeling of disconnection and lack of purpose.

Finally, people who are directed by their false self feel trapped in their life inertia. Their life is stuck on a course not of their choosing and they experience few healthy changes and little growth. They often feel like victims of their own lives and feel powerless to change them. As a result, they simply resign themselves to their life inertia and try to make the most of the path to which they are inextricably bound. Thus they are propelled through life on a course not of their liking and feel incapable of altering that course.

> Until you value yourself, you won't value your time. Until you value your time, you will not do anything with it.

> —M. Scott Peck, author and psychiatrist[10]

## Construction of the True Self

Ideally, all of the materials that are used as we develop early in our lives are of the highest quality and complement each other. Subsequently, the "construction process" proceeds smoothly and on schedule. What results is the creation of our true self, which is strong, stable, and resilient to the elements, like a well-constructed house. The true self is composed of materials that foster our values, attitudes, and beliefs, which ultimately pilot our lives in a certain direction. According to Dr. Daniel Goleman,[11] "The capacity to be true, as the saying has it, 'to thine own self,' allows acting in accord with one's deepest feelings and values no matter what the social consequences."

The construction of the true self occurs when parents expose their children to values, beliefs, and attitudes that are consistent with the true self. These parents have a healthy perspective on what kind of children they want to raise and understand what it will take to cultivate the emergence of their children's true self. This growth process encourages the internalization of constructive beliefs and attitudes—unconditional love, acceptance of imperfection, the value of effort—in which self-esteem becomes grounded in the qualities most important to the true self.

The true self allows children to assume a position of strength and abundance. They are confident in their self-worth, and this belief enables them to explore and take risks. Since their starting point is one of inherent value, they feel free to challenge themselves and grow. These children naturally strive to do their best with a primary goal to figure out their capabilities. All of their efforts are dedicated to building on the solid foundation of self-esteem that they already possess, as well as finding their untapped abilities.

When parents have finished their efforts in constructing their children's true self, around the time the child is moving from adolescence to adulthood, the true self becomes an independent entity that no longer needs parents to grow further. The values, attitudes, and beliefs that parents taught to their children become the children's own, and the true self becomes the place where love and validation are derived. Having rooted itself in children's psyches, the true self creates a life inertia at an early age that promotes the positive and life-affirming forces received from their parents and uses those forces to propel them along a healthy life trajectory. The true self can then pilot children's lives freely and without doubt, worry, or fear in a direction that both reflects and reinforces their true self.

The greatest thing in the world is to know how to belong to oneself.

—Michel de Montaigne, French Renaissance philosopher[12]

## Who Is the True Self?

The true self is composed of certain qualities, a belief system, and a set of rules that are inherent in every person. The true self lies at the core of who we are and who we can become. Unfortunately for many people, the true self gets buried so deeply under layers of a false self imposed upon them that they often don't believe that the true self still exists. Although the true self can be suppressed, it cannot be "killed." By understanding the true self, you can reconnect with it, empower it to reemerge from its imprisonment, push back against the false self, and reassert your true self on your life.

What lies behind us and what lies before us are tiny matters compared to what lies within us.

—Henry Stanley Haskins, businessman and Wall Street trader[13]

### Qualities of the True Self

Though there are unique aspects of the true self in each individual that derive from their particular upbringings, the true self possesses several qualities that seem to be universal. The true self allows these common attributes to emerge and grow in you.

The true self loves unconditionally. Love is given freely and generously to you by the true self. The true self doesn't barter or make love dependent on your actions. By living in accordance with the healthy values it has internalized, the true self accepts you for who you are and encourages you to become whom you aspire to be. Since you are confident in being loved by yourself and others, your self-esteem is grounded in unconditional love and is strong, stable, and resilient.

The true self is happy. Because the true self loves unconditionally, there is no fear of losing that love or pressure to gain that love.

As the cause of most unhappiness, this weight is lifted from you and it frees you to respond to life openly and without caution. You are able to find joy in all of life's many facets, risk failure when needed, and accept failure and sadness as well as success and joy with perspective and equanimity.

The true self accepts your imperfections. Mistakes and failure are seen by the true self as part of being a human being. Since flaws are not connected to your self-esteem, they are not a threat to your self-worth and do not hurt how you feel about yourself. Rather, imperfections are accepted and used as lessons and tools to grow and become a better version of you.

The true self is assertive. It knows what it needs to be happy and is willing to appropriately demand that those needs be met. This quality gives you permission to have your needs satisfied, relieving the fear that they won't be met. At the same time, the true self is realistic and understands that not all needs will be fulfilled on demand and shows patience until they can be satisfied.

The true self is realistic and reasonable. It appreciates the complexity of people and the world and doesn't expect to find simple answers. The true self understands that life is rarely black and white; it looks for gray areas and compromise to find sensible solutions to life's challenges. This attitude opens the true self up to a wide variety of perspectives and experiences. The true self is also flexible, allowing you to adapt to diverse situations and enabling you to change in accordance with the circumstances that are presented to you.

The true self is passionate about life. It derives joy from all of life's many facets, from the common to the exceptional. This passion enables you to throw yourself into whatever you do, producing a dedication and a work ethic that ensures high quality and great satisfaction in all of your efforts.

The true self is emotionally accessible. The true self encourages you to become familiar with, understand, and appreciate your emotions. Rather than fearing emotions, the true self revels in the strength and wide range of emotions that you can experience. The true self recognizes that only by feeling the full spectrum of emotions can you feel positive emotions such as happiness and exhilaration.

The true self is inquisitive. You are motivated to explore, learn, expand your horizons, and grow in ways that will enrich your life. You are curious about your inner and outer worlds and wish to expose yourself to all that life has to offer. If you are guided by the true self, you relish taking risks and testing yourself in new and challenging situations.

The true self is socially balanced. You have healthy friendships and enjoy being with others, but you don't need to be with others to gain validation. You also like to help others but do so out of the satisfaction that it brings rather than a need to please and receive love from others. Though socially active, you also enjoy being alone. Since the source of your happiness comes from within, you can be comfortable being by yourself and appreciate quiet time alone.

The true self is generous. Because the true self feels competent, loved, and safe, you are comfortable to give to others in many ways. You can open up and reach out to others without fear. Experiencing a surplus of love, you can share your love and care for others who have cared for you. This unconditional giving allows others to respond in kind and replenish your supply in an endless regenerative cycle of sharing.

The true self is driven to grow. Security and comfort do not mean that you are complacent. Rather, you are in a position of strength, which motivates you to challenge yourself and explore the limits of your capabilities. These challenges provide you with feelings of meaning, satisfaction, and joy as you fully realize your abilities and expand the boundaries of your world.

> People are like stained-glass windows. They sparkle and shine when the sun is out, but when the darkness sets in their true beauty is revealed only if there is light from within.
>
> —Elisabeth Kübler-Ross, psychiatrist and
> a pioneer of near-death studies[14]

### Belief System of the True Self

The true self believes you are worthy of love. This love is grounded in the belief in your inherent goodness and value. You don't need to prove yourself to the true self or earn the love it receives. You don't need to live up to a particular standard or expectation in order to gain love from the true self, especially from external sources such as other people and our culture.

The true self sees you as a human being who is worthy of love simply for who you are—the values you possess, the way you treat people, how you live your life. The true self accepts that a part of being a human being is that you are imperfect and that you will make mistakes and fail. This acceptance allows you to find peace and contentment in your life. It also encourages you to explore, take risks, and pursue success from a position of strength in which you are motivated to challenge yourself and realize your fullest abilities.

The true self believes you are competent and capable. The true self possesses a basic confidence in your abilities and the capabilities to be successful. This sense of competence removes the threat of failure and enables you to freely and positively pursue your dreams and goals.

The true self believes that you have control over your life. The true self has a fundamental belief that you have the ability to pilot your life in the direction you wish to go and live the life you choose. It enables you to take responsibility for both bad and good things that happen in your life and to make desired changes when needed.

The true self sees the world optimistically. This hopeful attitude creates a self-fulfilling prophecy in which you actively take steps to ensure that your life is heading in the direction you want. This optimistic perspective maintains your positive life inertia with beliefs, emotions, and actions that propel you toward an enriching life.

Because one believes in oneself, one doesn't try to convince others.
Because one is content with oneself, one doesn't need others' ap-

proval. Because one accepts oneself, the whole world accepts him or her.

—Lao Tzu, ancient Chinese philosopher and writer[15]

## Guidelines of the True Self

The true self creates a set of "guidelines" that help you initiate and maintain a life inertia that leads to a life that you want to live. I put "guidelines" in quotes because they don't have the rigid "I need to follow these rules" quality of the false-self rules. Rather, these are flexible guidelines that gently steer you along a positive trajectory. These rules encourage you to live a life that affirms your most basic true-self needs—to feel deeply, to connect with others, to experience the many facets of life, to engage in meaningful work and activities, to challenge yourself, and to grow.

Each person with a true self has particular rules that they developed. These rules steer their life in the direction of their choosing and ensure that their true-self needs are satisfied in the context of their own unique upbringing and life. At the same time, my work in transforming false selves to true selves has identified a set of true-self rules that are common.

*Guideline 1: I love myself.* This guideline acts as the foundation for all aspects of the true self. This simple statement carries with it far-reaching implications for how you pilot your life and the direction in which you steer it. This guideline acts as the impetus for a positive life inertia because it relieves you of all of the psychological and emotional forces that may propel you down an unhealthy path. It also encourages positive thought, emotion, and action that generate healthy forces to propel your life inertia.

*Guideline 2: I am my own best ally.* This guideline encourages you to act in ways that will facilitate achievement of your goals and realization of your dreams. Too often, Inertials are their worst enemies and create forces that resist a positive life inertia. By being your best ally, you can be sure that at least you are on your own side, even if the world is against you. As your best ally, you think, feel, and act in ways that drive your healthy life inertia.

*Guideline 3: Experiencing and expressing my emotions is not only acceptable but also essential.* Your emotions lie at the heart of your true self. Your willingness to experience and acknowledge your feelings fully—both positive and negative, without doubt, worry, or fear—frees you to face life without the threat of feeling bad. Your ability and comfort in expressing your emotions in honest, healthy, and constructive ways is essential to your true self. Being able to communicate what you are feeling to others enables you to let go of unhealthy emotions, build on healthy emotions, and create deep connections with people. Also, by fully expressing your emotions, you are free to fully express every part of you in all aspects of your life.

*Guideline 4: I choose the path of my life inertia.* The ability to choose begins with the belief that you have control over your life. The true self instills in you the confidence that you can pilot your life in the direction you want it to go. With that belief, you are able to see and create options for where you want your life to head. Making choices also involves having the courage to act on the choices that will steer your life in a healthy direction. Having a vision of what you want to accomplish, weighing the risks, considering the consequences, and then daring to make that choice enables the true self to pilot your life in a direction of your own choosing.

*Guideline 5: To be happy, to be my best, and to connect with others are the polestars that guide my life's direction.* These values are essential for the expression of your true self and act as the goals toward which you can aim as you pilot your life into the future. If you use these three values as your guide in what you think, what you feel, and how you act, all of your efforts will be directed toward creating a life inertia that will lead you in a positive direction.

*Guideline 6: All guidelines can be modified or ignored at any time to support my true self.* The guidelines of the true self are not dictates that are set in stone. They are not immutable laws that are punishable if broken. Rather, they are simply guides to help your life inertia move in the direction you want. Thus, the guidelines can be changed, violated, or replaced as your life's circumstances require so you can continue to be happy, to be your best, and to connect with others.

## Benefits of Allowing the True Self to Pilot Your Life

The true self provides you with an expansive view of yourself, the world, and the future. Because you are not guided by fear and the need to protect yourself, you can open yourself to all that life has to offer. You can view the richness and complexity of the world as opportunities to embrace rather than dangers to avoid. This "panoramic" and "telescopic" perspective also provides you with many inviting avenues that can be explored in the future.

Since the true self embraces life's many gifts, you have a strong sense of ownership of everything you do. You have passion for yourself, your work, your relationships, and other activities in which you engage. This connectedness motivates you to do your best in all of your efforts and generates great pride in everything you do.

Because the true self has confidence in your capabilities and worthiness to be loved, you have a fundamental trust in yourself and others. The true self has faith that you can make the right decisions that will steer your life in a healthy direction. With this trust in yourself, you are free to put appropriate trust in others. Rather than being distrustful or giving trust too quickly, you are selective in whom you trust and allow trust to build slowly. This trust in yourself and others enables others to be comfortable in trusting you.

The basic comfort that the true self engenders in you encourages you to connect with others. Without the threat of rejection, you are able to open yourself to healthier, more fulfilling relationships of all kinds including with family, friends, coworkers, and romantic partners. You are able to be vulnerable and put your heart out there in order for someone to respond to and connect with you. Your relationships take on a new level of depth and intimacy that provide emotional sustenance and social connectedness.

Since the true self is not shackled by *NEEDS!* and restrictive rules, you are not forced down a path that leads to unhappiness and you are not limited in your life's options. Rather, you have the freedom to choose the path of your life inertia. The true self offers you many options for fulfillment and joy. You have the power to recognize and act on the choices that are most in accord with your values and dreams.

The true self enables you to experience peace and contentment. There is no need for doubt, worry, or fear. Though life will always have bumps in the road, the true self provides a foundation of strength, ease, and comfort to which you can always turn to help you through the difficult times. Though you always will want to strive to live a richer and more satisfying life, you have a basic sense that "life is good right where it is."

The true self encourages physical health as well as psychological and emotional well-being. A goal of the true self is to foster overall physical health and wellness. You strive to have a healthy balance of physical activities and diet that produces energy and freedom from illness and injury. When physical equilibrium is lost, the true self understands that there are times when the body must step back, rest, and allow itself to rejuvenate without the fear of losing control.

The true self liberates you from doubt, insecurity, and fear. You have faith that your efforts will be rewarded and that your goals will be achieved. You are free to choose the path that will lead you to meaning, satisfaction, and happiness. You understand and accept that there will be obstacles and setbacks along the way. The true self allows you to embrace an attitude that fosters positive thoughts, emotions, and action. The true self will steer your life in a healthy direction.

Finally, the true self cultivates growth and healthy change. Because the true self is open to change, you are able to recognize and discard old, unhealthy patterns that keep you from the life path of your choosing. You have the power to make changes in your life that are consistent with your dreams and goals. You can pilot your life in new and exciting directions as they present themselves to you.

> By being yourself, you put something wonderful in the world that was not there before.
>
> —Edwin Elliot, professor and mathematician[16]

## Exerting Force against the Inertia of the False Self

When we are children, there is a battle for the "captain's chair" of our lives, which determines who we are and the path our lives will take. This confrontation is between the false self and true self. The winner will take the helm of our lives and determine which direction our life inertia takes. To be sure, our parents played a central role in this conflict. At the same time, our culture at large played a big part in this fight. The messages that our culture conveys to us about what we should value and believe can foster the construction of a false self and facilitate the imprisonment of our true self.

We could not win this "war of the selves" on our own when we were young. We simply did not have the awareness, experience, perspective, maturity, or resources to marshal an effective defense against such powerful forces. Our parents were our only hope, which meant that they had to be willing to fight with us against the forces of the unhealthy false self. Whether this battle could have been won outright is questionable given the omnipresence and potency of our culture's forces. However, society could be kept at bay by the alliance between our parents and ourselves if it started in the beginning and continued through childhood.

Unfortunately, our true selves were often casualties of this fight. Whether our parents simply did not have the "firepower" to resist society's defeating messages or, even worse, they joined forces with society, the true self lost control and we were taken over by a false self.

However, control of the helm of your life that may have been lost as a child can be retaken as an adult. Unlike when you were a child, you have greater resources in which to resist the strictures of your false self as an adult. You now have the opportunity to allow your true self to reassert itself in order to become captain and take your life in a direction of your choosing. You can lead the life you want. Much like a mutiny against an oppressive ship's captain, you can gather your forces, storm the bridge, regain the control that was lost, drive out your false self, and return your true self to the helm.

Much as an overthrow on a ship, this goal is not readily accomplished. Your false self has been steering your life trajectory for many years. It is strong and experienced and at first offers little room in which you can maneuver. The false self is ever vigilant, always on the alert for threats to its integrity. Your true self may initially lack the power to overwhelm the false self. So a direct assault on the false self will probably be unsuccessful. Instead, you must use guerilla and stealth tactics to fight back and slowly regain control of your life.

Your true self has several strengths that you can use to begin this offensive against your false self. The true self is at the core of your being; it is fundamentally who you are. Your true self actually has been around longer than your false self. It is motivated to reemerge and reclaim your life. Unlike the false self, which gets its power from the outside world, the true self gets its power from within—your values, attitudes, and beliefs—so you have more ready access to resources that will strengthen your true self. You can also block the false self from gaining resources by cutting off access from its suppliers in the outside world, such as the media. By reaching out to healthy forces around you, you can surround yourself with people who will help you strengthen your true self and resist your false self.

This battle is not an occasional confrontation between your two selves. Rather, it involves day-to-day combat with your false self and the life inertia it has created. You must constantly expose yourself to messages that will counter unhealthy false-self messages. This constant reinforcement of the true self allows it to gain the strength and resilience that will be needed to effectively overcome the defeating efforts of your false self. Consistent emphasis of the true self keeps its presence in the forefront of your mind, which enables you to more consciously make decisions and take action that are consistent with your true self.

> When you recover or discover something that nourishes your soul and brings joy, care enough about yourself to make room for it in your life.
>
> —Jean Shinoda Bolen, psychiatrist and author[17]

## Rebuilding Your True Self

The process of reconnecting with your true self is much like rebuilding a house that you own. Returning to the self-as-house metaphor I used earlier, the false self is really shoddy construction of the self. The false self was constructed with poor materials and inadequate construction. Your job is to tear down the false self and rebuild the true self. In some cases, your self-as-house may require a complete teardown, which is time consuming and difficult but necessary to change the trajectory of your life. Most likely, though, you simply need to do some renovations in which you deconstruct the false parts of the self that are interfering with your life and rebuild those parts with quality materials and construction. This renovation involves tearing down detrimental values, attitudes, and beliefs you have about yourself and the world and replacing them with healthy perspectives that are based on current and accurate perceptions that are consistent with your true self.

In order to grow . . . we have to let go of many things that have come to define who we are. . . . We often refuse to give up our view of ourselves and the world, in spite of the fact that many of the values, ideas, and self-definitions that sustained us during the first half of life will become obsolete and often antagonistic to the realities of the rest of our life.

—Kathleen A. Brehony, psychologist[18]

Dismantling your false self and rebuilding your true self involves exploring your inner world. You must fully understand and acknowledge who has been the captain of your life in the past and who you would like to steer it in the future. This process requires that you first explore your false self and gain insight into its qualities, beliefs, and rules that have governed you for all these years. You must then establish a clear vision of what your true self is and what qualities, beliefs, and rules you want it to possess.

After this period of internal discovery, you must act with your thoughts, emotions, and behavior and make deliberate choices that will allow your true self to emerge and regain control of your life. This process involves recognizing situations in which your false self causes you think, feel, and act certain ways. You then have to decide to resist those urges and respond in a way that is consistent with your true self. As you make more healthy choices, your true self will gain strength and your false self will lose its power. In doing so, these decisions will become easier because they are self-reinforcing. Over time, your true self will reestablish its dominance, alter your life inertia, and guide your life in a new and positive direction.

The process involves looking within to find a true core of self . . . accepting all feelings, not just the socially acceptable ones . . . knowing the difference between . . . [your] own voice and the voices of others.

—Dr. Mary Pipher, psychologist and author[19]

## Separate Who You Were from Who You Are

Much of the false self is based on who you were and how you were treated many years ago. So the false self treats you in the present the way you were in the past. The connection between the you of the past and the you in the present contributes greatly to the entrenchment of the false self in your life. For example, the false self treats you now like the immature and frightened child that you may have once been, despite the fact that you are no longer that child (though, thanks to your false self, you may still be immature and frightened).

The problem with this is that the false self forces you to think, feel, behave, and interact in the present like that child from your past. The false self keeps you shackled to those old beliefs because the false self can more easily control you by you keeping you a child. If the false self had to face the adult that lies within your true self, it would have a much harder time maintaining its dominance.

What is even more defeating and painful is that who you are now most likely holds little resemblance to who you once were. Yet your beliefs may be wholly out of line with your present reality. The reality is that your maturity, abilities, and strength make your true self eminently capable of responding to the world in healthy ways. Unfortunately, you are not acting on the world from that reality. Rather, you are responding to the world based on old beliefs that are controlled by your false self. So you are forced to act on the world in a way that is completely inconsistent with who you can be in the present. Moreover, the beliefs that the false self continues to impose on you and the way it causes you to think, feel, and act are not functional in your present life, nor do they bring you happiness.

Reasserting your true self involves clearly seeing who you once were and what values, attitudes, and beliefs you developed that led your false self to be in control of your life. Then you must understand who you are now and what values, attitudes, and beliefs lie at the core of your true self. This will help determine the direction you want your life to go now and in the future. Next you must align how you view yourself and the world with your true self. Your goal is to think, feel, and act in the world based on your true self and who you want to be, regardless of your false self and who you were in the past.

> The willingness to wrestle with your demons will cause your angels to sing.

> —August Wilson, American playwright and author[20]

## Know Your False Self

Your false self has directed your life since you were a child. Yet you probably don't know a lot about it. You know that it makes you feel bad and is taking your life down a path that you don't want to go. I believe that you must "know thy enemy" to defeat your false self. By familiarizing yourself with the qualities, beliefs, and rules of your false self, you make them more tangible, which better empowers you to challenge them. Earlier in this chapter, I described some of the attributes of the false self. Using those as your starting points, specify those that are unique to you and have the most negative impact on our life's direction.

## Values of Your True Self

> In order to be whole we must reclaim the parts of ourselves that have been neglected, prohibited, and repressed and integrate . . . them into our conscious life.

> —Kathleen Brehony[21]

Your true self may have been stifled for so long that you may not even know what it is or what it believes. The importance of identifying your true self cannot be overstated. Since your false self has been dominant for so long, you may have lost touch with what exactly it might be like to feel good about yourself and to treat yourself with respect and appreciation. Without having a clear vision of who your true self is, you will have a difficult time reconnecting with it.

The first step in rebuilding your true self involves identifying your true self and reacquainting yourself with it. Again, each of us has a true self that is unique to who we are based on our upbringing and our life experiences. Yet there are some shared qualities that I described earlier that you can use as a foundation from which to reconstruct your unique true self.

In learning about your true self, you must ask yourself several essential questions. First, what do you value? You must choose the aspects of your life that are most important to you and the role you want them to play in your current and future life. Typical values that I have seen include:

- Quality of life—what kind of overall life do you want to lead?

- Career—what kind of work will bring you fulfillment and meet your quality-of-life needs?

- Responsibilities versus freedom—what balance of structure and flexibility do you want?

- Activities—what avocations do you want to be involved in (e.g., religious, cultural, charitable, athletic)?

- Social interactions—what types of relationships do you want?

- Material needs—what possessions do you want in your life and what purpose will they serve?

For example, one value of the true self that is often squashed by the ambition of the false self is the desire for deep and enriching relationships. When identifying the values of your true self, you must also prioritize them. This ordering will help guide you toward the areas on which you want to focus during the reconnecting process.

A list of values that one of my clients came up with during this process includes quality work; physical, psychological, and emotional health; physical activities (sports, exercise, dance); family; friends; being a decent human being; caring about others; quality of life; balance; rich spiritual, cultural, and intellectual life (looking inside and outside of self); contributing to the world (giving something back); experiences rather than material possessions; freedom; open communication; intimacy; passion; and interdependence. What values resonate with you?

Another part of identifying your true self involves asking how you want to treat yourself and how you would like to feel about yourself. Typical responses to this include: unconditional love, respect, acceptance, kindness, and appreciation. These true-self ways of treating yourself are in sharp contrast to how you may now treat yourself: harsh, demanding, intolerant, and judgmental.

Common ways in which you would like to feel about yourself include feeling safe, contented, happy, optimistic, and calm. These good feelings probably differ greatly from how you may currently feel about yourself: unloved, inadequate, unworthy, and incompetent. These differences may seem self-evident, but if you are not now treating yourself and feeling about yourself the way you want, then perhaps they are not so obvious. By bringing the positive aspects of the true self to the fore and holding them in comparison to the way that the false self causes you to feel and to treat yourself, you have a clear picture of what you want and what you don't want. Only then can you move toward the vision that you have clearly established.

> Perhaps we shall learn, as we pass through this age, that the "other self" is more powerful than the physical self we see when we look into a mirror.
>
> —Napoleon Hill, author of *Think and Grow Rich*[22]

## Identify Desirable Qualities of the True Self

Your false self has many qualities that are undesirable and, by their very nature, steer your life along an unhealthy path. Qualities of the true self can act as goals toward which you want to strive to become happy and successful. These attributes—such as kindness, acceptance, and generosity—provide you with a clear recognition of and appreciation for the way you would like to view yourself and act in the world. You can use the qualities of the true self I described earlier to guide you in identifying the qualities you would like your true self to embrace.

### Establish New Beliefs of the True Self

Having clarified what values are important to you, how you would like to treat yourself and feel about yourself, and the qualities you would like your true self to possess, you are now in a position to create new beliefs that will guide your true self. You can begin this process by taking what you just learned about your true self and—using the belief I described earlier in the chapter as a beginning—create a series of "I believe" statements that reflect the fundamental beliefs on which you want to base your new life inertia.

### Change the Rules!

Rewriting and changing the rules that have guided your life for so many years is one of your most important challenges in reconnecting with your true self. You have lived with the rules of your false self for a long time; they are well learned and imprinted in every part of your psyche. Though they may not make you happy, the false-self rules are at least familiar, predictable, and manageable, which helps to maintain some small sense of equilibrium. In an odd sort of way, you have learned to count on them. They protected you from harm and minimized your pain. The thought of no longer having these rules can be unsettling, causing instability, uncertainty, and vulnerability.

Most of my clients find it relatively easy to identify their false-self rules because they have been present for so long. Yet they struggle with creating new rules that are consistent with their true self because the concept of rules that bring happiness are largely foreign to them. Ideally, the rules of your true self will evolve out of your previous explorations into the values, qualities, and beliefs of the true self. Your new rules should spring from and be consistent with the other aspects of your true self. Given those parts of your true self, you must ask yourself what rules (guidelines, actually) will enable you to live in accordance with them and allow you to be the captain who will steer your life in the direction you want to go.

To begin the process of embracing the new guidelines, you must be willing to reject the comfort that the false-self rules have provided you and recognize them for what they are: suffocating strictures that steered you down a life trajectory of unhappiness. Before your true-self guidelines become established and the lure of the false-self rules are still present, you must constantly remind yourself of what the false-self rules really are and deny them. You must trust the new guidelines and focus on the positive direction they will send your life trajectory.

At first, the false self will resist, and its rules will continue to impose themselves on you. But, in time, as your true self gains a foothold in your psyche, the new guidelines will become more familiar and comfortable. You will also see and feel the benefits of allowing them to guide you. Following your true self will become self-rewarding. With increasing use, the true self will move to the fore and gain power. In turn, the false self will fade into the shadows and lose its influence on you.

Natalie is a human resource director at a large investment firm. Growing up, she internalized the following rules that became a part of her false self:

- You must be competent.

- You must be self-reliant.

- Emotional expression is a sign of weakness.

- You must get along with others.

Natalie took these rules to heart, becoming very successful, independent, stoic, and skilled at resolving conflict. She also became a human doing who was lonely, never felt good enough, was unfulfilled, emotionally repressed, and unhappy. Natalie decided to rewrite her rules with the following guidelines:

- I will be happy.

- I will assert my needs.

- I will communicate my emotions appropriately.

- I will open myself up to others.

Natalie was able to change her rules and allow her true self to guide her. Today, she works for a small company in an area she loves, she is in a loving relationship, and she has never been happier.

## Connect with Your True Self

To begin the reassertion of the true self as the captain of your life, you must connect with its values, qualities, beliefs, and rules. A part of this process means simply sitting with these aspects of your true self (it helps to have them written down in some orderly fashion) and familiarizing yourself with them—you cannot follow something that you do not know. Much like meeting and getting to know a new person in your life, you must explore your true self and learn all about it. By reviewing what you have written about your true-self attributes, you have already started allowing them to sink into your psyche, becoming more comfortable with them, and beginning to internalize this renewed part of yourself without even realizing it.

Another helpful way to connect with your true self is to hold your true self up to your false self so you can see and feel the differences. By doing so, you can offer yourself a better view of the sharp contrast between the two selves. It is apparent in how each causes you to think, feel, behave, and interact with others. This clear picture of each self—and the divergent thoughts and emotions each engenders—should further gird you against the false self and encourage you to embrace your true self.

As part of this connecting process, you should allow yourself to experience the fit and comfort of the true self. Take a minute or two and close your eyes and begin appreciating your true self. Imagining different aspects of the true self, you can come to appreciate its many facets and see its benefits in your life. Much like trying on a quality piece of clothing, your true self will settle on you as you wear it and become something that simply feels like a part of you.

Life is a matter of choices, and every choice you make makes you.

—John C. Maxwell, author and speaker[23]

## Look for Another Trajectory

The false self offers you one unchanging path that your life inertia must follow. There are never deviations to the course that it takes. You are stuck on a trajectory not of your choosing, which has led you to a life of dissatisfaction and unhappiness. Asserting your true self involves recognizing that your life inertia doesn't have to propel you along one irrevocable path. Your life has many directions from which you can choose.

Looking for other new directions in which your life might go is your first step in actively establishing your true self. Having spent your entire life to this point on what seemed like a path you were destined to follow forever, you probably are not that adept at recognizing when you are presented with another direction your life might take. New trajectories often have signs that indicate their presence; however, you weren't able to read those signs when you were guided by your false self.

These new life paths arise when you come to a place in which your false self compels you in one direction that likely will lead to bad feelings and the perpetuation of false-self *NEEDS!* Though you have not been aware of it in the past, there is another direction you can take that is consistent with your true self. You can recognize these new trajectories when you experience some type of negative thinking ("I am worthless"), negative emotions (frustration, fear, sadness, or anger), or negative behavior (reacting to someone in anger). These experiences should be a signal to you that you have arrived at an opportunity to redirect your life inertia and that you can choose to take the path less traveled.

> Each path is only one of a million paths. . . . If you feel that you must not follow it, you need not stay with it under any circumstances. . . . There is no affront to yourself or others in dropping it if that is what your heart tells you to do. But your decision to keep on the path or to leave it must be free of fear and ambition. I warn you: look at every path closely and deliberately. . . . Then ask yourself and yourself alone one question. . . . Does this path have a heart?
>
> —Don Juan, Yaqui Indian shaman in
> *Teachings of Don Juan* by Carlos Castaneda[24]

For example, unbeknownst to Natalie, she experienced a fork in the road when she found herself wanting to contribute her ideas at a staff meeting but becoming very anxious each time she thought about speaking up. Natalie's anxiety stemmed from her false self's concern that her ideas would be rejected. This would represent to her that she was incompetent and not worthy of respect. To relieve her anxiety, Natalie stopped herself from saying anything. Taking a direction consistent with the false self caused two unhealthy things to happen. First, Natalie reinforced her false self by not speaking up because her discomfort went away. Second, Natalie felt frustration because she believed she was capable of making a meaningful contribution, yet did not.

At first, recognizing a new direction rarely occurs when you actually arrive at it. Early in this process, you may not recognize the fork in the road until long after you have gone down the false-self path. Only after you proceeded down the road a while, perhaps after the situation has concluded, will you have your first "Aha, that was a fork in the road back there" experience. Returning to Natalie, her first realization of a new direction occurred the evening following a particular meeting while she was preparing dinner. Though too late to change course, these first identifications are essential to sharpening your awareness of the forks.

As you gain experience in seeing the other paths you can take through hindsight, you will find that you begin to recognize them earlier and earlier. Instead of long after the situation, you will come to recognize them shortly after the event, then later during the event, then immediately following a new direction, until finally you recognize the fork as it is happening.

Let's go back to Natalie, who experienced the following progression in the subsequent weeks. First, she realized she had seen a new direction she could have taken as she was leaving a meeting. This progressed to recognizing the new path about ten minutes after she thought of speaking up and then right after she censored herself. After some time, she recognized the new direction as she was thinking about contributing in the staff meeting.

Learning to recognize these healthier paths as they arise is an important step in reasserting our true self. The next step, however, is more difficult. Recognition is not enough to ensure that you take the true-self trajectory, as this only gives you the opportunity to make the choice. Unfortunately, the false self is still dominant, though weakening, as you begin to identify and reconnect with your true self. In addition, your true self lacks strength and confidence. So you will go through a period during which you recognize the better path but still cannot take it. Do not be discouraged by this difficulty committing to the true-self road. Remember that the false self has been in control a long time and will not relinquish control easily.

Natalie experienced the satisfaction and frustration of this process. She was pleased that she was able to recognize her true-self path at staff meetings and in other situations, but she was disappointed that she couldn't get herself to speak up. Over time this frustration turned to righteous indignation for allowing her false self to control her in this way. Her righteous indignation turned to anger, and her anger turned to resolve.

It is at this point that you must take the leap of faith. You must decide that enough is enough. You must muster the courage to take a stand, resist the pull of the false self, and propel yourself down the path of your true self.

> You are the product of what you choose for yourself in every life situation. You do have the capacity to make healthy choices for yourself. . . . By being ever alert for turning adversity around, by improving your attitudes and expectations for yourself, and by fearlessly implementing risk-taking alternatives, you'll soon be gratified by the way your life can take a turn for the better.
>
> —Dr. Wayne Dyer[25]

Natalie took her newly found resolve and put it to practical use. She used several strategies to prepare herself and make the choice of taking the true-self fork easier. Natalie studied the agenda for the upcoming staff meeting and chose one topic on which she believed she had something useful to contribute. Then Natalie ran her idea by a trusted coworker and received positive feedback. Next she rehearsed what she would say so that she could communicate her idea clearly and succinctly.

As Natalie entered the staff meeting, she was determined to take the true-self path. When the topic Natalie chose came up, she listened to others' ideas, took a deep breath, and took her leap of faith. Though the false self resisted her attempt to take a healthy trajectory by increasing her anxiety, Natalie focused on what she had rehearsed and slowly and calmly articulated her ideas. After concluding her remarks, there were nods of agreement around the table and her boss suggested that she implement the idea immediately. Natalie walked out of the meeting unsteadily and collapsed in her office chair, relieved and exhilarated that she chose the true-self path and her decision was rewarded.

To facilitate this process, you want to start small. Rather than selecting a situation or person that has major false-self implications, you should start by choosing a less important area of your life that you want to change. By working on a new trajectory in less threatening aspects of your life first, you allow your true self to gain small increments of strength and confidence without great resistance from the false self. When you start small, you also increase the likelihood that you will be able to take the true-self path and that good things will happen when you do. These small steps confirm your leap of faith, give you confidence in your true self, and make it easier to take future true-self paths in more difficult situations.

In subsequent meetings, Natalie became a more active participant. Her coworkers began to seek her out for feedback, and her boss, who had been concerned about her lack of assertiveness and initiative, gave her more responsibilities. In a short time, she was promoted to a leadership position. As her true self became more dominant, Natalie began to recognize new directions in other parts of her life, including unsatisfying relationships, and began to choose the true-self forks in those areas as well. Natalie become more successful in her work and more fulfilled and happier in her personal life by allowing her true self to emerge and steer her life trajectory.

I do not want to underestimate how difficult it can be to reach the point at which Natalie arrived. It takes tremendous courage and commitment. Yet once you take your first true-self path, your life will be changed forever. With a firm foothold in your psyche, your true self will gain strength and your false self will lose its influence until your true self gains prominence. At that point, you will be on your way to propelling your life inertia in a new and healthier direction.

The journey of a thousand miles begins with a single step.

—Lao Tzu, ancient Chinese philosopher[26]

## Balance the Scales

Let's represent the relative impact of your false self and true self have on you as scales. Initially, the scales are unbalanced and weighted heavily toward the false self. Your false self has had a myriad of opportunities over many years to tilt the scales in its own favor. Every time your false self guided you in an unhealthy direction, the scales tipped further toward its direction. Each experience in which your false self caused you to feel inadequate, unloved, incompetent, or disrespected, the weight of the false self increased. Each time your false self punished you for failing to live up to its impossibly high internalized standards, the imbalance on the scales grew. Since you never had a choice, your true self had few opportunities to counterbalance the influence of the false self.

As part of reasserting your true self, you must begin to shift the weight of the scales toward your true self. This process involves several steps. First, you must assume that your false self is going to resist your efforts to rebalance the scale in an attempt to hold on to as much power as it can. Thus, it will be difficult initially to keep your false self from punishing you. So the second step in reversing the scales is to increase the number of true-self paths you take. Every time you make a true-self choice, you are adding weight to its side of the scale and giving your true self more power.

Your false self is very good at punishing you when you violate one of its rules, unfortunately. Your true self is not equally good at rewarding you when you do something positive. So you treat yourself with cruelty and alienation. To counter the punishment you receive from your false self, you must allow your true self to reward you for taking true-self paths. These rewards involve recognizing and appreciating when you think, feel, and act in ways that bring you happiness, like "chalking up a victory for the good guys."

As you take more trajectories that are consistent with your true self and your true self gains strength, you will find that you take fewer false-self forks. In addition, your false self punishes you less, which is rewarding because you no longer feel bad every waking moment of the day. Over time, as your true self grows and your false self atrophies, the scales will become balanced and then tip toward your true self until it becomes the Captain of Starship You. Finally, your false self becomes but a memory and an occasional nuisance.

## Trust Your True Self

One of the most difficult aspects of this process is learning to trust your true self. Remember, you don't know your true self well enough to have complete faith in it, just like when we first meet someone new. In contrast to someone you have just met, your true self has been trying to help you all along—you just weren't aware of it. Your true self has often communicated to you "the goodness of fit" of a person or situation. Unfortunately, you probably misinterpreted these messages because your false self intercepted them and construed the messages to fit its *NEEDS!* So what started out as a warning signal from your true self arrives to you as a "thumbs-up" after being reinterpreted by your false self.

Dean was a man who did not have a very successful history with women. He was raised by a demanding mother and grew up feeling unloved. As an adult, Dean projected this need for love onto the women he became involved with romantically. He would often meet a woman whom he felt very strongly about and dive into a relationship heart first before getting to know her very well. The problem was that he would have a strong physical and emotional reaction to a woman. Dean would interpret these powerful feelings as excitement, passion, and love. These emotions would cause him to believe that this woman was finally the one who would give him the love he so desperately needed and to disregard the signs that suggested otherwise. Dean would then invest himself in the woman and be crushed when the "real" her emerged and the relationship ended. This "failure" further reinforced his belief that he was unworthy of love.

Unfortunately, Dean's interpretation of his feelings was wrong. His true self saw the warning signs in the woman and sent him a powerful message of anxiety and discomfort. The communication was telling him to "get away from her as fast as possible!" In order to meet its own need for love, his false self intercepted the message and twisted it into one of strong positive feelings communicating "this is the one!" This situation resulted in an ongoing cycle of failed relationships that deepened Dean's feelings of worthlessness and reinforced the hold that his false self had on his life inertia.

Whether you call it gut instinct, intuition, or visceral feeling, your true self can act as a mechanism that tells you when a situation or a person is healthy or unhealthy. This sensation is trying to guide you in a healthy direction by telling you when there is a good fit and warning you when there is a threat. A part of reasserting your true self is learning to recognize, correctly interpret, and act on these signals in a way that will lead you along a healthy path.

As you begin to regain your true self, you must examine the signals you receive from your mind and body and consider how they relate to your false self. What purpose are those feelings serving in order to meet the needs of your false self? Is your immediate interpretation of those messages accurate? Then explore what the signals really feel like—they're usually uncomfortable—and see how they might be a warning. In time, you become adept at interpreting these messages accurately. You are able to resist the urges of the false self. You learn to accept the actual meaning of the true self. As such, you are able to act in a way that is in accord with your true self.

Intuition is a very powerful thing, more powerful than intellect, in my opinion.

—Steve Jobs, visionary leader and cofounder of Apple[27]

## A Final Thought about the
## True and False Selves

Though in time the false self will recede into the background of your psyche and your life, it will never be fully exorcised from you. The false self's habits and patterns have been a part of you for a long time and are too well ingrained for them to be fully expunged from your psychological system.

The false self is still present, and it may still trigger some of the same thoughts and emotions as it has in the past. The false self may still tug at you to get back on your life's old trajectory. The difference will be that the pull it has on you is no longer irresistible; the false self no longer holds sway over you. You no longer feel compelled to follow its unhealthy dictates.

Instead, your true self recognizes the compulsion of the false self, accepts it as a part of you, and asserts its dominance over the false self and your life. Your true self has changed your life inertia forever, and the false self will never again be able to regain control or return your life inertia to its old path. The strength of the true self has created a healthy life inertia that allows you to choose what is best for you in the present over what you needed in the past.

In a way, the presence of the false self now plays a healthy role in your life because it is a constant reminder of the life inertia you once had and the unhealthy trajectory it forced you along. You are able to look at how you once were, appreciate the effort you put in to altering your life inertia, and value how your new life inertia has changed your life for the better. Comparing your past to your current life further girds you to continue making choices that propel you in a positive new direction.

> Yesterday is not ours to recover, but tomorrow is ours to win or lose.
>
> —Lyndon B. Johnson, thirty-sixth president of United States[28]

# CENTERED IN THE UNIVERSE
## From Human Doing to Human Being

*Human being /yōōmən bEE-ingl*: A person who defines him- or herself based on his or her values, attitudes, beliefs, and efforts rather than on accomplishments.

An unfortunate byproduct of our achievement-oriented culture that feeds the emergence of a harmful false self is that it is made up of many people who did not have a balanced development of their self-esteem. They grew up in an environment that emphasized and rewarded accomplishment and success in lieu of instilling a strong sense of love and security. This belief is affirmed in research that has found many successful business executives are driven by personal insecurities to prove their worth through financial gains (e.g., Chamorro-Premuzic, 2013).

When our life inertia is driven by low self-esteem, we become the victims of a distorted and inaccurate understanding of how to gain competence and mastery over our lives, the second component of self-esteem. We don't just learn that our actions matter (which is very healthy), but that our actions are *all* that matter (not healthy at all). We can come to believe that being loved by our parents, and then by ourselves, depends on the success or failure of our actions. As a result, we come to believe that our self-worth is determined by our achievements.

The success of our actions becomes so influential on how we feel about ourselves that our understanding of "when we do good things, good things happen; when we do bad things, bad things happen; when we do nothing, nothing happens" transforms. We develop the belief that when we are successful, we are good; when we are unsuccessful, we are bad; and when we do nothing, we are worthless. This skewed perspective of what is an essential part of healthy self-esteem becomes a primary cause of low self-esteem. As a result, we cease to be human beings and grow up to become "human doings." Our self-esteem is based on what we do rather than who we are.

> To be yourself in a world that is constantly trying to make you something else is the greatest accomplishment.
>
> —Ralph Waldo Emerson,
> America essayist, lecturer, and philosopher[1]

Human doings only feel good about themselves when they are accomplishing things. They must be constantly validating themselves by getting things done. To prove themselves, they use some measurable criteria, which can range from financial or professional status to seemingly trivial things like how many miles they run or the cleanliness of their households. Human doings are often "list people" who wake up every day with a tally of tasks. They are not satisfied or happy at the end of the day unless they crossed off every item on the list. There is a temporary respite after the tasks have been finished, but that relief lasts only until they feel the need to get more things done and can add more items to their list and can continue to receive the validation they need to feel good about themselves. This pressure to complete tasks and for success puts human doings in a persistent, decidedly unpleasant, and never-ending position in which they are driven to accomplish things simply to buttress their fragile self-esteem.

Human doings live in a constant state of discomfort. They feel worthwhile only when they are doing something to validate their self-esteem. This ever-vigilant state that human doings are in causes them to feel as if they *must* achieve and be successful or they are worthless people undeserving of love. This relationship between achievement and self-esteem becomes the basis for their own self-love. Having internalized their perceptions of being a human doing from their parents or culture, they come to love themselves only when they are achieving success and experience self-loathing when they are not doing or when they fail.

These human doings create their life inertia to ensure that this primary need is satisfied. Most of their life's efforts are directed toward accomplishing things so they can validate their self-esteem and gain some modicum of peace. Again, if that peace is ever achieved, it is temporary; human doings never really feel any lasting contentment.

Though living as human doings often leads to some level of success, they never feel a strong connection with their efforts or have complete ownership over their accomplishments. Failure is so threatening that human doings can't fully invest in their efforts. If they do make that investment and they fail, they are devastated because failure is a judgment of their value as people. By distancing themselves from their efforts and successes, they protect themselves from that pain because they can tell themselves and others that they would have succeeded if they had given their best effort. Unfortunately, human doings can never experience the true exhilaration and joy of deep and meaningful success. Thus, human doings often have a persistent feeling of disconnection, ambivalence, and dissatisfaction in their pursuits.

Life as a human doing requires an odd contradiction in terms of the love they give to others and the love they give to themselves. Like most people, human doings love their family and friends for who they are, for being human beings—their values, the way they care for each other, their moral and responsible behavior. They don't value them because of what they have accomplished, their income, or their professional or social status. They give their love generously and unconditionally to those whom they care about. In other words, human doings paradoxically value others as human beings.

Yet human doings hold themselves to a very different standard. They don't love and value themselves for who they are, but rather for what they themselves do. Their self-love must be earned with constant activity and accomplishments for validation. In other words, though they love their family and friends for being human beings, they can love themselves only as human doings.

To love oneself is the beginning of a lifelong romance.

—Oscar Wilde, Irish poet and playwright[2]

Even when they do deem themselves worthy, human doings are misers at giving self-love. They mete out love to themselves in small portions, offering only enough to keep themselves wanting more and motivating themselves to do more to earn more of their miserly love.

Human doings often have negative associations with the idea of being a human being. They may love human beings in their lives dearly, but they don't fully respect them because they don't "do" very much. A client spoke of one of her best friends whom she recognized as someone who seemed thoroughly happy. Yet she admitted that she didn't really respect her because she didn't have a career and was "just" a housewife and mother. Like many human doings, my client viewed being a human being as an indication of incompetence and inadequacy. Human beings aren't good enough to be successful human doings.

Human doings often feel like their lives are asteroids hurtling uncontrollably through space. The asteroid continues along its inexorable path, causing them to feel trapped and unable to change its trajectory. They are caught on this asteroid that is their life. These human doings also have a sense of impending doom that sooner or later the asteroid will collide with another celestial body. Oddly, many human doings I have worked with have a reluctant wish for the crash to occur. At least, they say, the asteroid would finally stop!

## Meaning of Success and Failure

The self-esteem of human doings evolved in a way in which their successes or failures had an inordinately great impact on how they felt about themselves. This causes human doings to develop an unhealthy relationship with success and failure in their lives. It begins in school with academic, athletic, or artistic efforts, then generalizes to their relationships, and culminates in their professional pursuits. This relationship, paradoxically, has enabled human doings to "become" as a way of avoiding failure, which was simply unacceptable. Unfortunately, it also causes them to be very unhappy because there is never any joy in their successes, only relief of avoiding failure.

Growing up, nothing human doings did ever seemed good enough. They were never rewarded for their successes; in fact, they usually felt punished even when they were successful. When you came home with a 93 percent on an exam, did one of your parents ask why you got seven wrong? Human doings felt like their parents were constantly disappointed in them and they were never able to please their parents no matter how hard they tried or successful they became.

Much of the life of human doings has been directed toward striving to be "good enough." Every day, they wake up feeling like they have to prove themselves to their parents, themselves, and the world. They never feel like they deserve the successes they achieve. Even in success, they don't feel successful.

Though most parents intend to raise children who are focused on the future and success, they inadvertently cause their children to dwell on the past and failure. Instead of looking ahead to what they could achieve and its benefits, human doings peer over their shoulders at what they must avoid and the relief that provides them. The goal for these human doings was never success. Rather, their primary motivation was to successfully avoid failure.

In a way, human doings never really developed an understanding of or appreciation for success. In addition to viewing success as an escape from failure, they see it as a threat in and of itself. Over time, human doings come to see that success leads to even higher expectations from themselves and others, additional responsibilities, more pressure to succeed, more attention, and an increased likelihood of failure. Human doings have to make a choice between success, which they don't see in an entirely positive light, and failure, which has to be avoided at all costs. So rather than choosing success as a positive alternative to failure, human doings select success as the lesser of two evils. But that success provides little sustenance to them.

> Success is liking yourself, liking what you do, and liking how you do it.
>
> —Maya Angelou, American Poet Laureate[3]

## Unhealthy Reactions to Success and Failure

How parents respond to their children when expectations are not met has a significant impact on their children's future success and happiness. Melissa Kamins and Carol Dweck (1999) of Columbia University found that children who received "person criticism"—feedback related to their competence or value—attributed their failure to their lack of ability and showed negative emotions. As a result, they lowered their expectations and performed more poorly in the future.

> A great deal of unnecessary pain and grief is caused by this withholding, judging behavior on the part of parents. When has parental disapproval, in the form of shaming, humiliating, or withholding, ever been a positive influence on a child's behavior? It might result in obedience; but at what cost to the child, and to the adult that child becomes?
>
> —Jon and Myla Kabat-Zinn[4]

This type of feedback and punishment is what helps create human doings; they internalize these unhealthy forms of punishment and use this abuse on themselves. Human doings become adept at punishing themselves when they don't live up to their impossibly high internalized expectations. They berate and devalue themselves. Often the punishment that they inflict on themselves far exceeds the crime that they believe they committed.

This punishment could at least be counterbalanced if human doings were capable of rewarding themselves as effectively as they punish themselves. Unfortunately, as skilled as they are at self-punishment, they are equally inept at self-reward. Human doings rarely reward their accomplishments because, even in the face of objective success, nothing is ever good enough for them to deserve such praise. They are very good at finding fault and typically engage in the "yes, but" syndrome, in which they may be able to reluctantly admit that they have done a good job but always conclude their critique with a "but" and find fault with their efforts. It is entirely unacceptable to actually be nice to themselves and allow themselves the pleasure of self-affirmation. If human doings did that, they might become complacent and self-congratulatory and then they would be truly worthless people.

> The more criticism a child receives, the more likely he is to avoid trying the things that engendered the criticism. . . . The more you rely on external criticism, the greater the chance that your child will internalize these very same kinds of assessments and, before long, develop a self-picture that is based upon—you guessed it— being critical of himself.
>
> —Dr. Wayne Dyer[5]

## Red Flags

As you examine your life and determine whether you are a human doing, there are a number of red flags you can look for: conditional love, dangling carrot love, perfectionism, unhealthy expectations, being a bottom-line person, restricted self-identity, red flags internalized, and need for validation.

## Conditional Love

The vast majority of parents want what's best for their children. For most parents, this desire usually translates to a good education and a well-paying job. To ensure their children become high-achieving and successful people, parents set very high standards, place great emphasis on achievement, and push their children to be successful. These parents thought that making success central to child-rearing would make their children see its value and motivate them to work hard to become successful. In a way, they accomplished their goal, because success became very important to their children—just not in the way they intended.

Unfortunately, this well-intentioned, yet misguided, approach caused achievement to become excessively attached to children's self-esteem, so that the parents have unwittingly created human doings. Though some success will certainly be achieved by human doings, its source doesn't come from a healthy place because it is driven by the need to avoid failure and validate self-esteem. Further, its result doesn't offer the meaning, satisfaction, or joy that success should engender. You now may be the product of that upbringing—you are a human doing!

The danger of this parenting practice is that your parents made their love conditional on your success or failure. This is called *outcome love*, and it may have been communicated in open or subtle ways. Some parents actively reward success and punish failure. These parents create very clear outcome love, lavishing their children with love when they succeed and withholding love when they fail. They reward success by giving their love freely and expressively in the form of effusive praise and physical expressions of love, such as hugs and kisses. They also give outcome love materially by buying gifts when their children succeed. When they perceive that their children have failed, these parents show their disappointment by punishing the failure in the form of anger, verbal abuse, or disdain. They may also withhold love through neglect, emotional distance, absence of physical contact, and withdrawal of positive input and reinforcement.

Other parents may unknowingly create subtle outcome love that can have an equally devastating impact. Since parents experience their children's successes and failures vicariously, they often experience emotions similar to those of their children. Unlike obvious rewards and punishments, these emotions are often communicated subtly and nonverbally. It is natural for parents to feel happy and excited when their children succeed and to feel sad and disappointed when their children do poorly. When parents express these emotions, it is not always intended to be an expression of conditional love, but children may not yet be sophisticated enough to understand that parents are simply sharing a vicarious experience. Unfortunately, what children more often see is strong positive emotions from their parents when they succeed and strong negative emotions when they fail. This often inadvertent communication creates the perception of conditional love, regardless of intention, and produces many of the same difficulties in children as those resulting from malicious parents actively expressing outcome love.

Parents who offer outcome love implicitly believe in a "transactional" approach to raising children in which love is a payment for good work. These parents believe that children are not entitled to love; rather, children must earn it. If you are a human doing, it is likely that you were raised in a family that used one of these types of outcome love.

There is research that clearly demonstrates the very real and harmful impact of conditional love on children. The Columbia University researchers Kamins and Dweck (1999) discovered that children who believed their self-worth was dependent on how they performed on a task were highly self-critical, showed strong negative emotions, and judged their performances severely. This research supports that outcome love produces children who live in a constant state of fear. They are maniacally driven to succeed in order to receive their parents' love, yet have a powerful dread of failure and the anticipated loss of love. These children come to believe that they will be loved by their parents and, by extension, everyone else only if they are successful. These children grow up to be human doings who love themselves only when they succeed.

Unfortunately, all people will experience inevitable failures and setbacks as they strive to achieve success. These times are extremely difficult for human doings because they are so sensitive to even the smallest failures that they will be unable to focus on their many successes and maintain a healthy perspective on the setbacks. They may become depressed and anxious because of the threat to their self-esteem.

> Only love that continues to flow in the face of anger, blame, and indifference can be called love. All else is simply a transaction.
>
> —Vironika Tugaleva, author of *The Love Mindset*[6]

## Dangling Carrot Love

A more painful and defeating form of conditional love is *dangling carrot love*. This is love that is promised and held seemingly within reach by parents but always remains just out of the grasp of children and is never truly attainable. This notion came from my work with a young professional athlete who introduced me to a song by Alanis Morissette in which she sings of the "transparent dangling carrot." Much like the donkey who keeps moving forward in the belief that it will be able to reach the carrot tied at the end of a stick in front of it, children are impelled to keep trying to win to reach the love they desperately seek. Unfortunately, no matter how hard these children try or the level of success they achieve, it is never enough to gain the love from their parents that they want so desperately.

Parents who use dangling carrot love put their children in a hopeless position. Their children are never rewarded for their efforts; yet they are loath to give up. To do so would be to surrender the hope that their parents really do love them; that would be much too hurtful to accept. So these children keep striving and chasing that elusive carrot, however fruitlessly, to be good enough to earn their parents' love. The pursuit of dangling carrot love leads these children to become human doings in adulthood.

Parents communicate dangling carrot love through their consistent dissatisfaction with how their children perform. Even when these children are successful by anyone else's standards, their achievements are still not worthy of their parents' love. Why do parents use this defeating kind of love? Probably in the mistaken belief that if they give complete and unlimited approval of their children's successes, their children will learn that their efforts are "good enough" and they won't have to try as hard in the future.

Parents also express dangling carrot love by severely punishing failure in a way that makes love seem so distant as to be forever unreachable for the children. For example, a parent may completely withdraw communication with their child or show strong expressions of anger. The most extreme case of dangling carrot love I have ever seen came from the mother of a young athlete client. Over the course of a summer of competitions during which my client had some difficult losses, her mother smashed her daughter's equipment, abandoned her at a competition, told her daughter repeatedly that she didn't love her, and didn't speak a word to her daughter for a week on two separate occasions.

> Dangling a carrot in front of a donkey—or anyone else for that matter—is not nice, and not fair, unless you eventually plan to give it to them.
>
> —Vera Nazarian, author of *The Perpetual Calendar of Inspiration*[7]

## Perfectionism

If there is one quality that I have found to be evident in human doings, perfectionism would be it. Perfectionism is perhaps the most defeating aspect of conditional love that can lead to becoming a human doing. Parents can induce perfectionism in their children by never giving complete approval of their children's efforts. Children come to believe that nothing short of perfection is good enough for their parents, which means that anything less than perfection is absolutely unacceptable. Because of their need to gain the love of their parents, perfectionists push themselves unmercifully to meet their parents' expectations. Sadly, they internalize these impossible standards and punish themselves for falling short of perfection as they develop through adolescence and into adulthood.

> Perfectionism doesn't make you perfect. It makes you feel inadequate.
>
> —Maria Shriver, author of *Ten Things I Wish I'd Known*[8]

Perfectionism is defined as "the setting of excessively high standards of performance in conjunction with a tendency to make overly critical self-evaluations" (Frost, Marten, Lahart, & Ronsenblate, 1990, p. 449–68). Two types of perfectionism have been identified. "Healthy" perfectionism is characterized as fostering high goals, achievement, self-actualization, confidence, and success. Healthy perfectionists have high expectations and also show the ability to be flexible, adapt, and accept less precision when needed.

"Neurotic" perfectionism is distinguished by compulsive precision, neatness, and organization. Neurotic perfectionists set unrealistic expectations, demonstrate a rigidity in their thinking, have little tolerance for mistakes, are never satisfied with the fruits of their efforts, and show little enjoyment in their achievements. Neurotic perfectionists tend to associate mistakes with negative judgments of themselves and worry that failure will cause others to lose respect for them. They often lack confidence in their capabilities, question the quality of their efforts, and are highly critical of themselves. Neurotic perfectionism has been found to be associated with a variety of psychological problems including procrastination, depression, anxiety, poor stress coping, social phobia, and eating disorders (e.g., Pearson & Gleaves, 2006; Shafran & Mansell, 2001).

The divergence between healthy and neurotic perfectionists hinges on the severity of how perfectionists evaluate themselves rather than the high standards they set for themselves. Healthy perfectionists set high expectations for themselves but don't berate themselves for minor imperfections. Neurotic perfectionists hold themselves to the same standards but cut themselves no slack for anything less than total achievement of those standards.

> [Perfectionists have] standards [that] are high beyond reach or reason . . . strain compulsively and unremittingly toward impossible goals and . . . measure their worth entirely in terms of productivity and accomplishment.
>
> —Dr. David Burns, psychiatrist[9]

If your parents were perfectionists when you were growing up, it is likely that they held themselves to the same standards to which they held you because they were probably exposed to perfectionism and conditional love as children. Perfectionistic parents abhor failure, cannot accept their own perceived imperfections, and show great upset when they are unable to live up to their own impossible standards. For example, a parent may punish himself for failing to land a business deal or playing poorly in a round of golf. A parent may also become angry and frustrated when she is faced with obstacles on a work project.

If your parents did not appear to be perfectionists, yet set impossible standards for you, then there is another dynamic at play. Your parents may not have been able to accept their own imperfections but were unable to resolve these perceived flaws in themselves. As a result, they imposed impossible standards on you as a means of vicariously removing their own imperfections.

Parents communicate perfectionism in many ways. Research indicates that parents who raise neurotically perfectionistic children set very high goals and are excessively critical of their children (Frost, Marten, Lahart, & Ronsenblate, 1990). They also give their children consistent negative feedback about their achievement, and, not surprisingly, their children weigh these evaluations heavily in their own self-judgments. Children see the perfectionistic messages of their parents and internalize them. As such, their parents' neurotic perfectionism becomes their own.

Neurotic perfectionists are striving toward a goal that they can never, ever achieve. If you are a perfectionist, what is your life like? If you are like most perfectionists, you live in a constant state of fear of not being valued with a persistent belief that you are unworthy of love. Every morning you wake up with the need to prove to yourself and the world that you are deserving of love and respect. Each success is only the briefest respite from the fear of being inadequate and of not being loved. Every failure is a direct attack on your self-esteem. Perfectionistic children are caught in a trap of their parents' creation with little chance of escape as adults.

> When parents expect perfection, children can only feel inadequate and powerless to live up to their parents' standards.
>
> —John Gray, PhD, author of *Children Are from Heaven: Positive Parenting Skills for Raising Cooperative, Confident, and Compassionate Children*[10]

## Unhealthy Expectations

Unhealthy expectations are one of the most harmful ways in which parents use either outcome love or dangling carrot love.

Expectations can be thought of as standards to which we hold ourselves. Assuming you have internalized your parents' conditional love, your expectations provide the threshold that separates success from failure. They become the criteria for determining your self-worth. If you fail to meet your expectations, you are a failure. If you are a failure, you are a bad person. If you are a bad person, then you are not worthy of love from yourself, your parents, or others.

Expectations are assumptions that something will be achieved or is likely to happen. An expectation can make something uncertain seem more tangible, almost as if you already had it in hand. This perception causes tremendous disappointment when you fail to meet the expectation. It is as if something you already had was taken away from you, even though you never had it in the first place. Expectations are also all-or-nothing propositions—they're either reached or not—so anything less than complete fulfillment of the expectations is failure.

> Many people suffer all their lives from this oppressive feeling of guilt, the sense of not having lived up to their parents' expectations.
>
> —Alice Miller, author of *Prisoners of Childhood*[11]

Our expectations come from many sources. Growing up, you feel expectations from your parents, teachers, coaches, instructors, and society. Failure to meet expectations may entail not only letting yourself down but also likely disappointing many other people who had high expectations for you, no matter how well intentioned they might have been. The weight of all of these expectations is a tremendous burden on you, and a cross that you may bear into adulthood.

An unfortunate mistake that many parents make is to set expectations for circumstances in which children have little or no control. For example, an *ability* expectation is one in which you are expected to achieve a particular result based on your natural ability—"You'll do well in the chess match because you're so smart." An *outcome* expectation is one in which you are expected to produce a certain outcome—"I know you'll win."

There are few things more damaging to children than not fulfilling their parents' expectations. If you succeed in achieving an ability expectation placed on you, you will inevitably attribute your success to your ability. The downside to that attribution is that if you fail to meet an ability expectation, you likely will attribute your failure to a lack of ability—you weren't smart enough, strong enough, or skilled enough. This type of attribution is so harmful because ability is not within your control (we're all born with some threshold of ability in different aspects of our lives). You may come to believe that you are simply incapable and, as a result, unworthy of being loved by others or yourself.

> Too many children live with the feeling that they are not accepted for who they are, that, somehow, they are "disappointing" their parents or not meeting their expectations, that they don't "measure up."
>
> —Myla and Jon Kabat-Zinn[12]

Not meeting your parents' outcome expectations can be equally detrimental. Our society places great emphasis on competition and comparison, in which everything that we are and have is judged in relation to others. The problem here is that how you compare to others is also not within your control. At some point when you were young, you may have done your best but without performing as well as your classmates or teammates. As a consequence, you failed in comparison and thus failed to meet the outcome expectations your parents place on you. This is particularly unfair because children develop at different rates. A child who is less successful at ages ten, fourteen, or eighteen may surpass their peers at a later age.

Outcome expectations also become connected to outcome love. Children perceive that their success or failure in meeting their parents' expectations will determine whether they will receive their parents' love. This emphasis on outcome love puts you in a no-win situation. If you meet the expectation, there is no great joy—just relief that your parents still love you. If you don't satisfy the expectation, you are fearful that your parents won't love you.

The perception that nothing you do is good enough and the pressure you feel in response to these escalating expectations causes a heavy emotional toll. Research has found that parents who communicate unusually high achievement expectations produce angry children (e.g., Assor & Tal, 2012; Ablard & Parker, 1997; Ciciolla, Curlee, Karageorge & Luthar, 2017; Harwood, Keegan, Smith, & Raine, 2015).

> Parents are afraid that if father and mother do not place sufficient stress on winning, on high grades, on awards, then their children may not strive. The opposite is true. . . . Anxious parents who place emphasis on success often contribute to the very discouragement that prevents their offspring from becoming successful.
>
> —Shirley Gould, psychologist[13]

Expectations can be so defeating because your parents may establish a standard that is impossible to attain. As the boss of one of my clients once said about her, "The problem is that you expect to be perfect all of the time." Her perfectionistic belief and the expectations that it creates in her drive her down a self-defeating road. If she fails to live up to the expectation she sets for herself, then she will disappoint herself and everyone else. Not meeting this expectation will cause her to label herself a failure, which precludes her from seeing herself as a competent and capable person. Since she is so incompetent—and her competence determines her self-esteem—she quickly becomes unworthy of love or respect from herself, her parents, or anyone else.

> If you judge a fish by its ability to climb a tree, it will live its whole life believing that it is stupid.
>
> —Amos E. Dolbear, physicist and inventor[14]

## Being a Bottom-line Person

Bottom-line parents are those who place too great an emphasis on the outcome of their child's efforts to the exclusion of any other contributors to the child's development. Bottom-line parents communicate this focus in the hopes of motivating their children. Similar to the other red flags, too great a focus on an outcome burdens children with the weight of success and contributes to them becoming human doings.

Bottom-line parents treat their children like "little employees" and expect them to "produce" in the form of results and success. If the desired results do not occur, then these "bosses" show their displeasure. In this dynamic, children may perceive that their parents will "fire" them.

Children of bottom-line parents experience a painful realization when they become aware that their parents equate their achievements with their value as people. People who are raised as bottom-line children grow up to be bottom-line adults, in which they base their self-esteem on what they accomplish. Again, they become human doings. Unfortunately, meeting the bottom line is always an unwinnable game. Bottom-line adults always stay ahead of failure enough to not feel bad about themselves, but they never get far enough ahead to actually feel good about themselves. Thus, all of their energy is put into "keeping their heads above water" and avoiding drowning in failure.

> The child comes to the emotional insight that all the love he has captured with so much effort and self-denial was not meant for him as he really was, that the admiration for his beauty and achievements was aimed at this beauty and these achievements, and not at the child himself.
>
> —Alice Miller, Swiss psychologist[15]

## Restricted Self-identity

A person's self-identity comprises all of the describable attributes of a person. Typical components of self-identity include our values, attitudes, beliefs, capabilities, and roles. In parents' efforts to ensure that their children will grow up to be successful, they run the risk of raising children with a restricted self-identity. A restricted self-identity is one that is predominantly invested in a single area, which limits the sources of meaning and validation of self-esteem.

The self-identity of human doings is usually overly identified with accomplishments, without consideration for other ways of validating their self-esteem, such as relationships and other nonachievement-oriented areas.

Many human doings are raised with restricted self-identities. This limited identification with success places great pressure on them to succeed and creates an exaggerated threat to their self-esteem when they fail. Success allows human doings to view themselves as worthwhile, competent, and valued, but failure in their investment can result in feelings of anxiety, worthlessness, helplessness, and despair.

I have worked with many achievers who reached the highest levels of success. For a number of them, the single-minded pursuit of success resulted in a life with a facade of celebrity and wealth. Behind this veneer was discontentment, a series of failed relationships, and limited self-worth. For the others, this quest led to a future of unrealized dreams, dead ends, and lifelong dissatisfaction.

Oksana Baiul, the 1994 Olympic gold medalist in figure skating, exemplifies the child who became an adult with a restricted self-identity. With no parents or family to support or guide her, Baiul committed herself to her sport at a young age and had no life outside of figure skating. Her entire self-identity was based on her skating. As Brian Boitano, the 1988 Olympic champion, says of his friend, "Upbringing is so important to how young star athletes deal with pressure, and she didn't have any backup. . . . She needed good examples of how to be a responsible person" (Baiul, 1997, p. 57). After winning in Lillehammer, Norway, and turning professional, Baiul went into an emotional tailspin that culminated in committing herself to a treatment facility for alcohol abuse. During her stay, Baiul learned two things that most children learn from their families—self-respect and wisdom. She observed, "I thought I was a big shot, but I wasn't. I knew how to skate, but there was nothing else I knew. What a gift, to have a chance again to make a life" (Baiul, 1997, p. 43).

The antidote for the development of a restricted self-identity is to seek out opportunities to gain enjoyment, meaning, and validation in areas outside of your need for success. It is also helpful to create balance in your life by engaging in a variety of activities and experiences that you can invest in and find meaning. Your preoccupation with success will lessen as your self-identity expands and you find additional sources of validation for your self-esteem. Ultimately, you will experience greater peace and happiness.

### Red Flags Internalized

Through adolescence, the impact of parents declines as we become increasingly independent. The danger of being exposed to conditional love, impossibly high expectations, and the other red flags is that they become internalized over time. Your parents' beliefs and feelings become your own. This means that your parents still exert their negative influence on you even when they are no longer present.

Instead of parents no longer punishing failure by withdrawing their love, you withdraw your own self-love, leading you to punish yourself for not living up to your parents' standards, which have become your own. You no longer need your parents' expectations to create this pressure and discomfort as you create your own unhealthy expectations. The conditional self-love and internalized expectations shift from being about gaining your parents' love to allowing yourself to receive self-love. Conditional love of yourself perpetuates the cycle that your parents created and drives you toward success, but at a great cost. These internalizations interfere with your ability to find success *and* happiness, resulting in an adult life of human doing.

> The thoughts in your mind will always be more important than the things in your life. Choose happiness.
>
> —John C. Maxwell, best-selling author and speaker[16]

## Need for Validation

Internalizing all of these red flags puts you at a deficit in which you lack the feeling of being loved and competent, which is essential to happiness. This perspective creates in you a profound need for validation. Unfortunately, you are unable to satisfy this need from within and seek validation that you are good enough to be loved and valued from others. This means that you become dependent on others to feel good about yourself and to meet your need for validation.

In a way, this validation involves trying to get others to convince you that you are worthy of love, something that you don't really believe yourself. Because the validation you get from others is neither strong nor lasting, you must constantly reach out to others for validation. So you create a life inertia directed toward fulfilling a need that is insatiable and unrelenting but that ultimately can't be satisfied by others.

## Become a Human Being

Your goal is to shift from being a human doing to a human being. Human beings believe that the kind of person that they are is defined by their values, attitudes, and beliefs; their determination and effort; and how they treat people. They determine value based on who they are rather than what they accomplish. Human beings gain satisfaction and validation from being honest, considerate, and responsible, among other things. They also have complete control over what primarily affirms their self-esteem.

To shift from being a human doing to a human being, you must first change the way you view human beings. If you can't value human beings, you will not see becoming one as a worthy goal to aspire to. Human beings are, in fact, not people who are incompetent or incapable of being successful. Rather, they don't have the *NEED!* to achieve. Instead, they decide what makes them happiest and what they *want* to do. Then they *choose* to do what makes them most happy. This choice enables human beings to be successful—whether by creating an international conglomerate, raising a family, writing a novel, or following whatever path their heart guides them down—and find happiness in the process. This choice offers human beings a sense of peace and contentment that human doings can only dream of experiencing. Remember, the goal is to *be* successful, not to *do* successful. Doesn't that seem like a goal worthy of striving for?

### Redefine Success and Failure

Becoming a human being requires that you change the way you define success and failure. Your definition of success must be broadened beyond wealth, status, and other accomplishments. Definitions of success for human beings can include expending great effort in pursuit of a goal, gaining satisfaction and joy out of the process of accomplishment, pursuing creative avenues, or helping others. Ironically, rather than interfering with human beings' ability to succeed, extending the definition of success actually increases the likelihood of finding success that is meaningful to you. If you love what you do, are completely invested in your efforts, and are not threatened by the possibility of failure, the chances of success become greater. Human beings respond to success in a way that represents why we should strive for success in the first place: for the exhilaration and satisfaction of having our efforts reach fruition. In comparison, the best reaction to success for human doings is relief at having dodged the bullet of failure.

By broadening their definition of success, human beings narrow their definition of failure. Instead of an expanded and unhealthy definition of failure that would include disappointing others, not being perfect, feeling incompetent, and not being worthy of love and respect, a human being's definition of failure is limited to not giving his or her best effort, not enjoying the experience, and not being the best person he or she can be. This definition of failure is entirely within your control and doesn't carry the emotional baggage of the extended definition of failure. In this narrower context, the response to failure is one of disappointment rather than devastation for human beings. This less intense reaction allows them to let it go and use the lessons learned from failure to become more successful in the future.

> We are addicted to our thoughts. We cannot change anything if we cannot change our thinking.
>
> —Snatosh Kalwar, author of *Quote Me Everyday*[17]

## Accept Your Humanity

Part of being a human being is accepting your basic humanity, which includes the perception that no one is perfect. We all have flaws and that is what makes us human. Since we are flawed, failure is an inevitable part of life. If failure is inevitable, it becomes acceptable, part of the lived experience. From this perspective, failure loses its power to harm your self-esteem. With "being," there is no threat to self-esteem because there is no perfectionism, there is no fear of failure, and there is no fear of losing your self-love. *You cannot fail at being!*

## Broaden Your Focus

Living a "being life" requires that you make changes to the structure and process of your life. It means moving toward a life that is filled with less doing and more being. The first step in creating a being life is to broaden your focus. Most human doings have a single-minded devotion to one thing, usually school or career. They always have an agenda of what they need to accomplish, and the agenda drives them incessantly. By contrast, human beings have many aspects of their self-identity that bring meaning, satisfaction, and joy to their lives. Though they may still be committed to being their best in one area, they have balance in their lives: failure in one arena isn't a massive blow to their sense of self-worth because they have many sources of validation in their lives.

## Reduce Your To-do List

This wider focus involves reducing the number of items on your "to-do" list. Human doings are compelled by their need to do in order to gain validation and a sense of self-worth. As they check items off their list, they are driven to keep adding to their list in order to continue receiving confirmation of their worth. Thus they are caught in a vicious cycle of their own (and their parents') creation. They must come to realize that not completing the entire list will not make them an incompetent and unlovable person and that the world will not end. On the contrary, life will actually seem easier, freer, and less stressful. You come to learn that the sun continues to come up every morning even without completing your to-do list.

## Create More Balance

You must also create more balance in your life. As noted previously, although your single-mindedness may have enabled you to become successful, that dedication to one area has limited the sources from which you can gain satisfaction and fulfillment. By creating many areas of your life that are rewarding, there is less investment in any one area and less pressure on that area to meet your self-esteem needs. The ideal balance is one that meets all of your needs, which might include intellectual, social, physical, cultural, and spiritual pursuits. Having more balance in your life will make you a more stable person who lives a more meaningful, satisfying, and joyful life.

## Become More Flexible

Human doings typically have very structured lives to make sure they can complete everything before they collapse at the end of the day from exhaustion. Though structure can be quite efficient, it can also act as a prison. You become limited in what you do and how you do it. This structure provides you with a false sense of security and comfort because you create a sense of familiarity, predictability, and control in a life that is anything but these things at its core.

In contrast, human beings create a life with only enough structure to meet their most basic needs. This minimal structure gives sufficient order to the lives of human beings without limiting their options. They are also flexible enough to break out of their structure when an opportunity presents itself. Human doings need to plan to be spontaneous. Human beings are open to and comfortable with acting on spur-of-the-moment opportunities and see such experiences as healthy breaks from their otherwise orderly lives.

### Lighten Up

Human doings are generally very serious people. They have things to do, people to see, and places to go. "Don't bother me; I'm getting things done" is their attitude. This seriousness comes from living in a state of hypervigilance to any threat to their self-esteem.

In contrast, human beings understand that life can get pretty dull if things get too serious. So they have learned how to "lighten up." They are serious about serious things but don't need the melodrama of making the mundane more serious to make their life interesting and worth living. They know that laughter and good humor bring happiness and joy to a world that often takes itself too seriously. Human beings don't want to exacerbate the world's serious attitude.

> Humor is the greatest thing, the saving thing, after all. The minute it crops up, all our hardnesses yields, all our irritations and resentments flit away, and a sunny spirit takes their place.
>
> —Mark Twain, American author[18]

### More Is Just More

Human doings perpetuate the typically American attitude that more is better. Whether it is working more hours, accumulating more wealth, or buying more stuff, human doings think that if a certain amount is good, then more of the same is that much better. They think that if they aren't happy, then they just haven't gotten enough to be happy. As a college classmate of mine once asserted, "Anything worth doing is worth overdoing." Unfortunately, human doings appear not to have heard of the theory of diminishing returns. Human beings are aware of this concept. They understand that there are limits to everything and that too much of a good thing destroys the goodness of that thing. Human beings recognize that sometimes more is just more, not better. Remember when you had too much to drink at a party or ate too much at Thanksgiving dinner or spent too much money shopping? For a human being, this principle applies to everything in life.

## It's a Process

Becoming a human being takes practice. You may have been a human doing for most of your life. You have ingrained long-standing habits that cause you to react to the world as a human doing. You are very skilled at being a human doing. So to become a human being, you must practice "being" activities, which I define as any activity that doesn't involve goals, achievement, or outcomes. These are activities that we do for their meaning, satisfaction, and joy rather than to validate our self-esteem. Being activities are those that you cannot fail at or that you can gain from the experience without feel excessively bad for failing. The purpose of engaging in being activities is to simply enjoy the experience (which may or may not lead to success). Typical being activities include reading; spending time with friends; playing with your children; having a nice meal; listening to music; watching a film, play, or dance performance; or going for a walk (the list is endless). Being activities have no agenda, no clearly defined purpose, and no measurable outcome. Being activities also can include pursuing the achievement of your life goals because they are consistent with your values, hopes, and dreams.

Being a human being doesn't mean that you will be satisfied with being happy with yourself and lose interest in achieving or being successful. On the contrary, it liberates you from the fear of achieving because success and failure are no longer so centrally connected to your self-esteem. The removal of this threat allows you to pursue success from a position in which you *want* to seek out challenges, take risks, and fully realize your ability. There is none of the pressure—from you or others—that interferes with human doings becoming successful.

Beautiful things come together one stitch at a time.

—Donna Goddard, author of the *Circles of Separation*[19]

## Human Beings Still Do (Very Well)

Becoming a human being doesn't mean giving up what you do. Human beings aren't lazy or unmotivated. Rather, being means converting "doing activities" to activities that human beings do. Ironically, success is not really about what you do. In school, the arts, sports, and your career, no one has the market cornered on strategies that foster success. Most people do pretty much the same things. Rather, success comes from *being*—who you are, what you value, your work ethic, and your ability to connect and work with others.

However, you cannot just *be* to become successful. You must also *do*, but your doing must come from your being. In other words, your efforts must come from who you are, what you value, and what you dream of accomplishing. When functioning as a human being, doing something is very different than human doings doing something. Human doings are doing to feel safe, loved, valued, and validated. Their doing comes from a position of deficit and weakness. In contrast, human beings do to experience fulfillment on the journey, satisfaction in pushing their limits to see what they are capable of, and, yes, reveling in their successes. Their doing comes from a position of abundance and strength.

In a sense, human beings' achievement efforts are filtered through their being. The efforts that result are determined, confident, energized, and focused. Human beings experience a sense of happiness in their accomplishments that human doings can never feel. Human beings' efforts affirm who they are rather than protect them from what they don't want to be—a failure. Because of this connection with their doing, human beings are able to give everything they have to their doing and fully realize their abilities. It is this connection between who you are and what you do that separates human beings from human doings.

## Accept Yourself

One of the most damaging aspects of being a human doing is that you are unable to fully accept yourself for who you are. Your ability to accept yourself depends on whether you meet certain impossibly high expectations that you have internalized from your parents and to which you now hold yourself. As long as you are a human doing, you will never be able to accept yourself and you will live in a perpetual state of inadequacy, fear, and self-punishment.

> "You have peace," the old woman said, "when you make it with yourself."
>
> —Mitch Albom, international best-selling author[20]

### Expectations to Goals

Accepting yourself requires a shift in the expectations you set for yourself and the rigidity with which you hold yourself accountable. For you to accept yourself, you must cut yourself some slack. This transition begins by changing from expectations to goals, in which you give up unreachable expectations and adopt goals toward which you can strive. Instead of failing to meet expectations, you will make progress toward the goals you set for yourself.

### "Should" to "Could"

This shift also involves moving from "should" to "could." You may carry around a lot of rules about what you *should* do that governs every aspect of your life—thoughts, emotions, behavior, relationships. These "shoulds" act as strictures that you have to follow to meet your self-imposed expectations. These "shoulds" imprison you and force you to lead a life of confinement within those "walls," which can only lead to dissatisfaction and unhappiness. Accepting yourself means letting go of the "shoulds" and focusing on what you *could* do in your life, on the opportunities that are abundant in the world. These "coulds" provide you with possibilities that free you to seek your own path rather than to follow the internalized rules you have created for yourself. They also direct your focus from past limitations to future possibilities.

### "NEED!" to "Want"

You must also change from "*NEED!*" to "want." Conditional love—needing to gain validation that you are worthy of love—has become one of your most powerful *NEEDS!* Thus, most of your life has been devoted to fulfilling that *NEED!*, which has become limiting because there is no freedom to decide. Accepting yourself involves letting go of these unhealthy *NEEDS!* and deciding on what you *want*. "Wants" provide you with the freedom to decide and the opportunity to satisfy them.

### "Must" to "Choose"

Another transition is from "must" to "choose." When you were growing up, you likely felt that there were certain things that you *must* do—first to gain the love of your parents and then to gain your own self-love. You may have felt forced to do these things even if they did not make you happy. Accepting yourself allows you to *choose* what you do. These choices can be based on what is best for you and what makes you happiest. By releasing yourself from what you must do, you become free to choose what you want to do.

## Negative to Positive

Human doings also tend to have a negative perspective of their lives. They feel like they are always trying to get away from something that is chasing them—failure and the fear of being unloved—rather than looking and moving toward what will make them happy. This negative perspective causes them to look at their lives in terms of what is wrong rather than how they can make it better. Human doings see what is bad and avoid it in the future. Human beings see what is good and want to do it even better. Human doings see one bad thing and dwell on it. Human beings see nine good things and choose one thing to work on. The negative orientation of human doings colors their view of life in a way that fosters pessimism and perpetuates their unhappiness. The positive orientation of human beings brightens their view of their lives and produces a self-fulfilling prophecy of success and happiness.

Accepting yourself is a truly liberating experience. By creating a healthy relationship between your self-esteem and your achievements, you relieve yourself of the unattainable standards that have driven you in the past. You let go of the need to live up to those expectations and, by doing so, you remove the fear of not realizing those standards. Having released yourself from those shackles, you are free to fully express who you are and of what you are capable.

> Positive thinking (much like negative thinking) gets easier with practice.
>
> —Cole Todd, author[21]

## Give Self-love

It is impossible for human doings to give themselves love because nothing they do is good enough to earn it. There are always imperfections, mistakes, and failures that make human doings unworthy of their own love. For this reason, human doings seek out love from others that they are unable to give to themselves. Through ingratiation or intimidation, human doings try to manipulate others into providing them with the love and value they crave. What human doings don't realize is that others don't have the power to meet their need for love in a substantial and lasting way. The only thing others can do is give them a "booster shot" of love that lasts briefly without completely satisfying their need for love. Only we have the power to meet our most basic need for love. Even if others do give us their love, it is only icing on the cake. The cake is giving yourself love.

Human beings don't withhold this life-enriching love from themselves. They don't subject themselves to outcome or dangling carrot love. Instead, they give themselves *value love* that is conditional on how well they adhere to the values and principles that guide their life. Think of it this way: You can use self-love to value yourself and enhance and govern your life (or devalue yourself by withholding it). Human doings use self-love as a weapon. Human beings use self-love as a tool.

In contrast, you should be tough on yourself when it comes to acting in accordance with your values. For example, if you behave in a way that violates your values, something selfish or hurtful to someone you care about, you should "punish" yourself with feeling guilt and remorse. This value punishment will keep you from acting that way again. Value love nurtures the development of positive values and moral behavior, fosters healthy growth, and encourages success and happiness. You can embrace values such as accountability, discipline, hard work, compassion, respect, and generosity by showing disapproval—withholding self-love—when you don't demonstrate these values and by giving praise through offering self-love when you demonstrate these values. Just because your parents may not have given you this kind of love doesn't mean that you can't break your pattern of conditional self-love and use value love to enrich your life.

> Effective parenting centers around love: love that is not permissive, love that doesn't tolerate disrespect, but also love that is powerful enough to allow kids to make mistakes and permit them to live with the consequences of those mistakes.
>
> —Dr. Foster Cline and Jim Fay, authors of
> *Parenting with Love and Logic*[22]

## Set Success Goals

There are fundamental differences between expectations that you hold yourself to and goals you set for yourself. You need to understand the difference between expectations and goals in order to let go of the unhealthy influence of expectations. Goals are about possibilities. They are objectives that you can strive for that may or may not be reached. Goals are also flexible; they can be adjusted as needed. Goals are not overly connected to your self-esteem. How you feel about yourself is not riding on whether you achieve your goals. Unlike expectations that are either self-imposed or from others, which tend to create pressure, support for your goals from yourself or others tends to be positive. Others are behind you, encouraging you to pursue your goals instead of standing in front of your expectations, waiting and judging whether you meet them.

Because of the differences between expectations and goals, your reactions to whether you achieve your goals is very different from your reactions to meeting expectations. Goals lift and support you rather than weigh you down. When you set and strive toward your goals, you feel hope, inspiration, and excitement. When you achieve your goals, you feel pride and exhilaration. Since goals are not black and white, you certainly will feel some disappointment when they are not attained, but not the devastation that failing to fulfill expectations can cause you to feel. Despite setbacks, there is almost always progress made toward your goals. You can gain satisfaction from that improvement and that feeling acts to motivate you to continue to strive toward your goals.

## Healthy Expectations

Not all expectations are bad. The challenge is to set expectations that will help you become happy and nurture your self-esteem. I encourage you to be tough on yourself, but being tough does not mean being negative, critical, punitive, or demeaning. It does not mean punishing or devaluing yourself. Unfortunately, human doings mostly have expectations that motivate out of fear, anger, or hurt. These expectations and emotions may drive them to achieve success, but they also make them unhappy. Expectations should be positive and motivating. Ideally, they are grounded in high self-esteem and the desire to grow.

What expectations do you have for yourself? What is the primary motivation behind your expectations? Are they positive and healthy or are they negative and debilitating? To ensure that you hold healthy expectations, you must gain insight into the standards you hold yourself up to and the source of those expectations.

Jon Kabat-Zinn suggests that you ask yourself the following questions:

- Are my expectations realistic?

- Do they contribute to my growth?

- Am I expecting too much?

- Am I setting myself up for failure?

- Do my expectations enhance my self-esteem, or do they constrict, limit, or belittle me?

- Do they contribute to my well-being, to my feeling loved and cared for and accepted?

- Do they encourage important human values such as honesty, respect for others, and being responsible for my actions?

With these questions in mind, you should ensure that you set expectations only over that which you have control.

There are two types of expectations that are healthy and life affirming. First, *effort expectations* can be described as "giving it everything you have." If you meet these reasonable effort expectations, you will gain satisfaction that you did your best. In all likelihood, you will achieve some level of success. If you don't meet the effort expectations, you will learn what you need to do in the future to be successful rather than being crushed by the failure and attack on your self-esteem. Again, you may be disappointed, but you won't be devastated. Meeting your effort expectations will result in fulfillment in your efforts and will encourage you to set even higher effort expectations. Failing to meet your effort expectations will provide you with ownership of your efforts—you know why you weren't successful—and empower you to fulfill those expectations in the future.

*Value expectations* are those that emerge out of value love, which encourage you to behave in ways that are consistent with your values—for example, honesty, fairness, responsibility, and consideration of others. Meeting value expectations is also within your control. If you fail to meet a value expectation, you will feel bad about it and will be motivated to meet the value expectation in the future.

> Expectations can easily govern how we see things and our behavior without our really being aware of them. They can either be useful and positive and catalyze important openings, or they can be cruelly limiting and cause a great deal of suffering.
>
> —Jon Kabat-Zinn[23]

## Healthy Reactions to Success and Failure

Punishing yourself for falling short of impossible standards is a lose-lose-lose-lose proposition. You feel terrible and think little of yourself. Then your efforts decline and you very likely fail to meet those standards next time. Berating yourself usually only makes things worse. It is natural to be disappointed when things don't work out the way you want, but you shouldn't punish yourself excessively, even if it's a major setback. In other words, the punishment should fit the crime. You should not hang yourself by your thumbs for what is probably the crime of being human.

To this point in your life, failure has been entirely unacceptable. It has been a direct reflection of your inadequacy and worthlessness as a person. To reduce how much you punish yourself for perceived mistakes or failures, you must change the way you view failure. You must first accept that you will make mistakes and fail periodically. Importantly, *failure doesn't make you a bad person*. Instead, learn from the experience—figure out what went wrong and work to correct the failure in the future. See the failure as a challenge that you can overcome. You also have to recognize that there is often some success within a failure. Find the good things that happened along with the bad. Finally, you can find some satisfaction in having given your best effort. You will feel better about yourself, and, ironically, you will be less likely to commit the same crime in the future.

> Failure is simply the opportunity to begin again, this time more intelligently.
>
> —Henry Ford, automobile manufacturer[24]

You may have become very skilled at punishing yourself. You have had years of practice and you can make yourself suffer exquisitely. What you may not be equally good at is praising yourself when you do well. This means recognizing and acknowledging when you make positive changes, when you show progress, when you achieve your goals. Praising yourself does not mean ignoring areas that hold you back. Rather, it involves starting with what you have done well and then turning to areas you want to improve on.

You may suffer from the "yes, but" syndrome, in which you qualify a positive statement about yourself with some form of disparagement (e.g., "I got a good job evaluation, but my boss went easy on me."). Instead, in your evolution into a human being, you want to adopt the "no buts" position. With this attitude, you make an unqualified positive statement about yourself that ends with a period rather than a comma followed by a criticism (e.g., "I am so pleased that my boss gave me a good job evaluation").

Accepting praise also means allowing yourself to receive praise from others. When someone tells you that you did a good job, your likely response is to discredit the praise and point out all of the things you did wrong. You work to convince that person that you are not worthy of their praise. But people such as bosses, teachers, and coaches rarely give praise disingenuously. They usually give praise only when they believe it is deserved and worthy of acknowledgment. So to devalue their praise is also to attack their integrity and credibility. In return for their praise, all you need to do is provide a simple, yet seemingly difficult, response: "Thank you."

## Desire for Affirmation

Gaining a deep and resilient belief in your competence, value, and self-worth puts you in a position of strength in which you possess the internal capabilities to support and enhance your already good feelings about yourself. Unlike the need for validation that comes from having internalized conditional love and low self-esteem, healthy self-esteem allows you to have a desire for affirmation. You already have the capacity to love yourself and value your efforts regardless of whether you succeed or fail. Any positive feedback you get from others simply adds support to what you already know. This solid foundation frees you to create a life inertia that combines your fundamental belief in yourself with affirmations from others to further augment your already high self-esteem. This serves to continue to propel you along a life trajectory of your own choosing, and that will fulfill your hopes, dreams, and goals.

In the inner courtroom of my mind, mine is the only judgement that counts.

—Nathaniel Branden, Canadian American
psychotherapist and author[25]

## Twelve Rules for Human Beings

1. Let your attitude determine your achievement. Don't let your achievement determine your attitude.

2. Our emotions get in the way of doing for ourselves what we would like to do for others.

3. Don't be afraid to be a kid—have fun.

4. Don't let self-esteem get mixed up in achievement; achievement is different from life.

5. Don't run away from yourself. Wherever you go, there you are.

6. Faced with obstacles, do not ignore them, overcome them.

7. Confidence is born of proper practice.

8. Learn to forgive yourself.

9. The inability to forget is devastating.

10. Get into the process, not the result.

11. Doubt is the number one cause of poor achievement.

12. Follow your dream and enjoy the trip (Love, 1997).

## Part III
# OWNERSHIP:
# THE ENGINE THAT DRIVES YOU

Gaining control of your life inertia and shifting the trajectory of your life cannot be achieved without taking ownership. Drawing on our discussion from part II, ownership can come only from the true self. It is not possible to have ownership when the false self is in control because the false self is not really you; it is composed of the external forces from which you adopted the unhealthy perceptions and attitudes toward yourself and the world. Everything that the false self does is owned by others, not by you. Only when the true self emerges will you be able to connect with, gain ownership of, and become an active and fully engaged participant in your life. In doing so, you will be able to harness ownership as the engine to drive your life inertia in a new and more positive direction.

> Taking personal accountability is a beautiful thing because it gives us complete control of our destinies.
>
> —Heather Schuck, fashion mogul and author[1]

Ownership means that you feel that your involvement in your life—career, avocations, relationships—is truly your own. Your life is grounded in your dreams, goals, efforts, successes, and failures.

Ownership means that you make choices and decisions in your life that support and nurture your true self. Those who have ownership of their lives are deliberate in those choices and decisions because they are guided by their most basic values and their life is a positive expression of those values.

Ownership creates great caring about all aspects of your life because it is truly yours to make of it what you will. People who have ownership of their life have a great passion for it and participate in its many facets for no other reason than the value they place upon it. For example, participation in work, hobbies, and relationships gives them great satisfaction and contributes to how they feel about themselves and about the quality of the life they lead.

Ownership in their lives is expressed in two ways: philosophically and practically. Philosophical ownership relates to your raison d'etre (the why of your life) and the values that direct your life inertia, as well as the principles that guide your life inertia—in other words, how you live your life and why you live your life as you do. Practical ownership is the expression of that philosophical ownership. It is what you specifically do in your life, which includes where you live, what you do for work, who you spend time with, and to what activities you commit your time and energy.

Perhaps the thing that most separates those who have ownership of their lives from those who don't lies in the reasons behind their engagement in life and the source of their satisfaction and enjoyment. Because those without ownership are most concerned with success—or, rather, with avoiding failure—as a means of feeling loved and valued, they gain most of their validation from the *outcomes* that occur in their lives (e.g., career success or athletic achievement). Their false self relies heavily on outside benefits that accrue in their life such as accumulated wealth, social status, and attention from others. Very importantly, they are dependent on the outside world to give them their reason for being.

In contrast, those who have ownership of their lives gain most of their gratification from the *process* of life. They simply enjoy doing what they do. They love the process of life more than the outcomes and external rewards. Given that the true self is confident and comfortable with itself, their ownership enables them to enjoy the simple pleasures of engaging in life. They reward themselves for what they have gained from the experience rather than what the outcome may have provided. Their engagement in life confirms their reason for being. This ownership results in being the Captain of Starship You, in which you have the engine to drive your life along a trajectory of your choice.

# CHAPTER FIVE
## STARSHIP YOU
### From Dependence to Independence

The culmination of the trajectory your life inertia has taken you along, as described in chapters 3 and 4, will have been determined by the degree to which you have been able to define, understand, and act on your values and beliefs. It is also determined by whether you have given yourself the freedom to develop your true self and create a life that is personally meaningful.

Certainly, early in life, we are all highly dependent on our parents. As infants, we rely on our parents for nourishment, cleaning, and mobility. As we grow, we become more self-reliant in these basic areas of living and yet remain dependent on our parents for love, protection, and guidance. As we reach adolescence and move toward adulthood, we become less reliant on our parents and gain greater independence in all aspects of our life. This gradual process of separation prepares us for the demands of adulthood.

This evolution into independence is often a tug-of-war between children who naturally want to separate from their parents and parents who often want to maintain control of their children. This battle is particularly evident when parents co-opt their children's lives and foster reliance on them in their efforts to ensure that their children don't fail. It is this unhealthy dependence that causes the emergence of *NEEDS!*, the development of a false self, and the growth of human doings, all of which strengthen children's reliance on parents.

The distinction between contingent and independent people is the difference between those who grew up hurtling uncontrollably through a life not of their choosing and those who grew up actively captaining their life. Contingent people are unable to develop a healthy life inertia because their dependence on others precludes them from being self-actualized and happy adults. In contrast, independent people have developed through their upbringing the self-reliance and internal qualities that enable them to become fully engaged and self-determining adults.

> Instead of promoting healthy development, parents unconsciously undermine it, often with the belief that they are acting in their child's best interest.
>
> —Susan Forward, author of *Toxic Parents*[1]

## Contingent Adults

Contingent adults are those who grew up with an unhealthy dependence on others. This dependence produced low self-esteem that requires love and validation from others for these adults to feel good about themselves. This reliance on others fostered the development of a false self. Contingent adults were never given the chance to gain ownership of their lives because their parents took their lives away from them and never returned them. Subsequently, they adopted beliefs, established rules, and lived lives that were not their own.

Dependence on the outside world can manifest itself in many ways that range from subtle to blatant. I have identified five distinct types of contingent adults: the needer, the pleaser, the controller, the defender, and the observer. For the first two types of contingent adults, feeling loved and valued is paramount. The latter three are driven more by their need to protect their self-esteem. The key shared aspect of all contingent adults is that their outside world created their life inertia for them when they were children. As such, their paths were determined from a young age to be devoted to reaching out for love or defending their self-esteem from others. Remember, they were unable to alter their life inertia when they were young because they lacked ownership and agency over their lives. As a result, they maintained the same life trajectory into adulthood despite their discontent and lack of success.

Everything depends on upbringing.

—Leo Tolstoy, Russian writer[2]

In addition to describing the five types of contingent adults, I offer specific recommendations for recognizing the particular ways in which they rely on others and gain independence. Although the mechanisms of change for the five types of contingent adults are to create self-love and build self-esteem, the ways in which each type comes to the "epiphany" of their unhappiness differ greatly.

## Needers

Needers are "addicts" who are hooked on the most powerful narcotic available to them—the love of others. They are desperate for others' love because they are unable to give it to themselves. They seek out love and validation anywhere they can, regardless of quality or quantity. Because the strength of their *NEED!* is so great, needers prioritize satisfying their desire to be loved and, much like a drug addict, their *NEED!* must be met immediately. When they are unable to obtain their "fix," they experience psychological and emotional withdrawals in the form of doubt, self-punishment, sadness, hurt, anxiety, frustration, and anger.

The basis of their *NEED!* is feelings of worthlessness and being unloved by themselves. In addition to low self-esteem, needers have a fragile sense of themselves. This means they are vulnerable to misinterpreting even the most innocuous and unintended remarks as catastrophic attacks on their value as people. They are simply unable to experience self-love and turn to others to meet this need, which validates their self-worth. They think, "I must be worthwhile or people wouldn't meet my needs."

The force of this need is so strong that needers place significant demands on others in their life, including family, friends, and coworkers. Needers are considered "high-maintenance" people who constantly require attention. They ask—demand!—a lot of others but don't give back in kind. For this reason, needers can be exhausting to be with. They often require a great deal of energy; yet they don't reciprocate in any way. Thus they are difficult to be around for any length of time despite any of their good qualities.

To put it another way, needers were starved for love as children. It is likely that their parents were cold and distant. It was likely rare that their parents ever showed love in the form of spoken expressions, physical contact, or any other kind of positive affirmation. Added to this absence of positive feedback, needers may have been the objects of verbal or physical punishment. Extreme cases of needers were probably victims of some form of child abuse.

Few needers realize that they are needy people. They rarely make the connection between their difficulties in maintaining relationships and their neediness or lack of self-love. Needers may even put a positive spin on their neediness by seeing it as a sign of strength, since they are able to express and satisfy their needs. They can also give numerous examples of how others are more than willing to respond to their needs. A reality check is usually forced on them in the form of an "intervention," in which an important relationship implodes or a dramatic failure results from their neediness. In either case, needers are confronted with the knowledge that they are demanding, high-maintenance people who are difficult to be around.

Needers will face substantial challenges in letting go of their neediness. In many ways, needers have become spoiled due to their demanding nature. They have gotten what they want, when they want it, the way they want it for most of their adult lives without recognizing the price they pay for getting those needs met in such a greedy way. Being confronted with the reality of their behavior, needers are faced with the obvious and difficult choice of either becoming less demanding in their needs and developing healthier relationships with others or continuing their lifelong and immediately gratifying pattern of neediness. Whether needers have the ability to exert a new and healthier force on their life inertia depends on the strength of the message that family and friends convey to them when their neediness comes to a head, the potential hurtful consequences of clinging to their needy ways, and their willingness to explore, confront, and let go of the "demons" that have haunted them all of their lives.

Nowadays most people lead lives of noisy desperation.

—Raymond Radiguet, French novelist and poet[3]

## Pleasers

Pleasers are also addicted to love, but they get their fix in a much different way than do needers. Instead of demanding it from others, pleasers indirectly "bribe" people into giving them love through sacrificing their own needs for the needs of others. Pleasers are seen as model citizens who are exceptionally giving and supportive of others. They are popular and have many friends. When asked about pleasers, others uniformly give them the highest praise for their care, consideration, and generosity. They always have a smile on their faces and are always willing to lend a hand. For instance, pleasers will rearrange their own schedule to accommodate someone else's needs, regardless of the negative impact they may experience as a result.

Pleasers appear to be more concerned with the needs of others than they are about their own. They are thought of as giving, unselfish people who would do just about anything for others. But this apparent selflessness belies the true basis for why they give to others. In fact, pleasers are selfish people whose primary motivation behind their responsiveness to others is to meet their own *NEED!* for love. As long as others keep giving them love, pleasers will keep putting those people "first."

Pleasers are highly sensitive to having their needs met. They have developed an internal gauge of what they feel is an adequate "return on their investment." If they don't feel that others are paying them back properly—reciprocating with the love they need—pleasers are quick to pull their generosity away from those people and direct their giving to others more "deserving" of their apparent unselfishness.

In order to get the love they needed as children, pleasers did whatever they could to please their parents in order to feel worthwhile. Depending on their upbringing, children may follow one of two paths and become overachievers or attain significant social status. The path pleasers take depends on the nature of the love they received from their parents and the means by which it was gained.

Some pleasers were raised with conditional love that depended on whether they succeeded in their achievement efforts. The key aspect of this type of pleaser is that they did receive love, but only when they pleased their parents with success in school, sports, and other activities. So they come to believe that continuing to receive love as adults requires them to continue to achieve and be successful.

This type of pleaser often becomes highly successful in some area as an adult. Rather than gaining love in the traditional sense, these pleasers gain love through respect and appreciation for their achievements. Despite their success, pleasers are *rarely ever pleased with themselves.* This achievement-oriented drive provides them with some of the love and attention they crave while simultaneously being an unbearable weight that they carry. Always finding fault in their own efforts, they're unable to gain their own self-love and they continue to seek that love from others. They are caught in a vicious cycle in which each success provides them with a transitory sense of self-worth that dissipates quickly and is followed by the need to achieve success again and again and again in order to gain the love and affirmation they crave.

Other pleasers grew up in family environments in which achievement was irrelevant. Instead, it may be that one or both of their parents were very needy and didn't express love toward their children because they were so focused on getting their own *NEEDS!* met. So these pleasers learned that they could get the love that they themselves needed by meeting their parents' *NEEDS!* Entering adulthood, this pattern is continued as pleasers find that meeting the needs of friends and coworkers also gets them the love they need, just as it did when they were young. By being responsive to the needs of others, they find that they can meet their *NEED!* for love by having many friends. This type of pleaser may actually sacrifice professional success for social success in order to meet their *NEED!* for love in the adult world that they didn't receive from their parents in their child world.

In either case, the primary goal of pleasers is to keep the love flowing. Due to their *NEED!* for love, pleasers are uncomfortable with conflict and are known as peacemakers among others who are in conflict and in their own relationships. Their ability to resolve conflict among others is a strength; yet it acts as their Achilles' heel when the conflict is between themselves and another person. To again get the love they need, pleasers must resolve the conflict quickly and often subjugate their other needs to meet their *NEED!* for love. This suppression of other needs can cause underlying hurt, resentment, and anger in the relationship. Unfortunately, pleasers cannot allow themselves to express these feelings because it would cause more conflict and interrupt the flow of love; however, these negative feelings persist and must be expressed. The only outlet pleasers have is communicating their anger with passive-aggressive behavior in which they cannot be faulted for things they don't do.

Pleasers never learn that others cannot fundamentally meet their *NEED!* for love, no matter how much love others give them. Rather than providing self-love that is resilient and enduring, pleasers are unknowingly caught in a vicious cycle in which they can maintain only a small supply of love that requires constant replenishment.

Looking for love in all the wrong places.

—Johnny Lee, country music singer [4]

Pleasers don't need to be told that they have become contingent adults. At some point, pleasers begin to feel an uneasiness in their relationships with others. They gain an awareness of the inequity that is common to all of their interactions. Pleasers come to realize that they have been giving too much and getting too little without their needs getting met in any substantive and lasting way. They see the unfairness of this imbalance and learn that they have no one to blame but themselves.

There are several difficulties that pleasers face in shifting their life inertia and balancing their own needs with the needs of others. First and foremost, pleasers don't know how to identify their needs. They have been focused on others' needs and suppressed their own for so long that they are uncertain what they need to be happy. Second, pleasers question whether people will still like them if they don't sacrifice their own needs for those of others (again, this perception ties in with their sense of low self-esteem). Third, they doubt whether they are capable of satisfying their own needs. In order to stop their pleasing ways and to balance their needs with the needs of others, pleasers must come to some understanding of their needs and how they can fulfill them on their own.

For it is in your power to retire into yourself whenever you choose.

—Marcus Aurelius, Roman emperor and Stoic philosopher[5]

## Controllers

Controllers are the first of the three types of contingent adults who are more concerned with preserving their self-esteem than receiving love. Controllers satisfy this *NEED!* by maintaining absolute control over their lives in order to protect themselves from anything that might threaten their self-esteem. They are the stereotypical "control freaks" who experience debilitating distress when they feel any lack of control.

Controllers live in a constant state of threat to their self-esteem. Maintaining control is their only defense against this perceived threat and the only thing that enables controllers to experience psychological and emotional integrity and stability. Any situation, person, or experience that causes them to feel out of control triggers anxiety and agitation. The only way controllers can reduce this discomfort is to take or regain a firm hold on whatever aspects were triggering them. Because controllers don't understand the fundamental cause of their need for control, they attempt to satisfy their *NEEDS!* by controlling seemingly innocuous aspects of their lives such as driving directions, the course of a conversation, the orderliness of their home, or the leadership of a social group. Control over the minutiae of their life superficially mitigates their complete lack of control over more substantial aspects of their life. Most important, it masks their inabilities to validate their self-esteem, gain love, and feel like worthwhile people.

> The more control, the more that requires control. This is the road to chaos.
>
> —Frank Herbert, American science fiction author[6]

Controllers most often grow up in a family in which they had little or no control over their life. Their parents may have been dictatorial, overly strict, excessively punitive, and unloving. Controllers were not given options and had little decision-making power. As a result, controllers looked for small ways to gain a sense of control by focusing on the neatness of their room, the fastidiousness of their appearance, or the meticulousness of their schoolwork.

When controllers enter adulthood, their need for control manifests through inflexible rules, set routines, and a rigid lifestyle that continues to protect them from threats to their self-esteem. This regimentation creates an order in their lives that enables them to maintain a modicum of control of their lives and, with it, the smallest amount of self-esteem. Unfortunately, controllers pay a big price for this level of control. They are often lonely people who lack strong and healthy connections with others because they are unable to adapt or make compromises in their life that allow someone else to become a part of it. Professionally, their need for control may inhibit their professional growth and advancement due to inflexibility that limits their effectiveness in a work setting or alienates them from their superiors and coworkers. Exceptions occur when controllers possess a particular talent in some area that propels them upward in their career.

Controllers view having needs and reaching out to others as signs of weaknesses because they are governed by the need to appear strong. They see their self-control and apparent lack of needs as indications of strength. Sadly, their so-called self-control is actually a facade for a profound lack of control over their own ability to fulfill their most basic needs.

Controllers are often confronted by others who find their need for control to be intrusive and off-putting. Family, friends, or coworkers typically begin to communicate their discomfort with the controller in one of several ways. At first, they may try to subtly divert control away from the controller and toward themselves or someone else through alternative suggestions that counter the controller's directives. If this doesn't work, a group may create a united front and overpower the controller's will with force in numbers.

Although these strategies often wrest temporary control away from the controllers, it doesn't actually solve the ongoing problem because controllers remain unaware of their behavior. Similar to needers, one or more people (more than one is best to provide strength in numbers) will have to challenge the controller at some point and make him or her aware of the behavior and how it impacts those around them. Once again, the power of the message and the potential consequences of continuing on their current life trajectory will often determine the responsiveness of the controller.

## Defenders

Defenders build an impenetrable fortress to protect against anything that might threaten their self-esteem. Whereas controllers protect themselves with a need for control, defenders shield themselves from harm with an irrational need to be right. Being wrong is perceived by defenders as a direct attack on their personal value. Any appearance of being wrong about something, no matter how insignificant, confirms to defenders that they are incompetent people. Thus, defenders wear their "rightness" as armor against these perceived attacks.

Defenders *NEED!* to be right about everything; it doesn't apply only to important things. They must be right about how to work a VCR, tomorrow's weather, or a piece of trivia. Defenders also have to be right about issues that are a matter of opinion or taste that don't have a clearly defined right or wrong. These are topics in which two people can respectfully disagree and both can still be personally correct—for example, opinions about a movie, style of clothing, or type of automobile.

Because of the force of the perceived threat against their self-esteem, defenders protect their "rightness" with great determination, sometimes to the point of irrational vehemence. They can become agitated and upset when they are unable to convince others of their rightness. Defenders will often "beat a dead horse" to prove they are right. Ironically, a defender's need to be right can be so strong that sometimes being right isn't enough. In fact, someone else being right can be perceived as threatening as well. Therefore, defenders have to be right, the other person must be wrong, and that person must surrender to the rightness of the defender in order for the defender to be satisfied.

> Nobody, nobody can be sure they're always right. The ones who
> are fullest of themselves that way are the emptiest vessels.

> —Seamus Heaney, Irish poet and recipient of the Nobel Prize in
> Literature[7]

Not surprisingly, defenders are often raised in families in which
the dominant message they received was that everything they did
was wrong. This communication may have been accompanied by
anger, derision, shame, or rejection from their parents. They grow up
feeling stupid, incompetent, and unworthy. As such, this message becomes the foundation of their self-esteem and they shape their life to
disprove this internalized belief. They attempt to protect themselves
from this belief in two ways. First, defenders put up walls to shield
them from people, situations, or experiences that require them to acknowledge being wrong. Second, defenders actively confront people
whom they feel are attacking them.

Although there was protective value in being right during childhood, this approach to life doesn't serve defenders well when they
become adults. Other people often see defenders as hypersensitive
and combative. Their prickliness can turn an ordinary discussion into
a battle of good versus evil in which the defender must emerge victo-
rious. This thin-skinned quality of defenders makes people uncomfortable because they must always "walk on eggshells" around them.
Others often feel that they must be careful not to say something
that will threaten defenders and set them off. As you can imagine,
defenders have difficulty establishing deep relationships in all parts
of their life because they can't open themselves up to others and they
push people away with their overriding need to be right.

Because other people find defenders' need to be right so abrasive
and inappropriate, defenders often face backlash from those with
whom they are close. Family, friends, and coworkers may have accepted defenders' *NEED!* to be right and perhaps even made light of
it behind their back; however, at some point the defenders' *NEED!*
disrupts their relationships and others are no longer willing to

tolerate their behavior. Similar to controllers, others often start with subtle attempts at pointing out when defenders are wrong. Defenders will resist these passive attempts ardently, and a direct confrontation is usually necessary to wake up defenders to their *NEEDS!* and the negative impact they have on others. This intervention can be viewed as either a "slap in the face" or tough love, depending on who confronts the defender and how it's done. If the intervention is seen as an attack, defenders likely will gird themselves further from assault through digging into their "rightness," and the value of the communication will be lost. However, if the challenge is put in caring and supportive terms, defenders may be able to step back from their *NEEDS!* and see the veracity of the person's concerns. By gaining new awareness of their behavior, they can use these realizations to make changes to their life inertia to propel themselves along a new trajectory.

## Observers

Observers protect their self-esteem from harm by never fully investing themselves in anyone or anything. Observers come to believe that caring too much about someone or something puts them at risk for harm in the form of rejection or failure. As a result, they safeguard their self-esteem by keeping life at arm's length. This distancing ensures that observers never put themselves in a situation in which their self-esteem can be hurt.

Observers are often seen as cool, calm, and collected people who are able to survey life with a detachment that many people envy. They are not easily ruffled and seem to be pillars of strength among the "quaking masses." Unfortunately, this composure is actually a well-developed defense against a great fear of being deeply hurt. Although there are benefits, this detachment has a profound downside. By not fully investing in a career or an avocation, observers sacrifice their ability to experience deep, life-enriching exhilaration and satisfaction of having committed themselves fully to something and seeing the fruits of their labors rewarded with success. Not allowing themselves to care deeply for someone shields them from the pain of rejection, but they miss out on the happiness and peace that comes from caring for someone unconditionally and having those feelings reciprocated.

He will never have true friends who is afraid of making enemies.

—William Hazlitt, English essayist and renowned literary critic[8]

Observers experience upbringings in which they gave themselves fully to someone or something early in their childhood and experienced pain for it. Observers learned that when they care too much about something, it brings only sadness and disappointment. This belief can come from one dramatic experience, such as the death of a beloved sibling, or a series of smaller events, like being ridiculed and shamed by a parent who doesn't value something important to the soon-to-be observer. From these experiences, they learn that the best way to avoid feeling the pain of failure or rejection and protect their self-esteem is to not care too much about anything.

In adulthood, the observer's distance in responding to the world continues to protect their self-esteem, whether it still needs protection or not. It also places significant limitations on many aspects of their life. Despite their inability to develop deep and meaningful relationships with others, observers often have a circle of friends because they are experienced as strong and reliable. Though considered the "Rock of Gibraltar" by friends, observers are also seen as emotionally unavailable because they never open themselves up to others or express strong emotions. This emotional style particularly inhibits romantic relationships because prospective love interests aren't able to close the gap that observers create around themselves. Without that emotional accessibility, others are not comfortable being emotionally vulnerable themselves. As a result, others will keep their own emotional distance from observers.

Though observers are driven by the same fundamental need as controllers and defenders, they are treated much differently because they don't express this need in an overly intrusive or unpleasant way. Instead of feeling angry at or shunning observers, their family, friends, and coworkers want to break down the barriers and bring observers closer to them. Although people who care for the observers want to connect more with them, they feel the distance that observers keep between themselves and others. Observers are seen as good people who are emotionally inaccessible.

Persuading observers to let their guard down can begin by helping them feel safe with others. This security allows observers to gain trust, which becomes the foundation for them to open up emotionally. Family and friends can then model emotional vulnerability by sharing their own deep feelings for the observer and their feelings of distance from them. These steps can help make observers aware of their emotional distance. Building awareness may encourage them to explore why they maintain distance from people and how it may interfere with their happiness. In doing so, observers can come to see the value of deeper connections and feel compelled to exert force on their current life inertia to propel their life in a new and more engaged direction.

## A Final Thought about Contingent Adults

As you have read about the five types of contingent adults, you may have found yourself resonating toward some qualities of each type without connecting with any one type exclusively. This is because the types of contingent adults are not necessarily distinct and independent of one another. Rather, aspects of each type can be part of you. For example, you might alternate between pleasing others and demanding that your *NEEDS!* be met depending on the strategy that has worked with different people in the past. Similarly, the *NEED!* to be in control and the *NEED!* to be right often go hand in hand.

Further, the qualities of each type of contingent adult you experience at any particular time depend on the period of your life, the situation you are currently in, or with whom you are interacting. What is fundamental to all aspects of being a contingent adult is that you are driven by one of two basic needs: to feel loved and valued or to protect yourself from a perceived threat to your self-esteem. Either of these needs can be triggered and cause certain qualities associated with a particular type of contingent adult to emerge.

To clearly illustrate the qualities associated with the five types of contingent adults, my descriptions and examples may appear to be rather extreme. However, think of these qualities as a continuum rather than as polarities. In other words, you might possess these qualities to a greater or lesser degree and not exhibit their tendencies in the extreme ways that I characterize here. Yet these attributes still may take a toll on your lives, even in less extreme forms.

## Independent Adults

Independent children are those who are raised to have a healthy self-reliance while also being comfortable reaching out to others when needed. This independence results in a deep, resilient belief in their competence and value; in turn, this produces healthy self-esteem. Parents who raise independent children allow them to connect with their true self. These parents foster values, attitudes, and beliefs in their children that propel a healthy life inertia and encourage the development of independence in adulthood. Because these independent children are given the freedom to find their own life path and establish their own life inertia as they grow up, they gain ownership of their life. This ownership allows them to develop a passion for activities and a healthy connection with others. Independent children continue to express and expand their foundation of self-reliance into adulthood.

Children must be taught how to think, not what to think.

—Margaret Mead, PhD, American anthropologist[9]

## Qualities of Independent Adults

Unlike contingent adults, there are no "types" of independent adults. Rather, they all possess essential qualities that make them healthy, happy, successful, and connected people. Every chapter of *Change Your Life's Direction* offers a description of these qualities and how to develop them as an adult. Specifically, this book provides you with the five most important qualities that contribute to your emergence as an independent adult.

Foremost among these attributes is the self-esteem of independent adults; their belief in their intrinsic value as people and their ability to affirm their own self-worth. This quality alone frees independent adults from the feelings of inadequacy, the fear of being incompetent and unloved, and the need to look to others for validation, which ultimately only can be given to them by themselves.

Independent adults have ownership of their lives. They choose their life inertia and take full responsibility for the course that their lives take. Independent adults thrive on the accountability they have over their life. They know that they have the ability to control their life trajectory and make changes for the better, even though they must accept the onus of both their successes and their failures.

Independent adults are masters of their emotions; they recognize, understand, and express their emotions in ways that enhance their lives. Independent adults appreciate the full spectrum of emotions and realize that the only way to experience true happiness is to also be open to sadness, hurt, and anger. They don't shy away from emotions in themselves or others. They embrace the entire range of emotions as an essential part of having a life inertia that actualizes their true self and allows them to actively chart the course of their life path.

Independent adults know what gives meaning, satisfaction, and joy to their lives. They are directed by their true self and propelled by a healthy life inertia that enables them to separate old, defeating needs from those foundational to their health, well-being, and continuing growth as a person. They are able to resist the pull of their false-self *NEEDS!* and assert their true-self needs. Independent adults know what makes them happy. They use this knowledge to direct their life inertia and to seek out opportunities that bring them their greatest happiness.

Independent adults have the perspective and power to propel their lives in the direction they choose. They have faith that they can guide their life inertia and live the life that they choose instead of being a victim of their past life inertia. Independent adults realize that it is often a slow and difficult process that will ultimately reward them with a new and more positive direction for their life.

I am not what happened to me, I am what I choose to be.

—Carl Jung, Swiss psychiatrist[10]

## Developing Trust as an Independent Adult

One of the most difficult obstacles in making the transition from contingent adult to independent adult is the reliance that has been placed on others for so long and the consequent lack of trust in your own abilities and judgment. Because you have little experience in relying on yourself, you will be uncertain that you are capable of affirming yourself adequately and making good decisions without the guidance and support of others.

The only way to gain this trust in yourself is to take a leap of faith in relatively unimportant situations and allow your trust to grow as you find that you can, in fact, make good decisions. This process involves recognizing the options you have as you explore a change in your life trajectory. In situations in which you might have acted as a contingent adult in the past, you now can choose to affirm your own self-worth and make a decision that meets your need for happiness in the present rather than your *NEEDS!* from the past.

With each fork you take that fosters your growth into an independent adult, you will reinforce trust in your self-reliance (in other words, you learn that the rewards of being an independent adult outweigh the risks). As your trust in yourself grows and you're able to better provide self-love and affirmation of your self-worth, you will be able to use that burgeoning trust as a force to exert on your life inertia to change your life trajectory in a new and healthier direction.

Trust yourself. You know more than you think you do.

—Dr. Benjamin Spock, American pediatrician and author[11]

## Becoming an Independent Adult

As children, we were not given a choice in whether we would become a contingent person. Rather, we were victims of the way we were raised. We simply lacked the maturity or resources to opt out of a life inertia that fostered dependence. But now we are adults and have the ability to choose a path of independence over one of reliance on others.

There are some specific steps that you can take to facilitate the transition from contingent to independent adult. The first step in gaining independence involves recognizing the parts of yourself that are still dependent on others. In what unhealthy ways are you dependent on others? You may see some aspects of these five types of contingent adults in yourself. For example, you may see yourself as being emotionally inaccessible to others or as someone who pleases others but feels frustration and resentment at your own needs being neglected.

With these dependent aspects of yourself identified, you can explore how they developed in your upbringing. It is essential that you make these connections. Without understanding the origins of your dependent parts, you cannot sever the ties that maintain the past connections with you in the present. I am told often by people that simply realizing the reason they have acted a particular way for so long is a great relief. This understanding also acts as a jumping-off point from which you can begin to alter your life trajectory.

Once you know why you have these dependent aspects of yourself, you can examine what purpose they serve in your life. The reason you keep experiencing contingent thoughts, emotions, or behavior is that they satisfy an important *NEED!* Understanding what need the dependence meets is also a source of relief and a point of change because you can say, "Now I see why I keep doing that."

The final step in this exploration is to learn how the dependence interferes with your happiness. You may have been so focused on satisfying the *NEED!* for so long that you didn't realize how unhappy it made you. For example, needing to be right all the time may have protected your self-esteem, but it now alienates you from others. Understanding that your dependence, which may have met an important *NEED!* at some point in your life, now brings you great unhappiness can provide further impetus for change.

This process of gaining a greater awareness of your dependence helps in several ways. It removes the mystery from thoughts, emotions, or behaviors that have been a part of your life for years. You now have a reason for why you have done what you did for so long. This insight also makes the issue tangible, enabling you to more easily develop strategies to counter its influence. In addition, this knowledge can motivate you to change because it finally has become clear how it adversely impacts your life and makes you unhappy. With this understanding, you can begin letting go of your reliance on others and become an independent adult.

During the process, it will be difficult to stop thinking, feeling, or acting in a certain way without replacing it with something else. The next phase of becoming independent involves finding ways to meet your needs for being loved and protecting your self-esteem in ways that will break your dependence on others and simultaneously make you happy. Simply, this process involves building your self-esteem in such a way that you are able to give self-love and will not be dependent on others for feeling good about yourself.

Developing the ability to love yourself and raise your self-esteem allows you to stop protecting your self-esteem because there will be nothing threatening it in the first place. Further, developing self-love enables you to find affirmation from within rather than outside of yourself. Building your self-esteem will allow you to lower the walls you have built to protect yourself and to welcome others into your life without fear of being hurt. Strategies to accomplish this goal are discussed at length in chapter 3 and related ways to foster change are described throughout this book.

> If we don't look at how we were brought up and the legacy of that, it can come back to bite us.
>
> —Philippa Perry, British psychotherapist and author[12]

## A Final Thought about Independent Adults

Being an independent adult does not mean never putting your trust in or relying on others. Some dependence on others is a healthy and natural part of being an independent adult. As social beings, our culture is designed to foster some dependence on each other. Healthy dependence involves *interdependence*, and this is what makes it different from the dependence of a contingent adult.

Dependence means relying on others to meet your needs and to bring you happiness without their receiving anything in return. In contrast, interdependence involves being able to meet your own needs and find happiness within yourself while continuing to reach out to others. This dynamic adds a new layer and texture to your already satisfying and happy life while also enriching the lives of others.

## Life Lessons for an Independent Adult

1. There is no free lunch. Don't feel entitled to anything you don't sweat and struggle for.

2. Set goals and work quietly and systematically toward them.

3. Assign yourself.

4. Don't be afraid of taking risks or of being criticized.

5. Never give up.

6. Be confident that you can make a difference.

7. Be a can-do, will-try person.

8. You are in charge of your own attitude.

9. Be reliable. Be faithful. Finish what you start (Edelman, 1992).

# THE FORCE IS WITH YOU
## From Enemy to Ally

*Ally /ə-'lī/:* A person who provides assistance and support in an ongoing effort, activity, or struggle; someone who is on your side.

One of the primary reasons that Inertials come to me is that they are doing things that are not in their best interests. They are thinking, feeling, acting, and interacting in ways that are self-defeating to their happiness and their life. Inertials engage in negative and defeatist thinking. They experience predominantly counterproductive emotions such as frustration, anger, and sadness. Inertials behave in ways that actively sabotage their efforts and undermine their relationships. Inertials often know they're not on a good path in their lives. Typically, when I meet them for the first time, they have no idea why they continue on their current trajectory and haven't been able to change course. In other words, they have become their own worst enemy.

> I am my own worst enemy. This, more than any other trait, proves my fundamental humanity.
>
> —Dean Koontz, American author[1]

## Conflicting Drives

The question you need to ask yourself is "Why am I my worst enemy?" The answer to this question lies in a fundamental internal conflict that is common to all people but is accentuated in those with an unhealthy life inertia. We are motivated by two basic instincts: "thrival" and survival.

As evolved beings, we respond to what I call the thrival instinct. We want to be happy, fulfilled, and successful. We want to challenge ourselves and see what we are capable of. We want to grow, achieve our best, and live life to the fullest. For those of you who are familiar with Maslow's hierarchy of needs, this drive—which he calls self-actualization—lies at the top of all needs and is the last to be met.

At the base of Maslow's hierarchy is our survival instinct, which is primarily concerned with protecting ourselves from harm and ensuring our survival so that we pass our genes on and propagate our species. The survival instinct is the fundamental drive that safeguards us in physical life-or-death situations. It makes sense that this drive would be primary because if we can't stay alive, self-actualization can't be realized. Unfortunately, as humans have evolved, this survival instinct has affected us in ways that were not originally intended by the evolutionary forces from which they emerged.

The combination of technological and medical advances along with increased physical safety that has resulted from becoming socialized, domesticated, and modernized has largely removed immediate physical threat to life for most of us. In contrast to primitive human life, we are now live longer, healthier, and safer lives than ever before with rare threats to our physical safety. Thus, our survival instinct seems to have less value in modern-day society.

Yet as our survival instinct has become less important, its presence has not diminished. Rather, this drive has been redirected from *physical survival* to *ego survival* and aims to protect us from threats to our self-esteem. Given the diminished frequency of need to protect us from physical life-or-death situations, the "evolved" survival instinct now protects us when we perceive that our self-esteem is being threatened. This includes guarding us against the threats of feeling incompetent and unloved. Because this altered form of the survival instinct is still below the "thrival instinct" (or self-actualization) on Maslow's hierarchy, it continues to dominate our lives despite often causing more harm than good.

The survival instinct can safeguard our self-esteem from harm in healthy ways. For example, it helps us stay motivated after a disappointment at work. However, this need for protection is often misplaced and causes problems. The perceived threat to our self-esteem is simply not as great as threats to our physical safety; yet our reactions can be as immediate and intense. Moreover, the fight-or-flight response that was essential for our survival when our physical life was threatened is now usually counterproductive when our self-esteem is threatened. When our self-esteem is threatened, a more thoughtful and less extreme reaction most often produces the best outcomes.

This misdirected survival instinct lies at the heart of an unhealthy life inertia. As discussed in chapter 3, the self-esteem of those on an unhealthy life trajectory is grounded in insecurity about their competence and ability to be loved. Their self-esteem is highly vulnerable to hurt and the survival instinct acts to protect against that vulnerability. When we perceive a threat or potential harm to our self-esteem, our survival instinct is triggered and all thoughts, emotions, and behaviors are directed toward protecting us again the perceived danger. This modern-day survival instinct will do absolutely anything it needs to ensure that our self-esteem remains intact and unharmed.

As noted earlier, when we were young, we employed any strategy necessary to protect ourselves. These strategies often led us to become perfectionists or people pleasers and to adopt many of the qualities associated with a false self, which turns us into contingent people and, yes, our own worst enemy. Recall that what we now consider to be unhealthy approaches in adulthood were highly functional when we were children. Our way of being in the world as children enabled us to survive psychologically and emotionally in a hostile environment. We couldn't have known that this path would become so dysfunctional in adulthood. The external threats we faced early in life are no longer present but live on in our minds, in the attitudes and beliefs we hold, in the emotions that dominate our lives, and in the habits we continue as adults.

Herein lies the paradox of our survival instinct, which has become obsolete. Negative thoughts and emotions about a situation are interpreted by our survival instinct as imminent danger that we must confront or avoid. Evolutionarily speaking, these powerful messages cause us to behave in ways that theoretically serve to mitigate the threat and ensure our survival. The thoughts and emotions that make us our own worst enemy actually motivate us to fight against or flee situations that cause a threat reaction. But what worked in primitive times to help us survive doesn't work well in modern times to help us thrive. This survival behavior no longer serves our best interests because its reactions are usually extreme and unhelpful with threats to our self-esteem. Paradoxically, this survival reaction is "positive" (albeit a very qualified positive) because it provides immediate protection from the perceived threat to our self-esteem based on our experiences when we were young—that is, feeling disrespected and unloved. But this same reaction interferes with our ability to thrive because it is not appropriate for the present situation—for example, you get angry at your boss because a critical evaluation threatens your professional future. Thus, your life inertia is being driven by your survival instinct when your survival is no longer at stake; rather, you are ready to thrive.

> Get out of your own way. Often, we're our own worst enemy when working towards our goals.
>
> —Robert Kiyosaki, American businessman, author, and founder of Rich Dad Company[2]

Let's look at how this manifested for Michael. He was on a life course that was clearly self-defeating; yet he desperately wanted to be promoted to department manager at work. He felt that he had worked hard and earned this promotion. He applied for the position, which would be given to either him or a coworker whom he disliked. The day before the promotion announcement, Michael heard a rumor that his coworker was going to be given the position. This unsubstantiated news was a huge threat to his self-esteem, which triggered feelings of incompetence and worthlessness that he had carried since childhood. In an uncontrollable rage, Michael stormed into his boss's office and demanded to know why he was not going to be given the position. His boss informed him that, despite what he might have heard, the decision was going to be made that afternoon in a senior management team meeting. The next day, the position was given to his coworker and Michael was transferred to another department. Unfortunately, Michael's survival instinct resulted in behavior that likely cost him a promotion he deserved.

As long as this misplaced survival instinct controls the four life forces of your life inertia, the thrival instinct can never assert itself and take control of the direction of your life. You will continue to engage in thoughts, emotions, and behavior that ensure your survival but undermine your ability to grow and thrive. As a result, the goal is to remove the negative influence of the survival instinct on your four life forces and to gain ownership of and redirect them in a way that supports your thrival instinct to become the engine that propels your life inertia.

## Internal Conflicts

This fundamental conflict between the instinct to survive and the instinct to thrive creates other conflicts that further hinder your ability to change the course of your life inertia. One of the most prominent conflicts occurs in your emotional life. Inertials need to protect their self-esteem by avoiding any threat to their competence or value. Inertials are ruled by their emotions, which can be expressed in several counterproductive ways because they also have to protect themselves from threatening emotions such as frustration, anger, and sadness. Some Inertials block their emotions, creating an emotional numbness in their lives that safeguards them against feeling powerful negative emotions. They can't feel bad if they don't allow themselves to feel. Unfortunately, because people can't cherry-pick their emotions, this means that they also can't feel excitement, joy, or contentment. Alternatively, some Inertials experience overwhelming and unmanageable negative emotions. Their constant state of frustration, anger, or sadness keeps them ever vigilant and protected from threats to their self-esteem. Yet they suffer mightily from the deluge of unpleasant emotions that comes from that protection.

As a director of an advertising agency, Margot drove herself unmercifully. A lot of people counted on her, and her greatest fear was that she would disappoint them. To ensure that she didn't let them down, Margot pushed herself day and night. She got too little sleep, didn't eat well, and could never find time for exercise. Despite her strong, calm, and stoic presentation to others, Margot was a wreck inside and always felt on the edge of tears. Once when she was unable to complete a small project on time, Margot punished herself for days. She had problems at work and in her personal life, but she did her best to avoid them. Keeping her emotions bottled up inside her, Margot was her own worst enemy, and her self-defeating life was going to catch up with her sooner or later.

A conflict that occurs between the unconscious and conscious is also common among Inertials. The evolution of a false self requires a set of beliefs and attitudes to become deeply ingrained in your unconscious. These attitudes and beliefs emerge as habits and patterns outside of your awareness that direct your life inertia, without consideration for their usefulness or value. Your conscious mind must recognize these drives and exert deliberate force to override the unconscious forces that propel your life inertia down an unhealthy path.

There is also a conflict between past and present. The past exerts itself through the false self, which engages in self-defeating thinking, emotions, habits, and patterns that lead one to become an Inertial in the first place. The present is grounded in becoming the Captain of Starship You based on who you are now, taking control of the four life forces, and establishing a new direction in your life inertia.

I have no desire to suffer twice, in reality and then in retrospect.

—Sophocles, ancient Greek tragedian[3]

Another conflict involves the unhealthy and the healthy. Our drive to survive is meant to be protective and healthy in the most basic sense—it is intended to keep us alive. However, in an environment that lacks physical threats, this drive causes Inertials to think, feel, and act in ways that are ultimately unhealthy. This struggle is about harnessing the four life forces to propel our lives in the healthiest direction possible.

Fear and courage are also in conflict. There is no emotion more fundamental than fear. It overrides any other motivation or emotion that attempts to influence our thoughts and actions. Fear lies at the heart of the drive to survive: it is triggered as a means of avoiding the threat to self-esteem and of ensuring our safety. Fear keeps courage at bay. It doesn't allow courage to emerge because courage increases risk, which amplifies the threat to self-esteem. But courage also can be powerful, enabling us to confront the four life forces and wrest control of our life inertia from them. Courage can give us the determination and resolve to create sufficient force on our life to alter its direction to a new and more positive path.

Another conflict that arises is between protection and risk. The drive to survive is all about protecting ourselves from perceptions of incompetence and of not being valued, of emotions such as sadness, frustration, pain, and despair. The need to protect is fundamental to being an Inertial and takes precedence over every aspect of life that could present a threat to self-esteem. The drive to thrive involves risking failure, perceived incompetence, and being unloved in order to live life fully, feel deeply, and realize our capabilities. Risking means laying our self-esteem on the line. It involves knowing that risk is the only way to commandeer the four life forces from our past and to put Captain Starship You onto a new trajectory.

> Happiness is a risk. If you're not a little scared, then you're not doing it right.
>
> —Sarah Addison Allen, *New York Times* bestselling author[4]

The final conflict involves *failure and success*. As mentioned, Inertials live to avoid failure. They learned early in life that failure means that they are incompetent and unworthy of love. This unacceptable belief is the driving force in their life inertia. It guides their thinking, emotions, and behavior in ways that protect their self-esteem but lead them along an unhealthy trajectory. Captains of Starship You direct their lives toward success and happiness. They learned early in life that they were still competent people worthy of love from themselves and others, no matter whether they succeeded or failed. This belief frees Captains to take risks, experience the full range of emotions, and accept success *or* failure with equanimity.

> There is only one thing that makes a dream impossible to achieve: the fear of failure.
>
> —Paulo Coelho, Brazilian lyricist and novelist[5]

## Red Flags

Self-defeating behavior that reflects being one's own worst enemy expresses itself in many ways. Regardless of how it manifests, red flags are any behavior that interferes with your success, happiness, or relationships. What is most troubling about these red flags is that Inertials are largely unaware of what exactly they are doing or why they behave that way. Inertials often have a vague sense that they are not helping themselves but have difficulty making the connections among their past experiences, their current behavior, and how it leads them down an unhealthy life trajectory.

## Fear of Failure

Inertials typically have a profound fear of failure that is driven by the belief that failure will be followed by some sort of severe consequence. Common consequences include withdrawal of love, rejection, upsetting important others, losing social influence, experiencing shame and embarrassment, devaluing oneself, and having an uncertain future. David Conroy (2012), a leading researcher in this area, views fear of failure as a defensive reaction that arises from learning that being loved is dependent on succeeding; otherwise love will be withdrawn. Fear of failure has been associated with many difficulties including low self-esteem, decreased motivation, physical complaints, eating disorders, drug abuse, anxiety, and depression.

Children typically develop a fear of failure between the ages of five and nine years of age through interactions with their parents. One study found that daughters of mothers with a high fear of failure and sons of fathers with a high fear of failure experienced a high fear of failure (Elliot & Thrash, 2004). Children who had mothers who placed demands on them beyond their capabilities also learned to fear failure. Moreover, children with a high fear of failure tend to be raised in families with marital conflict, avoidant communication, hostility, and power struggles.

Children with a fear of failure also tend to believe that they are punished severely for their failures and are not adequately rewarded for their successes. For most children, seeking praise from their parents is their primary achievement motivation. For children with a fear of failure, their overriding motivation becomes avoiding criticism from their parents. This difference in motivation tends to create children who are submissive and remain dependent on their parents rather than becoming increasingly self-reliant as they move through adolescence. Fear of failure is one of the most powerful forces that propel children down an unhealthy life trajectory in adulthood. They have internalized the conditional love that their parents gave them, which lies at the heart of their fear of failure. Their self-esteem is based on their ability to avoid failure and gain both love from others and self-love. Most of their life's efforts in work, relationships, and other activities are devoted to avoiding failure.

> Success is often achieved by those who don't know that failure is inevitable.
>
> —Coco Chanel, French fashion designer and businesswoman[6]

There are three ways Inertials most commonly manage their fear of failure. The first way is avoidance; they do not engage in an activity if they believe that they will fail. Inertials believe that if they don't engage in an activity, then they are safe from failure. Injury, illness, damaged equipment, forgotten or lost materials, or just plain refusal to participate are common ways in which Inertials can avoid engaging in an activity in which they fear failure. Unfortunately, sometimes not engaging in an activity results in consequences similar to failure.

> Nothing ventured, nothing gained.
>
> —John Heywood, English writer and poet[7]

The second way to avoid failure is for Inertials to have a prepared excuse when they fail in an activity so that they don't have to take responsibility for failing. In doing so, they protect their self-esteem by not having to take the blame for why they failed. Since it is not their fault they failed, Inertials don't have to fear the perceived consequences of failure and can maintain their self-esteem.

The third way Inertials avoid failure is to achieve a degree of success. The goal of Inertials who have a fear of failure is to remove the threat of failure. They distance themselves sufficiently from failure to the extent that they can't be accused of failing or don't have to believe that they failed. To accomplish that goal, they get as far away from failure as possible by becoming successful. As long as Inertials are somewhat successful, they relieve the threat of failure and can continue to feel valued and loved. This approach maintains their self-esteem but robs them of the opportunity to enjoy their success.

Unfortunately, Inertials rarely achieve the level of success that's possible based on their capabilities because their motivation to succeed is secondary to their motivation to avoid failure. Once Inertials feel far enough away from failure, they lose their motivation, even if greater success is possible with a bit more effort. Additionally, some risk is usually necessary for high levels of success. By definition, risk means there is a chance of failure; therefore, Inertials are usually averse to taking risks because no level of success can outweigh the fear that taking risks will lead to failure. In other words, Inertials are more focused on the chances of failure than success so the risk isn't worth it. This inability for Inertials to maintain effort and take risks as they get further from failure and closer to success causes a constant state of frustration. They believe that they can be truly successful and don't understand why they can never seem to get all the way there.

### Self-hatred

Inertials often grow up dominated by self-hate. They don't hate themselves so much as they hate the failures that result from their internalized belief systems and rules. Since their self-hatred most likely came from their parents, at some level, their self-hate is an attempt to express hatred for their parents. They hate their parents for making them hate themselves.

As children, Inertials are conflicted about their feelings toward their parents. Their greatest need is to be loved by their parents. Their greatest fear is that their parents don't love them. Allowing themselves to acknowledge that their parents are actually to blame for their pain would require them to admit that their profound need for their parents' love was unattainable. In an attempt to reconcile this conflict, Inertials convince themselves that they deserve this self-hatred for failing to live up to their parents' standards. It is easier for children to blame themselves than to recognize their parents' standards were unrealistic. Additionally, rather than hating their parents, Inertials find an odd sense of control through their self-hatred. Continuing to believe that they can earn their parents' love if they just try hard enough allows them to maintain a level of control in the situation, which, in turn, provides a degree of relief from their pain.

At the same time, self-hatred is protective in several ways for Inertials. First, it removes the conflict that their parents are the ones actually causing them pain. If Inertials are to blame for their own pain, then they can absolve their parents of responsibility and still have a chance to be loved by them. Self-hate also preempts the withdrawal of love that Inertials expect from their parents for failing to live up to their standards. By buffering their pain in this way, Inertials actually feel better than having to acknowledge that their pain is unfair and wrong. Having a predetermined belief that they deserve punishment through self-hate allows Inertials to use their parents' withdrawal of love as confirmation of their already held belief. This takes away any chance for unexpected surprises. Again, resolution of their internal conflict in this way gives Inertials a false sense of control over their pain, which allows them to believe that they can lessen the pain since they are inflicting it on themselves, rather than it being administered by their parents. Sadly, hatred is more severe when it is self-inflicted because they hate themselves for who they are and also for treating themselves so badly.

Thou canst not think worse of me than I do myself.

—Robert Burton, English writer and scholar[8]

All attempts at expressing their self-hatred serve three essential purposes. First of all, Inertials experience temporary relief from their pain. Second, self-hatred often leads their parents to feel compelled to show sympathy, love, caring, and support for them. Finally,

Inertials can exact revenge on their parents by inflicting pain on them in indirect ways. For example, Inertials may intentionally fail at something, which will become a source of embarrassment for their parents.

Becoming an adult does not relieve these conflicts in Inertials. Instead, they are often exacerbated because they have been un-resolved for so long and there are now other responsibilities and stressors to manage. This discord impacts all aspects of their lives including their work, friendships, and intimate relationships. With the life inertia from their childhood still intact, Inertials act out those directives and spread them like a virus until they infect every corner of their lives.

This self-hatred manifests itself in adulthood in a variety of self-defeating ways. At a comparatively benign level, Inertials berate and devalue themselves for failing to live up to their now internalized standards; they are unmerciful in their judgments of themselves. In-ertials live in a constant state of fear that they will never measure up and earn self-love or the love of their parents. Even worse, they feel helpless to do anything about it, because no matter how hard they try, they are never good enough.

To this point, Inertials are simply unhappy. However, they may reach a point when the pain is too difficult to bear and it begins to negatively impact their lives. The pain may manifest itself in clini-cal depression and anxiety. This pain also can be expressed as anger, which offers Inertials a temporary catharsis of the pain that has built up inside of them. Ultimately, this situation only adds to their pain because the anger feeds their self-hatred.

> If that pain is blamed on themselves, on their own failures, it manifests itself as depression.... If that pain is blamed on others— on parents, peers or the culture—it shows up as anger.... In fact, anger often masks a severe rejection of the self and an enormous sense of loss.
>
> —Dr. Mary Pipher, author of *Reviving Ophelia*[9]

Substance abuse is another means of anesthetizing their pain. In a study of substance abuse, researcher Lynn Woodhouse (1992) discovered that most people who abused substances experienced emotional pain for many years from repressed fear, anger, self-hate, depression, and guilt. Depending on the type of substance used, drugs can either numb Inertials to their pain (e.g., alcohol or marijuana) or temporarily replace the pain with feelings of euphoria (e.g., cocaine or heroin).

Suicide is a final means for Inertials to escape pain that has become unbearable. Though relatively rare in the adult population, it can be seen as a viable alternative to their seemingly inescapable unhappiness for some Inertials who are pushed to the edge. Thoughts and fantasies about suicide offer vicarious relief from their pain. Suicide attempts offer a temporary respite from the pain and are cries for help to family and friends to give them the love they crave. And successful suicide renders them unable to experience that pain.

## Punishment Exceeds the Crime

One of the most common red flags for Inertials is a negative emotional reaction that is disproportionate to the apparent severity of the failure. Often the self-inflicted punishment by Inertials far exceeds the crime. Stemming from their self-hatred, Inertials experience frustration, anger, and self-castigation that far surpasses the magnitude of the failure. A project finished just past deadline, a few minor mistakes in a presentation, or a lost sale may all carry the same severe punishment.

Children of highly critical parents engage in extreme self-punishment because they have internalized their parents' responses to mistakes and failures. Parents who harshly criticize even the smallest mistakes communicate that these flaws are unacceptable in their children, even if the parents make the same mistakes. These children are also often perfectionists who will not tolerate any mistakes, as errors are a threat to their sense of competence and ability to gain love from their parents. These children come to believe that they must severely punish their mistakes to prevent repeating them in the future.

> The way you talk to your kids becomes their inner voice.
>
> —Peggy O'Mara, editor and publisher of *Mothering Magazine*[10]

This extreme self-punishment also may be a way in which Inertials protect themselves from withdrawal of their parents' love. These children expect to be chastised by their parents following failure, which triggers their fear of losing their parents' love. By punishing themselves more severely than their parents would, they preempt their parents' punishment because they have suffered enough. In addition to the hope that their parents will not punish them, these children hope their parents might show them sympathy and give them the love they crave because they see their children suffering.

These self-punishing children grow up to be equally self-abusive adults. In work, relationships, or other areas of their lives, these Inertials are unforgiving in the standards to which they hold themselves. Any failure to meet their expectations often results in extreme psychological and emotional punishment. These self-castigating adults continue to believe that, by punishing themselves adequately for their supposed mistakes and failures, they will avoid withdrawal of their parents' love—now internalized as self-love—and it will prevent them from being imperfect in the future. For example, a software sales director named Jack missed his quota for the month. Despite missing the mark by a mere 2 percent, he beat himself up emotionally. In the days following this "failure," Jack punished himself unmercifully, which resulted in a decline in his work and the morale and productivity of his sales team. He and his team emerged from this period battered and bruised by his emotions.

## Focus on Past and Failure

Hope is one of humankind's most ubiquitous positive qualities. Hope motivates us to dream, to strive, and to achieve. Hope allows us to believe in a better future and a better life. Yet Inertials are largely devoid of hope because hope requires looking forward when they only are looking backward. Inertials' attention is directed to the past and their behavior is guided by the past. All of the beliefs that make up the false self in Inertials are based in their past— conditional love, perfectionism. Their thoughts, emotions, and actions are guided by the rules that their false self created long ago. Their goal is to escape the past, but running from their past allows it to direct their future.

### Other Red Flags

Other red flags that have been or will be discussed in this book are also warning signs of being our own worst enemy. All of the red flags previously described—being a human doing, conditional love, perfectionism, unhealthy expectations, not knowing our needs, and being unaware of what makes us happy—interfere with happiness because nothing is ever good enough for Inertials to give self-love and experience happiness. Red flags introduced in later chapters are related to self-defeating behavior, including inappropriate emotions, lack of emotional control, and childish behavior.

> The more you nourish the old memories of pain, the more you obstruct the new lights and new truths.
>
> —Dr. Amit Ray, Indian author and spiritual master[11]

## Being Your Best Ally

A primary goal of Captains involves being your best ally, which means doing things that are in your best interests. Captains think, feel, and act in ways that foster their happiness and enrich their lives. They are their own best allies. They think positively and have an optimistic and hopeful outlook on life. They experience mostly positive emotions such as joy, excitement, and satisfaction and accept feeling frustrated, angry, or sad as a part of life. Captains behave in ways that actively cultivate their internal life, work, and relationships. They recognize and choose a life trajectory that leads them to success *and* happiness.

Stopping your self-defeating behavior and becoming your best ally involve removing the conflicts I described earlier in this chapter. In fact, every recommendation in this book helps eliminate the conflicts that interfere with you becoming your best ally and taking control of Starship You.

The first step in this process is to reduce the drive to survive. Since it is an instinct, this drive cannot be eliminated. In fact, you don't want to remove it completely because you still need this drive to protect you from real threats with which you are faced. Rather, you want to make it so that there are no "false alarms" that trigger our survival instinct unnecessarily. Think of this situation as similar to a fire alarm that keeps going off due to heat from the stove.

This sensitivity of the drive to survive can be reduced by limiting the perceived threat to your self-esteem. As long as your self-esteem does not feel in danger, this drive will not activate and you will not act in self-defeating ways. At the heart of this transformation is your belief in yourself as a human being; your basic goodness, value, worthiness of being loved, and competence. Unconditional love and a sense of competence make self-esteem strong and resilient, which makes it less vulnerable to harm. If you "hold these truths to be self-evident," then there can be no threat to your self-esteem and no need for the drive to survive to kick in. By minimizing the sensitivity of the survival instinct, you liberate the thrival instinct to gain control of Starship You and apply sufficient force to change your life trajectory. By relieving this fundamental conflict, the other internal conflicts that contribute to being your own worst enemy progressively resolve themselves and you become free to become your best ally.

You are no longer at the mercy of *NEEDS!* You are free to pursue your goals with courage and vigor without concern for failure. You are no longer guided by the mysterious and uncontrollable forces of your unconscious. Rather, you are able to regain the helm of your life and make conscious choices about the direction in which you want your life inertia to carry you.

You are no longer propelled by forces from your past. Who you were and how you once lived don't impact your life anymore. You are able to act on who you are and what you want in the present. You use that knowledge to pilot your life in a new and more positive direction. This release enables you to let go of unhealthy habits and patterns that have governed your life for so long. Unproductive thoughts, emotions, and actions that once guided your life inertia now have little impact. You are able to recognize and harness healthy forces that power your life as you pursue real success, happiness, and connection.

Fear no longer fuels your life. All of the things you lived in fear of don't threaten you anymore. You are able to assert your courage to explore and push your limits. With no more fear, you don't need to protect yourself, because the threat has been eliminated. You can now take risks to challenge yourself and grow. You are able to lay your self-esteem on the line because you are able to accept the consequences of your risks regardless of the outcome.

You are no longer afraid to fail because your self-esteem isn't threatened by failure. You recognize that you will fail periodically in your life and can accept that the possibility of failure is part of the process of challenging yourself and growing. When you do fail, it is disappointing but far from devastating; your self-love and sense of competence are no longer based on whether you succeed or fail. You are now free to turn your focus toward achieving success rather than avoiding failure. With this new emphasis, you experience the hope, enthusiasm, and optimism of no longer living your life in the shadow of failure. You clearly see the high probability of success and the unlikelihood of failure when you commit yourself to a path.

You had been caught in a life inertia powered by a vicious cycle of thoughts, emotions, and actions instigated by your own worst enemy—you! This caused you to do things that were not in your best interests. By moving your drive to survive to the background of your psyche and your drive to thrive to the forefront, you are now free to create a new life inertia driven by you as your best ally.

> Men go to far greater lengths to avoid what they fear than to obtain what they desire.
>
> —Dan Brown, American author of the Robert Langdon series[12]

## Part IV
# EMOTIONS:
# THE FUEL THAT PROPELS YOU

Emotions have always played an essential role in the lives of human beings. They guide the way we think, inform how we feel about ourselves and others, motivate us in various fundamental ways, direct our actions, and impact our interactions and relationships with others. Our emotions ultimately serve the vital function of compelling us to take action. Consider the following examples:

- Fear prompts us to flee from threats.

- Anger provokes us to fight for our lives.

- Frustration causes us to expend sufficient effort to gain control of a situation.

- Love impels us to find a mate and propagate our species.

- Disgust repels us from food that can harm us.

- Guilt, shame, and humiliation persuade us to act within socially appropriate boundaries.

- Disappointment inspires us to do better in the future.

- Despair prompts us to stop doing something that is fruitless.

- Inspiration urges us to persist in the face of setbacks and failures.

- Pride moves us to strive to do and be our best and to be held in high esteem by others.

- Hope bolsters us when we are faced with uncertainty and loss of control.

- Sadness helps us recover from a perceived loss and encourages social connection by eliciting empathy from others.

Emotions serve three fundamental purposes: survival, thrival, and belonging. First, emotions like fear, disgust, and anger aim to protect us from threats to our existence and are driven by our survival instinct. Second, some emotions enhance our lives and are driven by our thrival instinct, such as love, hope, pride, and inspiration. Finally, other emotions encourage us to abide by social norms and be good citizens, including embarrassment and guilt.

Not surprisingly, our emotions also fuel our life inertia. They act as the impetus for the actions we take in our lives. The type of emotional fuel that propels you partly determines the direction that your life path takes, and the more powerful the fuel (i.e., the more intense the emotions), the faster you fly and the more momentum you carry along your life course.

Our emotions are products of the other three forces that determine our life inertia. Our needs, *NEEDS!*, and values direct our life inertia, our self-esteem steers our life inertia, and our ownership drives our life inertia. All of these combine to determine the quality of the emotional fuel that ultimately propels our life inertia. It's not difficult to see how *NEEDS!*, a false self, being a human doing, living as a contingent person, and acting as our own worst enemy all provide emotional fuel that propel us along an unhealthy life trajectory. Conversely, living in accordance with our values, being guided by our true self, being a human being, living as an independent person, and acting as our own best ally will put emotional fuel in our tanks that sends us along a healthy life path.

If you have unhealthy life inertia, you will likely see that your fuel comes from emotions related to your survival. Your goal is to transition to tapping into the emotional fuel that comes from your thrival instinct. If your life isn't on a course of your own choosing or one that makes you happy, you will need to drain your tank of the toxic fuel and replace it with fuel that powers your life inertia in a new and healthier direction. This shift will require that you explore your emotional life, identify and jettison the causes of your noxious fuel, and replace it with an emotional fuel that propels your life inertia in a direction of meaning, happiness, and growth.

> Your emotions are the slaves to your thoughts, and you are the slave to your emotions.
>
> —Elizabeth Gilbert, author of *Eat, Pray, Love*[1]

# SAILING THE SOLAR WINDS
## From Threat to Challenge

*Challenge /ˈCHalənjl*: The situation of being faced with something that needs great mental or physical effort in order to be done successfully and therefore tests a person's ability.

I f I could boil down the explanation for the life inertias and the forces that continue to drive the lives of Inertials and Captains in different directions, it would come down to one simple distinction—whether they view life as an emotional threat or as an emotional challenge. Emotional threat fuels our life inertia in unhealthy directions and generates powerful momentum, which leads to resistance to change. Emotional challenge provides positive fuel that propels our lives in healthy directions. Gaining insight into the why, how, and what of this distinction is essential for us to regain control of and redirect our life inertia. Essential questions to ask ourselves are:

- What causes me to feel emotionally threatened?

- How does emotional threat express itself within me and in my life?

- How can I shift from emotional threat to emotional challenge?

As you answer these questions, you must understand and let go of the unhealthy emotional forces that have produced this threat response. You must recognize your old emotional habits and patterns generated by feeling emotionally threatened, which have not served your best interests. And you must use your newfound emotional capabilities to alter your life inertia in a way that will lead to a shift from Inertial to Captain and a healthy emotional life.

## Emotional Threat

Emotional threat lies at the heart of the negative emotional reactions that Inertials experience in their lives. The origin of the emotional threat is many parental miscalculations in childhood. As discussed in previous chapters, these missteps include parental overinvestment, conditional love, perfectionism, and fostering a false self. There are three fundamental fears that inform the emotional threat guiding the life inertia of Inertials. On the surface, Inertials have a fear of failure. You may recall that it is not failure per se that is feared; rather, it is the meaning attached to failure that causes the emotional threat. At a deeper level, Inertials have a fear of being incompetent. Again, it is the meaning they attach to the incompetence that causes the emotional threat. The deepest fundamental fear is what lies at the core of emotional threat and makes this fear such a potent fuel: the profound fear of being unloved, first by their parents and later by themselves. This state of emotional threat acts to perpetuate the self-defeating and unsatisfying life inertia in which Inertials are caught.

Inertials experience three powerful emotions—fear, frustration, and anger—that enable them to elude the emotional threat. Growing up, Inertials often felt the "fight-or-flight" reaction, wherein they could try to run from the emotional threat. However, they often had nowhere to run; the emotional threat of being unloved by their parents was unavoidable. Instead, they learned to fight. These "aggressive" emotions propelled Inertials to achieve success as a means of combatting and avoiding the emotional threats to their self-esteem—failure, incompetence, being unloved. A "fight" response, in the form of frustration and anger, acts to drive Inertials to overcome their fears.

Unfortunately, the emotions that help Inertials to meet their most basic need—protecting their self-esteem through success—also render them incapable of genuine happiness. Their hard-earned successes serve as a means of relief that they once again dodged the bullet of failure, but it brings them little joy or satisfaction Instead, Inertials' fears reassert themselves, and the relief is short-lived, as they are flung helplessly along their life trajectory. So Inertials rarely have a moment's rest. They are in a constant state of vigilance against emotional threat and always prepared with their "fight" response. Inertials are caught in a never-ending cycle of fear, frustration, and anger that is aimed at relieving the emotional threat but also brings profound dissatisfaction and unhappiness. Experiencing these emotions persistently for so many years often leads to depression and anxiety, resulting from feelings of helplessness and despair that are ever-present in Inertials' lives.

Additionally, Inertials have no real sense of ownership of their successes, which further exacerbates the emotional threat. Since the emotional threat comes from their false self, Inertials feel like they are working hard and trying to be successful for someone else, notably their parents and society. Thus, their fears are a very real part of themselves, but their efforts to overcome those fears are not their own. This lack of ownership is like having to withdraw money from your own bank account but only being able to make deposits into someone else's account. There is no direct benefit to you, but the costs are very personal.

Inertials often express inappropriate or extreme emotions. The emotions are often inappropriate because they are driven by their need to safeguard their self-esteem, so Inertials typically convey emotions that have a protective purpose. In addition, Inertials are in a frequent state of hypervigilance, which often renders their reactions to others out of proportion to the situation. Being on high alert makes Inertials increasingly sensitive to perceived attacks on their self-esteem so that anything that even remotely resembles a threat will be interpreted as such. In turn, this position produces a reaction with an intensity that is disproportional and out of place.

> People who keep stiff upper lips find that it's damn hard to smile.
>
> —Judith Guest, American author and screenwriter[1]

## Emotional Vicious Cycle

Inertials learned to approach life as a threat and developed their life inertia from this position of deficit and weakness—inadequacy, doubt, and fear. From this unenviable position, an emotional vicious cycle is created. Their life inertia perpetuates success while simultaneously building psychological and emotional barriers to happiness.

This frequent and consistent feeling of threat suggests to Inertials that they're incapable of overcoming the situation that is causing the threat ("I wouldn't feel this scared if I actually thought I could succeed"). So confidence plummets, negativity rules, and the threat grows. In itself, this lack of confidence is threatening and unacceptable to Inertials; yet they remain undeterred. Their lack of confidence drives them even harder to prove that their absence of confidence is unfounded.

Emotional threat also creates an ongoing state of anxiety, with all of the negative physical symptoms associated with fear—muscle tension, butterflies, shallow breathing, and muscle tremors—which further raise the specter of failure. The feelings of threat, loss of confidence, and anxiety create an increasingly uncomfortable state. This "perfect storm" of negativity leads Inertials to dwell on their unhealthy life inertia and feel an overwhelming sense of dread. It also makes it impossible for them to experience positive emotions such as hope, excitement, or optimism.

This apprehension increases with each negative thought, emotion, and experience that Inertials encounter as they descend into the vicious cycle. Over time, they morph into other, equally destructive beliefs ("I am an absolute failure"), perceptions ("Everyone sees that I'm a loser"), and emotions (e.g., sadness, despair, desperation), which further drive Inertials deeper into the vicious cycle. Each step into this emotional vicious cycle separately and cumulatively propels Inertials away from happiness.

As children, Inertials were in the difficult position of being afraid of failure without having the option of avoiding it directly. Their parents, subtly or forcibly, pressured them into continuing their achievement efforts regardless of their unhappiness and desire to avoid the predicament. This coercion intensified the threat response because Inertials have felt powerless to change their circumstances since childhood.

Being forced to strive for success because it was their only way to avoid failure led many Inertials to attempt to gain control through transforming their fear into frustration. This frustration acted to motivate them to focus on what they could control (achievement) in an effort to avoid their fears (failure). Expressing this frustration allows Inertials to let out their growing ill feelings. Although this frustration motivates them to succeed, it continues to cause Inertials even greater unhappiness because it provides only a temporary respite from the threat rather than actually solving the problem.

Unfortunately, Inertials' discontent grows with the presence of this powerful and persistent emotional threat. Their frustration shifts to anger as they continue to be stuck in a destructive life inertia that they didn't choose and from which there is no apparent escape. This anger furthers the "fight" response and is an attempt to continue using the negative emotions to meet their most basic need of protecting their self-esteem. Anger further motivates them to try to extricate themselves from the threat that has become an ever-present and unwelcome companion in their lives. Ironically, the anger interferes with clear thinking and purposeful effort, which only adds to Inertials' unwanted and self-defeating life inertia.

> Do not let another day go by where your dedication to other people's opinions is greater than your dedication to your own emotions.
>
> —Steve Maraboli, American author and speaker[2]

## Emotional Insecurity

The persistent emotional threat Inertials experience creates in them an emotional insecurity that impacts them in all aspects of their life. This hypersensitivity to threat makes Inertials susceptible to reacting to seemingly innocuous situations as if they were true threats. Others often see Inertials as on edge, uptight, or always "having their guard up." Inertials can have difficulty establishing deep and meaningful relationships and getting hired or staying employed because of their defensiveness. They defend themselves against rejection that they perceive as a threat to their self-esteem, so they aren't able to get close to people. In turn, others sense this diffidence and are reluctant to be open with them.

Emotional insecurity contributes to Inertials feeling "stuck" in their life trajectory. Their life inertia continues to propel them along a course that was determined years ago, which has been perpetuated by deeply ingrained, unhealthy emotional habits and patterns. Thus, there is little opportunity or hope for growth and change. Interestingly, the rational side of Inertials recognizes that they are trapped. Despite this awareness, their emotions have become so oppressive and the momentum of their life inertia so great that any attempt to muster enough force to shift their life inertia is repelled by the forces that protect their self-esteem. So Inertials are left feeling that they have no choice but to remain an asteroid hurtling uncontrollably through life rather than becoming Captain of Starship You, even though a part of them wants to break their present life inertia.

## Red Flags of Emotional Threat

How do Inertials determine whether there is an emotional threat? Inertials demonstrate their most noticeable red flags in how they respond emotionally to the world. Because they are in a state of hypervigilance, Inertials are overly sensitive to their own emotions and the emotions of others. Given that their "fight" response is constantly engaged, their tendency is to respond to situations that trigger emotional threat in an aggressive manner. Further, Inertials are often not "in touch" with their emotional experience and often have little control over how they respond to their emotions. As a result, their emotions often overwhelm them and cause reactions that protect their self-esteem but are ultimately self-defeating in most other aspects of their lives.

### Knee-jerk Reactions

When faced with an emotional threat, Inertials often respond in a spontaneous and reflexive manner, typically with some type of fight-or-flight reaction. The years of ingrained, unhealthy emotional habits and patterns cause them to react emotionally to the threat without thinking or considering a healthy and constructive alternative response. Unfortunately, while these knee-jerk reactions often make Inertials feel better temporarily, the long-term costs are usually significant.

These knee-jerk reactions rarely solve and almost always exacerbate the problem that produced the emotional threat in the first place. A knee-jerk reaction usually unsettles an already threatening situation and upsets other people involved in the conflict. The destructive responses often diminish Inertials in the eyes of those involved or onlookers. Finally, the goal to reduce the threat is not achieved and, in fact, is usually aggravated. Overall, the response is self-defeating. A simple, yet essential, lesson can be learned from the many downsides of responding to an emotional threat with a knee-jerk reaction: *Any time you react out of emotional threat, you lose!*

> The problem with a person who has knee-jerk reactions is that it often makes him look like a jerk.
>
> —Torry Martin, award-winning actor and screenwriter[3]

## Attack!

As previously stated, because Inertials are often in "fight" mode, their most common response to an emotional threat is to attack. On an emotional level, they believe that the best defense is a good offense. By attacking the source of the threat, Inertials relieve the threat in several ways. First, the cause of the threat often retreats from an aggressive reaction and thereby diminishes the threat, whether it's a person or a situation. Second, an attack response girds self-esteem by showing power and superiority over the threat. It also provides a renewed sense of control that is often lost when feeling threatened. Finally, a forceful response releases the strong negative emotions that build up and create the threat in the first place. For all of these reasons, an attack reaction in response to a threat has significant short-term benefits and is very self-reinforcing both emotionally and physically.

However, whatever immediate advantages it may offer, an aggressive reaction almost always has a substantial long-term downside. An attack response is a form of self-defeating behavior that sabotages future needs and goals. Such a reaction inevitably hurts the relationship with the person from whom Inertials experienced the threat and toward whom they directed their emotional assault. Whether in a personal or a professional setting, that person will likely distance him- or herself from the Inertials and be less open and cooperative in the future. Ultimately, an attack response does more harm than good and keeps you from achieving whatever outcome you desire most.

## Defend!

Because of their upbringing, not all Inertials will attack when they experience an emotional threat. If they were raised in a family in which emotional expression of any sort was discouraged, these Inertials inhabit a "flight" mode in which they attempt to run from, rather than confront, the threat. When Inertials run from the emotional threat, the direction of the negative emotional response is inward, and they do harm to themselves instead of to the one who committed the perceived assault. Another way to look at this defensive response is to think of the defense as turning the attack response on oneself rather than others. Though there is less harm done to the relationship in the short run, the long-term internal damage can be significant.

Defending against the threat involves completely internalizing the negative emotions that the threat provokes. Whatever hurt, frustration, or anger that Inertials may feel about the situation, they focus those emotions on themselves rather than directing them outward onto the actual cause of the threat. Inertials inflict this assault on themselves, which only does more harm and further hurts their self-esteem.

In some ways this internalization can be beneficial. It preserves the relationship or situation that caused the threat, since the response is never expressed outwardly. In this way, Inertials continue to receive positive feedback from others, which validates their self-esteem and may reduce the threat. This defensive response may also provide Inertials with self-punishment that they subconsciously believe they deserve, which they are preempting. Thus, Inertials experience an increased sense of control that was lost when the threat arose. Also, by turning their focus and emotions inward, they erect a defensive perimeter in an attempt to repel the assault of the threat.

This defensive reaction causes long-term damage by repressing the strong negative emotions triggered by the emotional threat rather than resolving them. These negative feelings continue to gnaw away at Inertials, inflicting even more pain. These feelings damage their relationship with the person or situation that caused the threat because the situation remains unresolved. Without the other person realizing it, the relationship is hurt and there is no awareness or acknowledgment from either party that can act as the basis for repairing the damage. The result is that the unresolved threat perpetuates itself internally as well as in interactions with others.

## Ventilate!

Some Inertials are unable to direct their response to the threat itself. This may occur because expressing strong negative emotions to the source of the threat may be even more threatening, such as anger directed back to a parent. Rather, their reaction is directed toward a target unrelated to the threat or is unfocused. This response can be best characterized as a "rant-and-rave" outburst. The short-term benefit of this form of emotional ventilation is that, since it is not directed at the source of the threat or at themselves, harm to any relationships associated with the threat is less likely. Ranting and raving acts as an immediate cathartic for the strong negative emotions that they experience. This reaction also provides Inertials with a distraction and temporary relief from the threat.

However, responding to a threat with ventilation creates its own set of problems. A tantrum highlights the complete lack of control Inertials have over the emotional threat and perhaps their lives. This realization further threatens their sense of competence and acts as an additional attack on their self-esteem. A childish outburst also communicates volumes to others. It suggests immaturity, an inability to manage stress, and a lack of emotional control. Such a reaction to a threat hurts Inertials' relationships with others because it diminishes others' impressions of them and causes people to question Inertials' ability to be trusted and relied upon.

> When you react, you let others control you. When you respond, you are in control.
>
> —Bohdi Sanders, author and martial art master[4]

## Big Deals

One of the most ubiquitous red flags I have observed among Inertials is that they may react to seemingly minor situations as if they are big deals. Their emotional reactions seem disproportionate to the apparent circumstances and are often one of the previous types discussed. Big deals are characterized by a complete break between the reality and the perception of the situation. To the outside observer, the circumstances seem entirely benign. Regardless of how innocuous the situation may appear, it is experienced by Inertials as disruptive, upsetting, and potentially disastrous—it is a big deal!

Big deals are prompted by a threat to self-esteem and result from three types of threats. The two main triggers of big deals are the perceived loss of love from others or yourself and the inability to meet expectations or the fear of disappointing others. The third type of threat involves the perception of incompetence triggered by real or perceived failure, loss of control, feeling overloaded, or being under time pressure.

As with other red flags, big deals serve the very important function of protecting self-esteem. They act to divert attention away from the real problem. By focusing on the circumstances of the big deal—which really isn't a big deal—Inertials are less aware of the actual cause of the emotional threat. Big deals enable Inertials to delay or avoid facing the real threat. If Inertials are responding to the circumstances of the big deal, they pay less attention to the cause of the threat and put off having to deal with it. Also, Inertials justify their strong reaction by making something a big deal. It would look pretty bad if they got upset over a little deal, but a big deal deserves a big response. Further, a big deal acts as an excuse if they fail. The original threat signals to them that they may fail. Making the situation a big deal gives them an excuse if they do fail because it was too big a deal for them to handle in the first place. Inertials can say, "I would have succeeded, but this thing was such a big deal and it was beyond me."

Big deals are always self-defeating. A typical response is impulsive, urgent, and intense reactivity. Inertials stress out and may exhibit one of the red flags just described. They subsequently feel terrible and experience strong negative emotions, such as sadness, frustration, anger, panic, or despair. In this state, there is no way Inertials can have a positive response, so they end up "shooting themselves in the foot" by making it a big deal. Their intense reaction to the big deal keeps them from finding a solution, which often makes the big deal even bigger because they feel helpless to reduce its size. The irony is that reacting to little deals as if they are big deals results in the creation of actual, real-life big deals. The cumulative effect of creating and reacting to big deals is that Inertials affirm what they have always believed, which adds further momentum to their unhealthy life inertia.

Big deals also have a big impact on Inertials' relationships and interactions with others. Other people notice when Inertials treat a seemingly minor situation as a big deal. They see them losing it emotionally and think, "What's the big deal? Why are they reacting that way?" All others see is Inertials overreacting. When Inertials make life a big deal, they show others that they can't handle the normal challenges of life. People in their lives may come to believe that Inertials can't be counted on when things get tough. Others may then distance themselves from Inertials because they don't trust them to react appropriately in a crisis.

Strong feelings are fine, it's the overreaction that messes us up.

—Albert Ellis, American psychologist and creator of
Rational Emotive Behavior Therapy[5]

## Responding Positively to Emotional Threat

It's unrealistic to expect that that you will never again experience emotional threat once you begin to exert new forces on your life inertia and make the transition from emotional threat to emotional challenge. Some of the emotional threat you experience is deeply ingrained in your psyche and will take time to mitigate and remove completely as a force in your life inertia. Also, some emotional threat is an inevitable part of life. If you care about something in life, you will care too much about it from time to time, and this overinvestment will lead to a threat response. It is inevitable that you will periodically face emotional threats. Most important is how you respond to the threats when they arise, as this response will determine what kind of impact they have on your life inertia.

### Recognize the Threat

The first step in responding positively to an emotional threat is to recognize your reaction to a threat. Often, our reactions are so habitual that we have no conscious awareness of the threat or of our reactions to the threat. In some cases, the emotional threat reaction is so strong that it overwhelms us psychologically, emotionally, and physically to the extent that it renders us incapable of stepping back from the threat and making conscious and deliberate decisions about how we want to respond to it. Without this recognition, there is no way for us to intervene and stop our unhealthy reaction to the threat.

The best way to "short-circuit" your instinctive reactions is to know the situations in which they most frequently occur. In all likelihood, you experience emotional threat in the same situations and with the same people; it's called "having your buttons pushed." Reflect back on your life and identify those situations and the people that produce an emotional threat reaction in you. You likely will see a pattern emerge. You can then see your emotional threat reaction coming and consciously intervene and alter your emotional response before it takes control of you.

### Accept the Threat

For many Inertials who experience emotional threat, the problem is often their perception of the threat rather than the threat itself. They might believe it is wrong to feel threatened, so they feel bad about it. A common remark or thought is "I just shouldn't feel this way." It's bad enough to have to deal with an emotional threat on its own. Adding feelings of frustration, anger, embarrassment, or shame makes it even worse. These feelings can create an emotional vicious cycle that compounds the emotional threat many times over. You feel bad about feeling bad, which makes you feel even worse, which further increases the threat and harm done.

The first step in overcoming an emotional threat is to accept it as a part of your life (though one that you are determined to change). When you feel an emotional threat, cut yourself some slack. Reducing or eliminating the self-judgment eliminates the added pressure of feeling the threat. As a result, you will have less internal turmoil and conflict. This change in perspective alone makes the threat less menacing and more realistic. By not adding the insult of a cacophony of negative emotions to the injury of the emotional threat itself, you will feel better and take away much of the power that the threat has over you.

## Understand the Threat

With the emotional threat in its proper perspective, you are now in a position to better understand the threat. Common emotional threats include many of the issues that have been discussed so far, including fear of incompetence, feelings of worthlessness, feeling unloved, or lacking respect. Other emotional threats are lack of confidence, fear of rejection, and worry about embarrassment. Knowing the cause of the emotional threat allows you to face something specific and clearly defined rather than an amorphous feeling of anxiety and discomfort.

Emotional threat often occurs in response to something that someone says or does that you perceive as a personal slight since you connect it with disrespect and feelings of being incompetent or unloved. In understanding the threat, you must distinguish between whether the person's words or actions were intended to be hurtful or if they were harmless, but you interpreted them as an assault.

If you cannot see how you might have provoked the person and his or her words or actions were clearly malicious, you should rely on the third agreement of Don Miguel Ruiz, the author of *The Four Agreements*: "Don't take anything personally." More often than not, what people say or do is more about them than about us. If they are being aggressive, it should tell you that they are responding to an emotional threat of their own. By following Ruiz's agreement, you disengage your self-esteem from the remark or action, the emotional threat is removed, and you can act in whatever appropriate manner you choose.

If the comment was benign but interpreted as hurtful, you may be hypervigilant to any possible attacks on your self-esteem. In this case, Ruiz's agreement wouldn't apply because it is about you and to place the onus of the harmless words or actions on the other person would be unfair. You must look to yourself to understand how an innocuous statement could trigger an emotional threat reaction in you.

Emotional threat can also be caused by situations in which your competence is tested. Whether it is a project at work, participation in a sport or game, or another activity that reflects on your capabilities, your involvement in an activity that causes you to believe that you may fail prompts an emotional threat reaction to protect your self-esteem.

Regardless of the type of threat, you want to identify and understand its source. Once you know the cause of the threat, you can recognize it when it arises again and choose a healthier response. Over time, you can work to let go of the cause so that the emotional threat reaction stops arising.

### Respond to the Threat

You want to keep from responding in one of the ways described as red flags. A strong indication of emotional maturity is the ability to stifle the compulsion to defend against the threat by attacking or withdrawing. An impulsive reaction will invariably be emotional, defensive, angry, hurtful, devaluing, and unproductive.

Being impulsive will do more harm than good. For example, if a person makes an intentionally cruel comment, you want to avoid lowering yourself to their threat-induced behavior. This is because if the remark was unintentionally hurtful, then you will unfairly hurt them while portraying yourself in a poor light through a knee-jerk emotional reaction.

The best first response to an emotional threat is to take a break. This should involve some sort of distancing from the threat, such as stopping the threatening task or walking away from the threatening person. Rarely has damage ever been done when a person walks away from a threatening situation and later returns with a cool head and a calm heart. Taking a break allows the negative emotions that were provoked by the threat to dissipate and for you to look at the situation rationally and dispassionately.

You can then decide what is the best "big-picture" path to take. The goals of responding positively to an emotional threat are to relieve the threat and resolve the problem that caused it. A response that is detached, calm, supportive, valuing, and productive will accomplish those goals. In deciding on the best course of action, you want to ask yourself what kind of response will remove the emotional threat and produce good feelings and a good outcome. This is the greatest challenge when faced with emotional threat. When you are feeling threatened, it is often difficult to see "the forest for the trees" and come up with a positive response. If the situation allows, it can be useful to seek out feedback from others about a good response and to test your ideas about a best reaction. You want to walk away feeling like a win-win situation has occurred. If another person is involved, the relationship will be either maintained or stronger than before.

> It is not the actions of others which trouble us, but rather it is our own judgments. Therefore, remove those judgments and resolve to let go of your anger, and it will already be gone.
>
> —Marcus Aurelius, Roman emperor and Stoic philosopher[6]

## Transforming Big Deals into Little Deals

The first step in transforming big deals into little deals is learning to distinguish between a "really" big deal and a "faux" big deal. Really big deals are experiences of great importance with significant consequences. Really big deals involve any situations that will have an important impact on you. The upside of a really big deal is substantial, and its downside would be significant. Issues related to health, money, family, and friends are often really big deals, such as losing your job, getting a divorce, or having a family member become ill. Another aspect of really big deals is that their importance and influence are obvious to everyone. The threat lies very clearly on the surface. There are no underlying issues or hidden agendas. There is never an incongruence between the appearance of the situation and its impact.

What is ironic about really big deals is that we usually respond much better to them than we do to faux big deals. Perhaps this positive reaction occurs because we realize deep down that it really *is* a big deal with real consequences, and if we don't handle it well, we or others will suffer because of it. Due to the potential consequences, most of us respond to really big deals as emotional challenges. We stay calm and keep our emotions under control. We maintain a clear head and are able to think rationally and deliberately. Our foremost goal with really big deals is to find a solution, so we break the enormity of the big deal into more manageable steps—a series of little deals—and methodically work through each toward a resolution.

In contrast, faux big deals are experiences that appear to be of little importance and have seemingly minor consequences, yet are interpreted as very threatening. Faux big deals are never about the superficial issue at hand. Instead, the situation triggers an emotional threat related to some underlying concern (e.g., need for control, not being perfect, disappointing others). Unlike really big deals, there is a disconnect between the reality of the situation and what is perceived. As a result, the reaction is as if the faux big deal is a really big deal even though it doesn't look like a big deal to anyone else.

Despite the fact that faux big deals are not really big deals, Inertials usually respond much worse to them because they view them as emotional threats. Inertials become absorbed in their emotions, experience fear, and are focused on the superficial aspects of the situation that are causing the threat rather than seeing what the actual threat is. Because Inertials are overwhelmed with visceral sensations, including strong emotions and anxiety, they lose their ability to think clearly and to make conscious decisions. They tend to react impulsively and often in a self-defeating manner (see the red flags described earlier). Inertials' primary goal is to remove the emotional threat, relieve their strong negative emotions, and once again feel safe and intact.

> We live our lives as if they were one big emergency! We often rush around looking busy, trying to solve problems, but in reality, we are often compounding them.
>
> —Richard Carlson, American author, psychotherapist, and motivational speaker[7]

## Understanding Little Deals

The next step in developing healthy responses to emotional threats is to transform big deals into little deals. In order to do this, you must understand the nature of little deals. Unlike faux big deals, little deals are perceived as emotional challenges. Little deals are uncomfortable because they have a minor threat value, but they are not overwhelming. *Little deals are a challenge to your capabilities, but they are not a threat to your self-esteem.* They communicate that the demands of the situation slightly exceed your ability to manage them. Without these challenging qualities to little deals, they would not be deals at all.

Given that little deals possess a small amount of threat, you will feel some discomfort; however, you will not be wholly threatened by them as you are with faux big deals. You realize that you will have to step up and meet the demands of the situation if you are to overcome it. You have confidence that if you do the right things, good things will happen. This recognition motivates you to be fully committed and to do the things that will enable you to prevail over the little deal. Because little deals are an emotional challenge, you are able to keep the situation in perspective. You are able to stay calm and focused, think deliberately, and use your emotions to help rather than hurt you.

### Preventing Big Deals

Changing faux big deals into little deals involves removing the original emotional threat. Letting go of the emotional threat that creates faux big deals is what much of this book is about. Gaining control of the four life forces that propel your life inertia removes the emotional threat and, in doing so, alters your life trajectory. In addition to the internal changes that I advocate, there are a number of practical changes you can make to reduce the likelihood of a faux big deal arising.

You can first identify the situations that tend to cause faux big deals in your life. As I have already indicated, situations that cause people to feel out of control, overloaded, and under time pressure are commonly related to faux big deals. They trigger red flag reactions that include feeling incompetent, unvalued, unworthy, and unloved. If you possess those red flags, when you are running late, behind schedule, or are feeling stressed, you are more likely to experience emotional threat related to your self-esteem. Knowing what your triggers are for faux big deals will enable you to take active steps to prevent those feelings from occurring.

An unrealistic belief that most people who experience faux big deals have is that we can get things done faster than is actually possible. This belief alone causes most of the faux big deals in our lives. Ways to reduce the likelihood of faux big deals are as follows: You can schedule fewer things in your day so that you don't feel overloaded. You can also give yourself more time for each task, so that a faux big deal isn't created due to time pressures. You should also plan ahead so that you give yourself enough time before you begin another task. This recommendation is particularly important when other people are involved, such as children, a spouse, coworkers, and friends. You can also prioritize your responsibilities and specify what tasks must get done and what tasks can be put off to another day. If you don't cross everything off your list, you will be pleased for having accomplished the important tasks rather than feeling like a failure for not having completed the entire list.

Finally, you should expect the unexpected. Most of us have such deeply ingrained habits that, even though we know what will happen—we will be late, feel time pressure, and create a faux big deal—we continue to put ourselves in situations that lead to faux big deals. By knowing yourself and your habits, you can expect what will happen when you put yourself into certain situations. Based on your past experiences, you can also plan for unexpected occurrences to arise and choose not to be "freaked out" when they do occur. For example, children always take longer to get ready to leave the house than parents expect; yet they rarely give themselves and their children the extra time that is needed.

## Reacting to Big Deals

Despite our best efforts to reduce the likelihood of experiencing faux big deals, they will occur from time to time. Big deals are a normal and inevitable part of life and we will never completely remove them from our lives. As noted previously, part of being human involves being susceptible to some emotional threat. No one is completely immune to becoming overinvested in something or to the emotional baggage we carry with us from our childhoods. As with many aspects of life, it is not about whether we experience faux big deals, but how we react when they arise.

It's not what happens to you, but how you react to it that matters.

—Epictetus, Greek Stoic philosopher[8]

When you begin to experience a faux big deal, your goal is to stop it from engulfing you and becoming a really big deal. What you don't want to do is react impulsively in response to the emotional threat. Rather, start by recognizing that you are making the situation a big deal. Next, take a break to regroup. Take a deep breath and relax yourself to counter the emotional and physical reactions to the threat. Make a conscious choice to react differently than you have in the past. Recognize that the pressures that caused the faux big deal are self-imposed; if you can get yourself into the pressures, you can get yourself out of them. Understand the underlying threat that is creating the faux big deal, such as feeling incompetent or disrespected. Then regain a healthy perspective in which you realize that the situation that you have made a faux big deal doesn't have to be. Refocus on your goals and figure out a solution to the problem that is causing the faux big deal. Finally, make a deliberate choice to turn the faux big deal into a little deal that is challenging and manageable.

There are several key questions you can ask yourself to facilitate this transformation from a faux big deal to a little deal.

1. "Is this a really big deal or a faux big deal?" If it is a really big deal, do what's best because the consequences demand it. If it is a faux big deal, recognize this fact and act accordingly.

2. "Is this helping?" Making situations into faux big deals is usually self-defeating, so remind yourself that faux big deals make the situation worse.

3. "Is this necessary?" If it is a really big deal, then it is necessary, and the situation should mobilize you to action. If it is a faux big deal, the answer is no, and you should choose another response.

4. "What is the real issue?" The apparent situation is rarely the real issue. As long as you focus on the surface

concern, the faux big deal will continue. You must recognize the emotional threat underlying the situation. If you can understand the cause of the threat, you can address it directly.

5. "What is the best reaction to resolve this situation?" When you answer this question, you will create a clear path through which you can identify a new, healthy response to choose rather than making the present situation a faux big deal.

## Signs of Progress on Faux Big Deals

As you make the transition from faux big deals to little deals, you should monitor changes that indicate progress. Practical positive indications of change include reducing the number of tasks you try to accomplish in a day, allowing yourself more time to get places or complete tasks, and changing priorities in your life (e.g., spending more time with family and less time at work). As a result, you will have fewer emotional "meltdowns" and less conflict with others. You also will notice that you are having increasingly fewer faux big deals. At some point, you will realize that you have done something you probably have never previously experienced: had a day with only a few faux big deals.

It's helpful to monitor internal changes that occur during this transformation. Not holding yourself to an impossible standard and lowering your expectations to more realistic levels are good indicators. Not berating yourself or feeling bad about situations that formerly caused faux big deals are also good markers. Being more accepting of yourself and others is another positive sign. You will find that you are dwelling less on things that are of little importance and are able to focus on areas that really matter in your life. You will also feel less pressure in your day-to-day life, which translates into less stress and more peace. Because you are not wasting so much energy on faux big deals, you will become aware of how much energy you have to devote to more important things in your life. At a basic level, you will experience fewer negative emotions such as frustration, anger, and disappointment, which are part and parcel to the lives of Inertials. In turn, you will feel more positive emotions like pleasure, contentment, and happiness, which are much more common among Captains.

## Emotional Challenge

The life inertia of Captains is guided by emotional challenge. Everything that Inertials run from, Captains embrace and pursue. Unlike the descent into the greatest depths of fear that Inertials experience, Captains ascend to the greatest heights of success, connection, and happiness. Captains who never experienced life as an Inertial were secure in their parents' love growing up and developed a healthy self-love as they grew into adults. This affirmation freed them to explore, challenge themselves, and gain satisfaction in all aspects of their lives. As a result, life is not seen as a series of ongoing "life-or-death" experiences, but rather a life-affirming journey into possibilities and all that life has to offer.

For Captains, emotional challenges and the subsequent opportunities that they create are an expression of a fundamental belief in their capabilities, in their value as people, and in their deserving of love and respect. Captains see themselves as competent people with the confidence to succeed in the endeavors to which they commit themselves. This confidence also inures them against the potential devastation of inevitable failure that they will experience as they pursue their dreams and goals.

At the same time, Captains are not unhealthily driven to succeed, because they don't *NEED!* to succeed—or, rather, avoid failure—to feel good about themselves. Without this compulsion that Inertials feel constantly, Captains experience satisfaction and contentment in their lives. They also have the ability to take a break from their pursuits and just enjoy being themselves and doing what they love to do.

Because their life inertia is fueled by emotional challenge, Captains have ownership of their lives. Whatever they think, feel, and do comes from their deepest values, beliefs, and convictions. This ownership gives Captains a healthy connection with their lives, and their lives provide them with many enriching experiences as a result. Their successes bring them great exhilaration and add momentum to their life inertia. Their failures are taken in stride as a natural part of life's ebbs and flows.

Emotional challenge is expressed in the strong desire for Captains to push themselves beyond their perceived limits, to achieve their goals, and to grow as people. Their belief in being loved and competent enables Captains to sustain a life inertia that is propelled by a positive attitude, high but realistic expectations of success, and satisfaction in their efforts. Emotional challenge motivates Captains to seek out new experiences and actively find success, connection, and happiness in all aspects of their lives.

> Emotional immaturity is searching for love outside you. Emotional maturity comes from realizing you are the source of love.
>
> —Collette O'Mahony, author of *In Quest of Love*[9]

Captains create a life inertia from a position of abundance and strength—love, competence, and confidence. This healthy perspective gives them the courage to explore, risk, and take advantage of opportunities that present themselves. Their goal is to achieve success and find happiness in the process. All of their efforts are directed toward pursuing the challenge that will lead to attaining that goal. This position of strength initiates an emotional upward spiral that drives Captains to success, happiness, and connection with others.

Because life is challenging rather than threatening, Captains are confident in their capabilities and have a fundamental belief that their efforts will be rewarded. This positive attitude allows them to feel relaxed and energized instead of fearful and anxious. These feelings create excitement and enthusiasm that further encourage Captains to seek out enriching experiences. This upward spiral of positive thinking, emotions, and actions generates more positive emotions like joy and contentment, which continue to propel their life trajectory in a healthy direction.

### Developing Emotional Challenge

An essential part of changing your life inertia is altering your emotions from a toxic fuel to an enriching fuel that will power your life along a positive life path. A key to changing your emotional fuel is to shift your emotional reactions from threat to challenge. In doing so, you change your emotional life from one filled with negative emotions—such as frustration, anger, sadness, and hurt—to one replete with positive emotions including joy, contentment, excitement, and pride.

One of the basic causes of Inertials' life trajectory is the overinvestment of their self-esteem in their lives, which turns any important life experience into one of life or death. Much of this book is devoted to helping you understand how this mindset developed and how it has led to you becoming an Inertial. The goal is for your self-esteem to maintain a reasonable distance from everything you do, however important it might be. Most simply, developing emotional challenge involves removing the "too" from anything related to your self-esteem. You care enough to want to commit to your life, but you don't care *too* much; this way failing to live up to your expectations or achieving your goals will not be a crushing blow to your self-esteem. Regardless of the outcomes, you will have learned much and become a better person from your life's experiences. This distancing creates a position of strength and challenge from which you can live your life. This shift requires that you develop a healthy perspective about the relationships among your self-esteem, who you are, and what you do. The remainder of this section introduces a variety of ways in which this separation can be facilitated.

Your emotional state affects the way you think and thus the choices you make.

—Claudia Velandia, author of *Wake Up!*[10]

## Essential Beliefs for Emotional Challenge

The ability to view life as an emotional challenge is grounded in essential beliefs that you hold about yourself. Drs. Aubrey Fine and Michael Sachs[11] offer a nice summary of those beliefs (I have added numbers 1 and 7 and the parenthetical comments):

1. I am loved (sense of value)

2. I am capable (sense of competence)

3. It is important to try (value of effort)

4. I am responsible for my day (sense of ownership)

5. It is okay to make mistakes (accept imperfections)

6. I can handle things when they go wrong (respond to adversity)

7. I enjoy what I do (value of passion and happiness)

8. I can change (being a master)

By adopting these simple beliefs, you remove anything in your life that you perceive as a significant threat to your self-esteem. With this threat removed, all experiences can be approached as an emotional challenge, and that shift generates an immense force on your life inertia.

## Perspective on Mistakes

The perceptions about mistakes that you adopted as a child had a dramatic impact on whether you became an Inertial or a Captain.

Parents of Inertials conveyed that mistakes were bad and reflected poorly on both their children and the parents themselves. As children, Inertials were placed in the untenable position of being expected to be successful—which inevitably involves making mistakes—and knowing that they would be criticized for their mistakes. As children on their way to becoming Inertials, they became fearful of making even the smallest mistakes because they were a direct threat to their self-esteem. Inertials come to believe that if they make mistakes, they are incompetent people who are not worthy of their parents' or their own love.

> Mistakes are a fact of life. It is the response to the mistakes that counts.
>
> —Nikki Giovanni, poet[12]

These beliefs may drive Inertials to overcome their mistakes (e.g., perfectionism, need for control), but they pay a great price for avoiding these small failures that are so deadly to their self-esteem. Mistakes are like poison-tipped arrows raining down upon Inertials, because they drive themselves so hard to succeed that they are bound to be hit by some arrows. The only antidotes are to punish themselves for these small failures and to distance themselves from the poison of mistakes with ever-increasing success. Though these remedies keep Inertials from facing ego death and ensure some degree of success, the poison is so toxic to happiness that it perpetuates their emotionally threatening and unfulfilled lives.

The negative perception that Inertials hold about mistakes seems incongruous considering that the world's most successful people make mistakes routinely. In every scientific inquiry, sporting event, dance performance, and musical recital, people at the top of their fields make mistakes on a regular basis. Because they make mistakes, it would seem expected and acceptable that everyone else does too. What many people do not realize is that one of the things that makes the greatest achievers in the world so successful is not that they do not make mistakes; it is that when they do, they react in a way that serves to improve their efforts.

The development of emotional challenge involves changing the way you view mistakes. You must let go of the unrealistic and destructive perspective that mistakes are a threat to your self-esteem. To become a Captain, you must acknowledge that mistakes are a natural and necessary part of life. You must see the benefits of mistakes in your pursuit of captaincy. You must learn that mistakes are only failures if you do not learn from them. Living a rich and satisfying life is simply not possible without making mistakes.

We learn from failure, not from success!

—Bram Stoker, author of *Dracula*[13]

## Change Your Emotional Inertia

Making the transition from emotional threat to emotional challenge may be the most important change to make toward becoming the Captain of Starship You. This shift involves a fundamental change in the emotional force of your life inertia. What has made you an Inertial has been the old emotional baggage that fueled your life inertia and caused you to act in a self-defeating manner. This emotional inertia, which was created many years ago, no longer has any healthy function and is what causes emotional threat.

You are at an inflection point in your life trajectory in which you are presented with an opportunity to change the source of your emotional fuel. You can continue to have your life inertia fueled by past emotional energy or you can choose to change the content of your emotional fuel by making the transition from emotional threat to emotional challenge. If you choose to continue with the same emotional fuel, it will continue to lead to emotional threat and unhealthy reactions to important situations and people, which keep you unhappy. You will continue to repress the feelings of hurt and sadness that emotional threat evokes and transform those feelings into emotions that are more familiar, controllable, and comfortable, such as frustration and anger. This emotional threat reaction will continue to immediately relieve the threat and protect your self-esteem. This is like putting a Band-Aid over a bullet wound: it will stop the bleeding temporarily, but it doesn't heal the wound. As a result, infection and future suffering are inevitable.

Alternatively, you can shift from emotional threat to emotional challenge. This shift allows you to let go of the causes of emotional threat, develop healthy reactions to the world, and create a life inertia that will put you on a more positive and healthier course in your life. Changing your emotional fuel and creating emotional challenge allows the deep wounds that have festered inside of you for so long to heal. It allows you to be open to the fullest range of your deepest emotions. Using this new fuel tank of emotions, you will be able to experience your negative emotions authentically without fear and truly revel in your positive emotions of emotional challenge and your new life inertia.

Emotional awareness and expression are generally frowned upon in our society. As a result, you may have grown up in a family that discouraged emotions, which means you may have little comprehension of your own emotional life. You may have established rules against emotions at a young age as a means of protecting your self-esteem, and these rules may have directed your life inertia into adulthood. Changing your emotional fuel begins with changing those rules you hold toward emotions, thus enabling you to understand and embrace their true nature and all emotions have to offer.

> If you fuel your journey on the opinions of others, you are going to run out of gas.
>
> —Steve Maraboli, American writer[14]

## New Attitude toward Emotions

Emotional threat may have taught you to associate feelings and expressing your emotions with feeling bad. In the past, any time you felt strongly, your emotions may have been predominantly negative and unpleasant. You may have come to see emotions as a sign of weakness that others can take advantage of. To avoid this pain, you developed rules against emotional expressions such as "I will not allow myself to feel sad or angry" or "I can never express what I really feel." Rules like these protect you in several ways. They shield you from the past emotional pain and keep you from future pain. The rules prevent you from feeling vulnerable and out of control. They ensure that anger toward others is not expressed, which would cause them to withdraw their love. Ultimately, the rules protect your self-esteem from the pain of feeling incompetent and unloved.

These strong emotions are denied but are not relieved. Rather, they are buried deep inside where you believe you won't feel them. Nonetheless, they fester, leak out in subtle ways, and take their toll. Powerful emotions that are turned inward are felt as sadness, anxiety, and depression. Though ostensibly aimed at protecting you from some powerful threat, creating this artificial disconnect from your emotions constructs a self-made prison in which you become trapped. You are unable to establish emotional connections with others, so this prison becomes one of solitary confinement. Just as the prison keeps you in, it keeps other people out. Because of the walls you have built around yourself, others are unable to get close to you. Finally, the prison doesn't allow you to express fully other aspects of yourself such as your ideas, creativity, and abilities in many areas. This inhibition causes you to live in a state of perpetual frustration, lack of fulfillment, and unrealized dreams.

To shift to emotional challenge, this attitude and its accompanying rules and prohibitions must be changed. Rather than seeing emotions as a sign of weakness, you must accept them as indications of strength. Despite how it sounds, this change is not a great leap. Expressing emotions in healthy and constructive ways requires courage because it means you are being vulnerable. People who are weak do everything they can to keep from feeling vulnerable. In contrast, only those who are strong and whose self-esteem is resilient are able to expose themselves emotionally.

You must come to realize that emotions are allies that can provide you with a richer and more satisfying life. Instead of weapons, emotions are tools that you can use to cultivate happiness in your relationships, work, and other activities. As tools, they serve to help you meet your needs, rather than you attempting to serve them to achieve their means. You have control over your emotions, and you can choose what emotions you experience. When you feel negative emotions, you can choose how they affect you and how you respond to them. So your emotions and, by extension, your life are your choice.

You must also understand that emotions are two sides of the same coin. You can't feel just the pleasant emotions and ignore the unpleasant ones. To experience emotions like joy, satisfaction, contentment, and happiness, you must be willing to feel frustration, anger, and sadness. You must accept that the unpleasant emotions are a necessary part of a rich emotional life. They will not be pleasant, but they also will not be devastating. In fact, a deep and meaningful life is not possible without the ability to express all of your emotions in healthy ways.

Pity those who don't feel anything at all.

—Sarah J. Maas, *New York Times* best-selling author[15]

The ability to fully experience and express your emotions is an essential part of being a Captain. It is perhaps the final piece of the puzzle. To become truly successful, you must be willing to take risks. To take risks, you must be willing to make yourself vulnerable. To make yourself vulnerable, you must believe in yourself. This belief comes from self-esteem that is strong and resilient, which allows you to experience and express your emotions without fear or concern.

Once you are aware of the spectrum of emotions and can accept unpleasant emotions, you can start to build emotional understanding.

This involves several key steps. First, you must gain access to the full range and depth of your emotional life, which goes beyond what you feel on the surface and reaches what you really feel deep inside. Second, you need to understand the layers of emotions you experience and their causes. What exactly do you feel and why do you feel those emotions? Importantly, you must acknowledge the "okayness" of your emotions, as well as accept and welcome all emotions into your life. Finally, you can learn to express the full range of emotions in ways that are relieving and constructive.

> But feelings can't be ignored, no matter how unjust and ungrateful they seem.
>
> —Anne Frank, German-Dutch diarist of Jewish origin[16]

## Let It Out vs. Let It Go

You have become very good at letting your emotions out. Whether you let them out by yelling at someone, crying, or berating yourself, letting them out has been a necessary survival skill that served several purposes. Letting it out relieved the vague, yet powerful, feelings that accompany emotional threat. It also allowed you to avoid facing the real emotions underlying the threat. Most important, letting it out protected your self-esteem from the pain of what those fundamental emotions meant to you.

Unfortunately, as I have discussed, letting it out is a temporary and ineffective solution that doesn't offer any long-term benefits. Letting it out leads you to believe that you are responding to emotional threat in a way that is helpful and positive. To yourself, you might think, "I may not have dealt with that perfectly, but I sure feel better." The problem is that the emotional threat remains to rear its ugly head the next time you perceive that your self-esteem is under attack. Even worse, the immediate relief that letting it out provides reinforces this reaction, causing it to become a habit and discouraging the adoption of other, more constructive ways of handling the emotional threat.

An essential part of making the transition from emotional threat to emotional challenge is learning to let your emotions go. This release of unhealthy emotions, rather than simply relieving them temporarily, is what emotional understanding is about. Gaining insight into your deepest emotions, identifying their source, connecting them with your present, and then shifting your current emotional trajectory are all necessary steps to changing your life inertia.

Time doesn't heal emotional pain, you need to learn how to let go.

—Roy T. Bennett, author[17]

## Surface Emotions

When you feel emotional threat, you are not feeling the emotions that are actually causing the threat. In fact, most people can't put a finger on their feelings when an emotional threat presents itself. Rather, they feel an amorphous emotional discomfort. Only when the threat becomes stronger and more immediate do the emotions begin to take shape. Usually, when the emotions are expressed physically, through behavior like a raised voice or tears, you are able to label these emotions as anger and sadness, respectively.

Most of us learn our dominant emotional response to threat from our family. For example, if one or both of your parents expressed their emotions with anger, then you likely learned to do the same. Likewise, if hurt and crying were most frequently used, you may have adopted these emotional reactions. Alternatively, if emotional expression was frowned upon, then you probably learned to turn your emotions inward. Regardless of the specific means of expression, these surface emotions keep you from experiencing the underlying emotions that caused the emotional threat. All you knew was that expressing the surface emotions made you feel better (or perhaps just less bad).

However, surface emotions often bear little resemblance to the underlying emotions that caused them. Superficial emotions such as anger or sadness are simply overt reflections of a fight-or-flight reaction to the perceived emotional threat. These outward emotions are so powerful because they protect you from the deeper, more unsettling emotions.

No matter how you let your surface emotions out, you never reach the deeper emotions that really need to be relieved. Rather, your reactions to the superficial emotions keep you from having to face the underlying emotions and their causes—thus their protective value. Consequently, those core emotions are pushed down and bottled up. They slowly build up and act as a great weight on you. Much of what you feel physically actually may be an expression of those primary emotions that have no outlet. These emotions can cause you to feel tired, lethargic, melancholy, unmotivated, anxious, agitated, restless, or tense. You may have fantasies about running away, but you realize the difficulty with trying to escape your problems is that you always take yourself with you. Even without knowing the real perceptions and emotions that lay beneath the surface emotion, you know that you need to relieve the pressure you feel and unburden yourself of the emotional weight you carry in any way possible.

Instead of reacting to the emotions associated with the threat, you must be willing to sit and experience the discomfort. Accept the surface emotions for what they are and what they are not. They are clues and conduits to the deeper emotions from which the emotional threat is warning you away; they are not significant emotions themselves. Once you are able to experience and understand these superficial emotions, you will be in a position to move below them and explore the depths of your emotional world.

## Underlying Emotions

The greatest challenge in letting go of the emotional threat is to get in touch with the core emotions related to the threat. This step takes considerable courage because your life inertia was created to avoid having to face these very emotions. It is here that the leap of faith that I have discussed previously plays such a vital role. As an adult, you have far more capabilities and resources than you did when you were young. Taking the leap of faith requires you to trust that you are now equipped to face underlying emotions and that you will be okay. Facing these deep emotions is a necessary and healthy step in changing your life inertia. It also allows you to use more positive emotional fuel to propel your life away from superficial emotions and the experiences and perceptions that precipitated them. In fact, confronting these core emotions is your first act of emotional challenge.

Now that you have learned that what you are feeling on the outside is not the same as what you are feeling on the inside, when you experience an emotional threat you must ask yourself, "What am I really feeling?" The answer to this question will open the door—and sometimes the floodgates—to the depths of your emotional life. It initiates the transition from emotional threat to emotional challenge.

There is no magical way to connect your surface feelings with this deep well of emotions. You must simply experience the surface emotions and then give yourself the opportunity to feel beyond them. Where is the frustration coming from? What emotions underlie the anger? What feelings are at the root of the sadness? Try completing the following sentence: "Underlying my [sadness, frustration, anger], I am feeling _____." As you allow the deeper emotions to surface, you must acknowledge and accept them. Though this process will be difficult, gird yourself in the knowledge that you are taking a significant step in changing the source of your emotional fuel.

Reaching these long-buried emotions can be both a terrifying and a motivating experience. Terrifying because these emotions are primal and powerful. They have composed the core of your emotional life and have been locked deep inside of you for years. These emotions have been the fuel that propelled you in the direction to become an Inertial. Fear of these emotions may impel you to push these emotions back where they came from because they are so uncomfortable. I encourage you to push through that discomfort because you are likely to find something surprising—and relieving.

When you allow yourself to fully experience these underlying emotions, you find out that they aren't as strong or terrifying as you thought they would be because you are a different person than who you were as a child. You have greater maturity, a different perspective, more skills, and better resources that turn down the volume on emotions that once screamed at you in the loudest voice possible.

This moment is also motivating because the experience of the emotions is difficult, yet never as overwhelming as the anticipation. This realization often acts as a great impetus to explore further. In time, you will become comfortable with these emotions and you will be able to accept them as a part of you. This acceptance alone saps much of the influence these emotions have on your life. Instead of fearing these emotions as they run your life, you can allow them to be a part of you, which renders their impact diminished in the future. Also, exposing the emotions to the light of day makes them more tangible and manageable because they lose their "fear-of-the-unknown" quality.

> You'll never cross an emotional bridge, if you keep rushing back to the other side.
>
> —T. F. Hodge, author of *From within I Rise*[18]

## Underlying Perceptions

Most often, the deeper emotions are caused by long-repressed, yet ever-present, perceptions that you developed about yourself and your world as a child. For example, perceptions and beliefs like "Failure is unacceptable," "I must be in control," or "My parents don't love me." These perceptions were formed from experiences early in your life that you perceived as threatening. They may have involved your relationship with your parents or other meaningful experiences. The superficial emotions that you experience in the present are intended to protect you from the deeper emotions and the subconscious perceptions that caused them in the past.

These underlying emotions are most often grounded in fear and pain: fear due to the perception that "I am incompetent and worthless," and pain from the perception that "my parents don't really love me" and that "I don't love myself" as an adult. We come to believe we are incapable, of no value, and unlovable through the development of the false self.

These perceptions lie at the heart of being an Inertial. Your recognition of them is essential to letting go of their impact and replacing them with perceptions that are based on who you are in the present. Knowing what you feel and why you feel this way can reduce the impact these emotions and perceptions have on your life inertia. These realizations alone finally answer the question: "Why have I been making myself so miserable for so long?" With this knowledge, you now have the power to change those perceptions and emotions and alter the trajectory of your life.

The challenge for you is to figure out how to uncover these hidden perceptions that have directed your emotional inertia for so long. There is no single way to do this. This discovery can come from introspection and reflection, relevant readings, podcasts, blog posts, workshops, or seeing a therapist who can guide you in this journey. Regardless of which road you choose, you must start with courage, an open mind and heart, and the realization that it will be difficult. Keep the faith that the destination will be worth every step you take.

## Connect Emotions and Perceptions with the Past

Once the underlying emotions have been acknowledged and experienced and the underlying perceptions have been identified, the next step is to understand where the emotions and perceptions came from. This process involves looking into your past for the relationships and experiences through which you first developed these perceptions and felt these emotions. You must ask yourself, "When did I first feel this way?" and "Who or what caused me to feel this way?" The answers to these questions are essential steps in changing your emotional fuel and exerting a healthy force on your life inertia.

Most often, the sources of these underlying emotions are found in the relationships that people had with their parents. For example, the feeling of being unworthy of love may have come from a parent who was cold and punitive when you didn't live up to his or her expectations. These core emotions also may have come from a traumatic event or a series of experiences. These can range from the death of a family member to a personal illness or injury, being the object of bullying or abuse, a persistent state of loneliness, or other emotionally indelible experiences.

You will never be able to completely remove these connections from your psyche. Unlike a tumor, which can be surgically removed, past experiences, perceptions, and emotions will always be a part of you. The goal is not to eradicate them from your system but to sever the emotional ties to those experiences that have fueled your life inertia since you were a child and adversely affect your life now. Once you have cut the emotional connections, the memories of the experiences still will be present. The difference is that they will be less vivid, influential, and painful because they won't carry the emotional resonance that they once did. The emotions will still be there as well, and they will surface from time to time when you are faced with a situation similar to those that originally caused the emotions. The important thing is that those emotions will not dominate your life as they have for so many years. Rather, other thoughts, emotions, and actions that are based on who you are in the present will emerge and override the old, unhealthy patterns. This is when the quality of your emotional fuel changes and then can propel your life in a different direction.

Making these connections can be a truly liberating experience, as you finally have answers to questions that have been confounding you for most of your life. You have probably known for years that something was not quite right. You may have had the sense that there were forces within you that have held you back and that continue to propel you along a life trajectory that is neither healthy nor constructive. Until now, you could never identify those forces. Now, the mystery is finally solved! You understand why you have been thinking, feeling, and acting as you have for all these years. Where for so long there was no rhyme or reason for doing things that were obviously not in your best interests, now you have a clear and reasonable explanation.

> In order to move on, you must understand why you felt what you did and why you no longer need to feel it.
>
> —Mitch Albom, international best-selling author[19]

### Separate Past from Present

After connecting the deep emotions you feel with past experiences in your life, you want to connect those experiences and emotions with who you are in the present; explore how those experiences and emotions from the past have shaped who you are and how you think, feel, and behave in the present. You will likely find that much of your current life is guided by those early experiences, perceptions, and emotions, even though there is little resemblance between the person you were then and the person you are now. You will likely be shocked by the power of those connections between the past and the present and by your inability to break those unhealthy connections up until now. Fortunately, you are now in a place in which you can leave those old emotions behind and begin to develop healthy emotional reactions grounded in the present and who you want to be in the future.

## Corrective Emotional Experience

At the heart of changing your life inertia and altering the trajectory of your life is the realization that you are the Captain of Starship You and that you alone can harness your emotions to fuel your journey. Having command of your life provides you with the ability to choose the path you want rather than the destructive one that you have been following for many years, which has led you to becoming an Inertial.

Directing your life in a new and healthier direction begins with a corrective emotional experience, in which you are faced with people and situations similar to those you had in the past but that you respond to in positive and healthy ways. This new direction in your life is based on who you are now and what is in your best interests for the future. For example, in the past you may have experienced situations at work in which you felt incompetent. In these circumstances, your life inertia propelled you down a path of hurt and withdrawal. By committing to a corrective emotional experience, you choose to see the situation as an emotional challenge that requires courage and assertiveness. The response from your work colleagues will also change and become positive and encouraging, which will make you feel effectual and supported.

The beauty of corrective emotional experiences is that they are self-reinforcing. You will be rewarded for taking a new direction in a particular situation with better feelings about yourself, more positive emotions, supportive reactions from others, and doing what is best for you now and moving forward. Each time you engage in a corrective emotional experience, you are using your emotions to exert force on your life inertia. The cumulative effect of more and more corrective emotional experiences is a stunning blow on your life inertia that shifts your life trajectory.

## Open Up Emotionally

Another part of changing the course of the life inertia you have felt trapped in for many years involves opening up to other people emotionally. This step requires faith in your ability to respond with emotional challenge and courage to take the risk and make yourself vulnerable. Only with experience, familiarity, and positive results will you become comfortable in opening yourself up to others. It begins with taking a leap of faith and trusting that good things will happen.

The journey to understand begins with a leap of faith.

—Dannika Dark, *USA Today* best-selling author[20]

Unlike Inertials, who experience emotional threat and live a life of emotional insecurity, those who experience emotional challenge are able to live a life of emotional vulnerability. This emotional openness involves the capacity to feel your deepest emotions, both pleasant and less so, fully within yourself and to share those feelings with others. This opening of your heart, in turn, invites others to return the vulnerability in kind, thus enriching your relationships. As a Captain in command of Starship You, you feel comfortable choosing to be vulnerable in order to experience life to its fullest. You learn that there are potential risks to being vulnerable, but you also know that only by laying your self-esteem on the line will you experience all that life has to offer.

The ability to be emotionally vulnerable begins with having the capacity to be a human being rather than a human doing. This ability means being able to acknowledge and accept all aspects of yourself including the good, the bad, and, yes, the ugly. It also involves never being connected with anything to such an extent that your self-esteem is at risk. Emotional vulnerability likewise means that you are grounded in the present and who you are now, rather than in the past and who you once were.

What happens when people open their hearts? They get better.

—Haruki Murakami, Japanese writer and best-selling author[21]

Emotional vulnerability has numerous benefits. Instead of merely surviving, your most fundamental drive becomes to thrive, challenge yourself, and grow in every part of your life. This motivation provides you with the impetus to open yourself to your entire emotional world. You can allow yourself to fully experience the spectrum of true emotions. You no longer have the need to protect yourself from negative emotions such as sadness, pain, frustration, or anger, because you accept them as just another part of your emotional life. You can reach out to others as well as be accessible to others, thereby creating strong relationships with people. You can welcome others into your emotional world and allow them to impact you both positively and negatively. This vulnerability engenders trust in other people and encourages them to open themselves to you.

Emotional vulnerability does not mean that you are naive or indiscriminate with whom you make yourself vulnerable. Part of your ability to be emotionally open comes from your understanding of people and the potential consequences of vulnerability. With this understanding, you are selective both with whom you are vulnerable and regarding the degree of vulnerability that you offer. If your vulnerability is betrayed, you have the emotional strength to handle the betrayal. You naturally feel bad, but it is not a devastating blow to your self-esteem.

Much like all aspects of changing the emotional fuel that propels your life inertia, opening up to people emotionally is a process that you should allow yourself to proceed through slowly. The primary barrier to opening up to people is that past experiences have taught you that if you are vulnerable, then you will be hurt by others. You must learn that this is not always the case. In fact, there are wonderful benefits to being open with others. In time, you must learn to see the value and to enjoy the emotional openness.

To change your beliefs and gain trust in emotional vulnerability, you must explore the newfound openness slowly and in a way that will validate the risks you are taking. You should begin being emotionally vulnerable with people you trust and in whom you have seen emotional openness before. Carefully selecting certain family and friends who will reciprocate your vulnerability is essential. At first, you want to offer only small bits of yourself rather than fully baring your soul. For example, you may tell a friend whom you trust, "I am feeling kind of sad today," rather than "I have been angry at my mother for years." With this initial emotional risk, look for her reaction. If you chose wisely with whom to be vulnerable, her response likely will be positive and empathic toward your feelings. She also may share her own feelings with you.

With each success of emotional vulnerability, you will become increasingly comfortable with your emotional openness as it is reciprocated with vulnerability, warmth, and emotional connectedness from others. With each experience of making yourself vulnerable, you are changing your emotional fuel and, in doing so, exerting force on your life inertia.

At the same time, you must realize that not all of your emotional experiences will be affirming. There will be people who do not respond to your openness and may actually turn it against you. It is imperative to accept that this is a risk you take for being emotionally vulnerable and to remind yourself that such encounters will not be devastating. Rather, you can keep these experiences in perspective and weigh them against the benefits of being emotionally open. Also, as you become better acquainted with being emotionally vulnerable, you will become more skilled at selecting those with whom you are open and the degree of openness that is appropriate. With practice and feedback, you will become skilled at knowing when and how much you should be emotionally open with people.

## Respond to Others with Emotional Challenge

Developing a positive emotional response allows you to change the way you respond to others emotionally. Instead of being self-protective, you can be self-enhancing. Rather than needing to put your needs ahead of those of others, you can appropriately put your needs aside and respond openly to the concerns of others.

When there is ill feeling, conflict, or another negative emotional reaction, your natural inclination is to defend yourself against the perceived attack by reciprocating with your own threat. This response prevents you from hearing the real message behind the conflict. It puts the other person in a defensive position as well and creates a downward spiral of bad feelings and discord. Emotional threat also doesn't allow the other person to step back and recognize their behavior or decide that their reaction wasn't the most appropriate.

Emotional challenge enables you to do what is right not only for yourself but also for others. You are free to take the moral high road instead of being dragged down to another's level and becoming a part of the problem; you can help lift them up to your level and be a part of the solution.

Emotional challenge liberates you from the need to respond in kind; rather, it allows you to hear what the other person is trying to communicate beneath the frustration, anger, or hurt that lies at the surface of the message. You are able to understand your behavior and emotions, as well as the meaning underlying both. You can see that their reaction is not about you, but rather reflects a threat that they perceive that may or may not be related to you.

Understanding that your emotions are not a reflection on you but rather an internal conflict that you are experiencing and expressing allows you to choose to respond in a way that leads to a win-win situation. By not buying into the ill feelings expressed by the other person, you disarm the confrontation before it starts. Since you don't respond with your own threat response, you allow the other person to pause and evaluate their reaction and perhaps choose to change the way they feel and how they respond to you. You can also help them to distill what the real problem is and find a solution that serves both of you. This high road ends with the other person feeling good about the outcome of the interaction and you building greater rapport and strengthening your relationship with him or her for the future.

Rather than being your thoughts and emotions, be the awareness behind them.

—Eckhart Tolle, spiritual teacher and best-selling author[22]

# Breaking Emotional Habits

You may have finally let go of the unhealthy emotions that have fueled your life inertia for many years, but that does not mean that your emotional reactions will change immediately or permanently. Though the emotional connections that triggered emotional threat may have resolved, the thoughts and behaviors that were the most common reactions to the threat have become deeply ingrained as emotional habits over the years. Emotional habits can be understood as automatic reactions that were instilled through repeated exposure to situations that share common qualities. For example, you may have felt unworthy of love when you were growing up each time your father devalued your achievements. When this happened, you felt great anger toward him; however, it was unacceptable to express your feelings to him, so you turned your anger toward yourself. Over the years, any experience that caused you to feel that others were not appreciating your efforts triggered anger that you internalized, which created an emotional habit.

Having let go of the old emotions and perceptions that caused the threat reaction, emotional habits no longer serve a purpose. Because there is no longer a threat to self-esteem, there is no need to continue protecting yourself. Despite letting go of the emotional threat, you still may react in an emotionally unhealthy way because the emotional reactions when faced with an emotional threat have become emotional habits. For you to use your emotional fuel to propel yourself in a healthier direction, you must retrain yourself and develop new emotional habits that are based on who you are at present; what thoughts, emotions, and behavior will be in your best interests; and what will help you achieve your goals and make you happy.

Changing your emotional habits is a progressive process of awareness and action that will culminate in a complete shift in your emotional inertia. The first step involves recognizing situations that triggered an emotional threat response and caused the unhealthy emotional habits to develop. It is the recognition of these past associations that creates opportunities to develop new emotional responses. At first, you will not recognize the new direction that your changed life inertia can take you. Because the inertia behind your emotional habits is so strong and entrenched, you will continue along your old life trajectory for a period of time. Only afterward will you recognize the opportunity you had to use your new emotional inertia to change course.

As you separate yourself further from your past and the old emotional threat loses its potency, you will come to recognize your new emotional inertia sooner and sooner. You will see the new direction you want to go and know it is much better for you, albeit too late. Then you will see the opportunity to change course approaching rather than after it's too late. Still, you may not be able to leverage your new emotional fuel to take the good direction. You will see the chance and still go right past it because your emotional habits are so well entrenched. This situation can be frustrating, but it is important to recognize that you now have an opportunity that hadn't been there for many years, and it will appear again. You now truly have a choice about what fuel will propel your life inertia.

The next step in this progression involves recognizing the new course as you near it and actually stopping at it. While at this point, you likely will have an internal battle between the old emotional habit and your new emotional response. You will want to go down the healthy life path, try to change direction, and even force yourself to change course. The old emotional habit will still be strong, so don't be disheartened if you aren't able quite yet to leverage your new healthy emotional fuel to change direction.

During this process, you are likely to feel frustrated and get discouraged by your inability to quickly and easily replace old emotional habits with new ones. These feelings are normal. In fact, these feelings are probably remnants of the old emotional baggage you had of having to do everything perfectly the first time. You must resist these feelings because they will only slow the retraining of your emotional habits and reinvigorate your old emotional baggage. Most important, you must continue to persist in the retraining process and persevere in the face of the slowness and difficulty of the change process. Stay confident in the knowledge that your old emotional habits will die in time and you will develop new, healthy emotional habits. You will be able to choose the new course in your life in the near future and it will get easier.

As time passes, the internal battle will continue, but the tides will slowly turn. With each experience, your old emotional habits will lose their power and your new emotional habits will gain strength. Then one day it will happen. You will see the opportunity to change your life direction ahead, you will prepare yourself, you will use your new healthy emotional fuel to propel you along a new life trajectory, and you will stay on it! Finally, your persistence and perseverance will have paid off. You will have let go of the old emotional habits and replaced them with new, healthier emotional habits that will further fuel your new life inertia. You will be one step closer to being Captain. To paraphrase poet Robert Frost, it will make all the difference.[23]

## Don't Forget the Positive Emotions

Although the majority of part IV focuses on negative emotions and how you can overcome them, it is of equal importance to learn to experience and express positive emotions and how they can contribute to altering your life trajectory. An unfortunate byproduct of an upbringing that emphasized strong negative emotions or no emotions at all is that positive emotions were rarely experienced. Negative emotions have their place because they act as warning signals for people and experiences that can harm us, so negative emotions can indicate to us what to avoid. But positive emotions are as important because they communicate what to seek out and look forward to. Love, excitement, joy, enthusiasm, contentment, and happiness are the emotional goals toward which we should strive and are the emotional rewards for our efforts in all aspects of our lives.

Just as experiencing and being guided through negative emotions can help you gain emotional maturity, so, too, does feeling and learning about positive emotions. You have opportunities on a daily basis to create, express, share, and talk about the positive emotions that you feel. There are no rules for expressing positive emotions. There are no techniques for learning positive emotions. You learn about positive emotions by allowing yourself to experience and express them in your daily activities, work, and relationships. When you are happy, show it. When you are excited about something, share it with someone. When you thoroughly enjoy something you are doing, tell someone why. When you feel content, describe the feeling to someone. Most important, when you are with others whom you care about, express your love in any way you can. By experiencing and expressing positive emotions, you steadily remove the negative emotional fuel and replace it with positive emotional fuel. You can then use that good emotional fuel to exert force on your life inertia and propel your life in a new and healthier direction.

## Benefits of Emotional Challenge

The culmination of this difficult, sometimes painful, and ultimately rewarding process is a life propelled by emotional challenge. Acting on and responding to life as an emotional challenge has many benefits that enable you to become Captain of Starship You and move your life in any direction you want. Since you no longer live in fear, you are able to take complete ownership of your life. This ownership enables you to choose the path your life takes and gives you the power to change your life in the future if you so decide. Being responsible for all aspects of your life allows you to fully revel in life's successes and bounce back from life's setbacks.

Emotional challenge encourages you to be an active participant rather than a passive observer in your life's journey. You can be proactive in guiding your life inertia instead of reacting to what life gives you. This active involvement allows you to engage yourself in your life without reservation or hesitation. With emotional threat removed, you can open yourself to the full range of your emotional life. You will feel more deeply and experience life more richly as a result. At the end of this journey of emotional liberation, you will feel completely alive—free to explore everything that your inner and outer lives have to offer, open to all experiences and people—and that is the definition of being the Captain of Starship You.

But this story? This one's mine.

—Carmen Maria Machado, American short story author[24]

## Let Go

To let go does not mean to stop caring, but to not care too much.

To let go is not to cut yourself off, but to open yourself up.

To let go is not to dwell on what might be, but to enjoy what is.

To let go is not to blame, but to take responsibility.

To let go is not to fix, but to heal.

To let go is not to deny, but to acknowledge.

To let go is not to judge, but to accept.

To let go is not to punish, but to cherish.

To let go is not to control, but to be free from control.

To let go is not to regret the past, but to live for the present and future.

To let go is to fear less and to risk more.

To let go is to not strive for perfection, but to seek excellence.

To let go is to pursue success rather than to avoid failure.

To let go is to achieve what you deserve and to deserve what you achieve.

To let go is to feel exhilaration rather than relief.

To let go is to give and to receive love.

To let go is to feel happiness and peace.

# CHAPTER EIGHT
# SEEING THE CONSTELLATIONS
## From Child to Adult

**Adult** /ə'dəlt/: A person who is fully developed and mature; capable of reasoned thought and rational decision making; possessing emotional control.

One of the most consistent observations I have made in my work with Inertials is that many experience delayed emotional development. In other words, many Inertials exhibit emotional behavior that is more characteristic of children than adults. For example, they throw a "temper tantrum" when they become frustrated or they sulk when they don't get their way. Though Inertials exhibit substantial maturity in some areas—for example, intellectually or culturally—they often demonstrate underdeveloped emotional capabilities. This slowed emotional growth appears to be related to the amount of inappropriate investment their parents had in them when they were young and to many of the issues already discussed in *Change Your Life's Direction*.

Parents of Captains foster emotional development in their children. These children often show emotional maturity beyond their years. Their parents use achievement as an avenue for teaching their children about emotions. These parents provide their children with opportunities to learn about and gain mastery over their emotions. For instance, after their child receives a poor grade in school, these parents allow them to feel the disappointment and hurt of failure without additional punishment. They also acknowledge and affirm what emotions their child is experiencing. These parents then offer their child a positive and healthy perspective on those feelings and show them how to deal with the emotions on their own.

In contrast, parents of Inertials interfere with healthy emotional development. These parents protect their children from their own emotions in the mistaken belief that emotions—particularly "bad" ones such as frustration, anger, and sadness—will hurt future achievement. Because they are not allowed to experience their emotions, these children develop little awareness or understanding of them. As a result, they often exhibit emotions that are inappropriate or disproportionate to the situation. Without normal emotional "training" with support from their parents, these children are kept from learning healthy and mature ways of responding to their emotional life.

Early in a child's life, parents devote most of their energy to their child's emotional development. Parents normally provide their children with opportunities that allow them to acquire experience with emotions and to gain emotional maturity. These experiences then act as the positive fuel that allows children to begin their lives on a healthy trajectory.

However, when parents lose perspective and become overly invested in different aspects of their children's lives, the emotional fuel becomes toxic and it propels their children down an unhealthy life path. These parents become so focused on facilitating their children's success that they stop paying attention to their children's emotional development. This shift in emphasis ensures that children do not have the experiences necessary to gain emotional maturity. So these children are sent off on a trajectory early in their lives that ill prepares them for the emotional challenges that are a natural part of life.

As soon as the child is regarded as a possession for which one has a particular goal, as soon as one exerts control over him, his vital growth will be violently interrupted.

—Alice Miller, noted psychologist[1]

These "Inertials in training" lack the emotional maturity to respond positively to the emotional demands they will face in their lives. Perhaps most significant is that they are emotionally handicapped as they enter adulthood. These children lack the basic tools of emotional life that will allow them to become socially and professionally successful, happy, and connected to others. As noted by Dr. Daniel Goleman (1995), these include self-awareness, self-control, empathy, and social skills. In a very real sense, Inertials are children inside of adult bodies and their lack of emotional maturity inhibits all aspects of their adult lives.

Certainly, children are expected to act like children for much of their childhood. However, as they enter and move through adolescence, there should be a decrease in childish behavior and an increase in adult behavior. Given that Inertials weren't allowed to engage in this emotional training, they continue to demonstrate childish means of managing their emotions and are not equipped to learn from the opportunities they have to replace them with appropriate adult emotional coping behaviors.

To summarize five hundred volumes of psychoanalytic literature: No matter what your age, we remain our parents' child. The gnarled dynamics of parent-child relationships continue deep into adulthood.

—Joshua Halberstam, author of *Everyday Ethics*[2]

## Emotional Immaturity

The emotional immaturity of Inertials is evidenced in many aspects of their lives. The way they interpret the world, what they think, the emotions that dominate their lives, the quality of their relationships, and how they act on and react in their lives are all reflections of their emotional immaturity.

> Men are not angered by mere misfortune but by misfortune conceived as injury. And the sense of injury depends on the feeling that a legitimate claim has been denied. The more claims on life, therefore, that [they] . . . make, the more often [they] will feel injured and, as a result, ill-tempered.
>
> —C. S. Lewis, British novelist and scholar[3]

### Immature Attitudes and Perceptions

The life of a child is one of self-absorption and immediate gratification. From an early age, children are the center of their parents' universe and demand much of their attention to have their needs met. This self-focus can lead to attitudes that interfere with children making a healthy transition to adulthood, which leads to their development into Inertials. These attitudes tend to be highly self-centered and harmful to normal emotional development. There are three areas that inform this problematic attitude: egocentrism, the drive to receive love and approval, and absolutism.

*Egocentrism* is the inability to understand another perspective than their own. If the need for special attention in infancy and childhood doesn't dissipate as children age, they may remain in an egocentric state and come to believe that all of their needs will be satisfied on demand. Attitudes such as "The world revolves around me" and "I want it *now!*" are common among children who are not making a healthy transition to adulthood. When parents consistently respond to children's demands without delay or thought, children never learn to grow out of their "I-am-the-center-of-the-universe" attitude.

Egocentric children can get away with this attitude through at least adolescence because their parents are always going to want to do what they think will make their children happy. However, such self-centeredness begins to be frowned upon in adolescence and is not sustainable in adulthood. Family, friends, coworkers, and acquaintances will simply not tolerate this kind of self-absorption. Egocentric children turned Inertials will find themselves becoming increasingly alienated and alone.

> In order to be profoundly dishonest, a person must have one of two qualities: either he is unscrupulously ambitious, or he is unswervingly egocentric. He must believe that for his ends to be served all things and people can justifiably be shifted about, or that he is the center not only of his own world but of the worlds which others inhabit.
>
> —Maya Angelou, American poet and activist[4]

The second area of consideration that maintains this self-centered attitude is the drive to receive love and approval from parents and others. To get the love they need from their parents, some children develop attitudes such as "I must please everyone" and "I must be liked by everyone." They come to believe that they will receive the love they need to feel good about themselves by pleasing others. Unfortunately, it is impossible to please everyone, which means these children will never receive the love they need and they will end up disappointed.

> The need for universal acceptance is instilled in our children at an early age. This prevents them from forming their own concept of self-respect, and instead substitutes a fear of being unloved.
>
> —Dr. Stanley Krippner, noted psychologist[5]

If children become overly dependent on others to have their needs met and to be loved, they can develop unhealthy beliefs about themselves and rules about the world, such as "I must be perfect" and "Failure is unacceptable." These attitudes lead to perfectionism, fear of failure, and emotional threat, all of which lie at the heart of being an Inertial. These children are caught in the trap of experiencing very negative emotions, which they are unable to deal with in a positive and constructive way.

Absolutism is the final attribute found in the attitude of Inertials. They often view the world as black and white; they either have their needs met or are neglected, they feel loved or are unlovable, they are perfect or completely flawed, they are a success or they are a failure. This dichotomous thinking serves a protective function by simplifying life and reducing the number of threats that they must face. At the same time, it creates an inflexible world that offers little margin for error. This rigidity limits Inertials in their options to two and traps them in an internal world in conflict with the uncertain, enigmatic, and "gray" nature of the real world.

> Mortals, everything is so black and white with you.
>
> —Kami Garcia, American writer[6]

## Immature Reactions to Failure

Perhaps the most immediate negative emotion Inertials experience following a perceived failure is an intense variation of disappointment. Disappointment involves the feelings of thwarted desire, loss, and discouragement when people fail to achieve their goals. Most people perceive their failure as situationally related and thus not an emotional threat. The disappointment they feel is a helpful emotion (though, admittedly, unpleasant), as it spurs a "fight" response, which acts to increase motivation to avoid the failure in the future, thus preventing subsequent disappointment.

In contrast, Inertials experience failure as confirmation that they themselves are failures. As a result, it is seen as an emotional threat to their self-esteem. Inertials experience an unusually intense and aversive form of disappointment with a much different reaction to it. Their emotional response is better characterized as devastation because the failure is perceived as a direct reflection of their self-worth.

This intense reaction of devastation is so significant that it produces a "flight" response in which Inertials lose their motivation to persevere in the face of the failure. Ironically, Inertials feel so threatened by failure that they often react in ways that increase the likelihood of failure and further devastation. A common response to failure is for Inertials to punish themselves unmercifully. They also tend to either avoid similar situations to the one in which they experienced the failure, thus avoiding the possibility of future devastation, or sabotage themselves by not giving their best effort. Both of these responses make future failure more likely.

Failure can cause Inertials to feel incompetent and inadequate, which will lower their self-esteem if it's persistent. Some disappointment following failure is normal, but Inertials can be seen moping around the house, looking downtrodden, and feeling sorry for themselves for far longer than is appropriate to the situation.

### Immature Reactions to Frustration

One of the best ways to judge emotional immaturity in adults is to look at how they respond when they don't get their way or when they experience obstacles in their path to their goals. For example, how do they respond when a friend changes their plans at the last minute or when they are having trouble finishing a work project? Inertials have a very low tolerance for frustration when they don't get their way. Remember, they never learned to effectively delay gratification or manage their feelings when they didn't get what they want. When frustrated, they tend to either lash out at the source of the frustration or give up easily when the frustration doesn't resolve itself quickly.

These kinds of unhealthy responses to frustration act as a significant obstacle in adulthood. Immature emotional reactions to frustration that might work in childhood (e.g., their parents helping them to overcome the cause of the frustration) will cause the opposite reaction in adulthood (e.g., alienation and withdrawal of support by friends and colleagues). In general, adults are resistant to meeting the needs of emotionally immature adults. Think of how an airline gate agent responds to an irate traveler as compared to a calm and cooperative flyer.

## Immature Anger

One of the most noticeable ways in which Inertials distinguish themselves is how they deal with their anger; it is often inappropriate and out of proportion to the situation. At the heart of this anger lies their learned belief that they should get what they want when they want it. Their anger is also impacted by their inability to effectively manage the frustration they feel when they don't get their needs met. Unfortunately, Inertials communicate their anger in ways that distract from the fact that their needs aren't being met and focus on the negativity and intensity of the emotions.

The most common way in which Inertials deal with their anger is the "fight" response. They attack and express their anger openly to its cause. This anger is typically uncontrolled, unfocused, and unrelenting. It acts as an immediate emotional release for other strong, pent-up emotions that Inertials are experiencing. A common and unfortunate outcome of their anger reaction is that the recipient of the anger reacts in kind with anger of his or her own. Not only does the cause of the anger remain unresolved, but it also harms the relationship between the two people involved.

As children, anger is modeled by our parents. Inertials tend to experience mutual expressions of anger with their parents in which they feed off of each other to create a vicious cycle of conflict, aggressiveness, and ill feelings on both sides. The result is that both the children and their parents feel bad, their feelings toward each other are diminished (at least temporarily), and they are unable to resolve the problem that led to the children's anger in the first place. This pattern of dealing with conflict with others is carried over into adulthood and Inertials maintain similar reactions and difficulties with friends, partners, and coworkers.

Alternatively, if children experience severe punishment as the result of expressing their anger, they may be afraid to express it openly and suppress it out of fear of reprisal. Children may turn that anger inward and punish themselves, which leads to low self-esteem, perfectionism, depression, or anxiety. Outwardly, they appear to be sulking or brooding, but inside they experience a torrent of hurt and anger. They may express their anger in subtle ways such as a loss of motivation, self-defeating behavior, and passive-aggressive behavior as a way to "get back at" those whom they perceive to be the cause of their problems.

Parents often give in to their children's anger because giving them what they want allows their anger to dissipate. Unfortunately, this response exacerbates the problem by reinforcing the children's beliefs that they can get whatever they want simply by acting with anger. A pattern of surrender by parents in response to their children's anger sets an unhealthy precedent for the effectiveness of anger as a tool—or weapon—for immediate gratification. The children will learn to use this situation to their advantage throughout their childhood and into adulthood as Inertials.

> A child thinks and acts like a child. But when you are grown, you act and think like an adult. Too many people are still childish and immature and fail to realize it's a setback in their lives.
>
> —Amaka Imani Nkosazana, author and poet[7]

## Immature Language

Growing up in a family that does not foster emotional maturity leads to children who can communicate their emotions only in childish and emotionally immature ways. These children learn to express their emotions in ways that ensure that their needs are met. For example, they engage in fits of anger or prolonged episodes of sulking to manipulate their parents into giving them what they want. Their communications are unclear because their language is infused with strong emotions. Recipients of these messages have a hard time responding constructively because the emotions obscure the intended communication. As a result, misunderstandings are common and any reasonable resolution is difficult to achieve.

In addition to the emotional tone of the communication, immature language includes the vocabulary that is used. Inertials tend to use mostly "I" statements that focus on getting their needs met. From a deeply unsettled emotional state, these statements tend to be demanding and threatening. Inertials' vocabularies also tend to include absolutist words and phrases such as "must," "should," "need to," and "have to."

As children, Inertials learn to listen for a similar language from those with whom they are in conflict (usually their parents). The communication they have with others is filtered in a way that reduces the emotional threat and meets their fundamental emotional needs of feeling loved and valued. Because they have come to associate emotions with feeling bad, the words they hear with their inflections and tones are sifted through a filter for emotional threat, potentially bad feelings, and an inability to deal with them. Rather than clearly hearing the intended messages, Inertials tend to interpret the communication from others in ways that are most protective in the short term, which tends to interfere with arriving at a mutually beneficial solution. Inertials' responses to what they hear often lead to an "I win" reaction. In the long term, however, this results in greater emotional turmoil and a no-win situation for both parties because it does not consider the other person involved.

As children evolve into adults, this emotionally immature language becomes entrenched and eliminates the opportunities to learn an adult emotional language. As you can imagine, Inertials carry their emotionally childish vocabulary and intonations with them into their adult lives. Sometimes people can appear to have a firm grasp of the emotionally mature vocabulary, but their true emotional language becomes evident when they feel an emotional threat. When their self-esteem is under siege, people revert to ingrained emotional habits, which, for Inertials, are emotionally immature language.

Though effective in childhood, the grown-up world is less indulgent of emotionally immature language, and it causes problems in all aspects of Inertials' lives. Others are often resistant to communicating with those who are unwilling or unable to speak an emotionally mature language. They are even more likely to reject those who speak a language that is uncomfortable and disruptive. Moreover, just as it is harder for adults to learn a foreign language, adults who speak a childish language also will have difficulty learning an emotionally mature language once they are well into adulthood.

### Immature Decision Making

Decision making is one of the most noticeably harmful qualities of Inertials. Children tend to make decisions that are impulsive, short-sighted, focused on immediate gratification, and often lacking adequate deliberation because of their lack of experience and perspective. They rely on the "if it feels good now, it must be the right decision" approach to decision making.

These decisions are usually seen as rash by others. They may produce some short-term benefit, but there is almost always a long-term price to be paid. This impetuous decision-making style is aimed at meeting their most immediate needs, which are often protecting their self-esteem. Children tend to ignore the long-term ramifications of their decisions, which are also usually selfish and oblivious of others. Children don't consider the needs of other people involved in the decision-making process or their effects on others when the decision has been made.

This kind of decision making is common among children; however, if this decision-making style continues into adulthood, it can cause significant problems, as is often the case with Inertials. Since their decision making is often directed at immediate and selfish outcomes, other people come to mistrust these emotionally immature Inertials. Others question whether these childish adults can be relied on to stay calm and make good decisions that are in the best interests of everyone during a crisis. Inertials will have difficulty finding others who are willing to make a commitment in the face of such mistrust and uncertainty.

Most people grow old, but not everybody grows up.

—Nishan Panwar, author[8]

## Emotional Overprotection

One of the most common causes of emotional immaturity in children are parents who protect their children from experiencing emotions. These parents do everything they can to make sure that their children don't feel emotions, especially so-called "bad" emotions such as frustration, anger, disappointment, and sadness. They mistakenly believe that feeling unpleasant emotions will stunt their child's self-esteem. For example, after receiving a poor grade on a test, a mother does everything in her power to placate, cover up, or distract her son from feeling bad in the misguided belief that this approach will make him happier and more successful in the future.

Not only do some parents protect their children from potential emotional disturbance, but they also bend over backward to cater to their children's emotional needs. In this case, the misguided belief is that negative emotions will hurt their child's development. They avoid situations that might cause their child to feel bad. For example, if their child loses a tennis match, the parent might blame the opponent for cheating rather than giving the opponent credit for being a better player.

Sadly, this protection from emotions produces the opposite effect. Without the awareness and understanding of emotions that come from experiencing them, children never learn how to positively handle the many emotional challenges they will face as they progress through childhood and into adulthood. The inability to experience and understand negative emotions makes it impossible for children to fully feel and appreciate positive emotions. Like two sides of the same coin, children cannot experience one side of emotions without experiencing the other side.

As adults, these formerly emotionally protected children become Inertials who lack the experience and skills to use their emotions in positive and healthy ways. Instead, they continue with ineffective emotional habits they learned as children that are now more destructive than constructive. In adulthood, Inertials continue to use their harmful emotional fuel to power their life inertia along a decidedly unhealthy trajectory.

> This is the tragedy of modernity: as with neurotically overprotective parents, those trying to help are often hurting us the most.
>
> —Nassim Nicholas Taleb,
> Lebanese American scholar and essayist[9]

## No Emotions

I have worked with families in which emotions were largely nonexistent in their lives. It's not that they didn't express negative emotions; it's that they didn't express *any* emotions. The parents in these families were often raised in "emotionally detached" or "cold" families and never came to grips with their own emotional lives. They simply passed on this emotional practice to their children without realizing it.

This absence of emotions in a family—whether anger, sadness, joy, or love—can be as harmful to a child as a family consumed by strong negative emotions. Without the expression of emotion, children will not feel loved, which is the most important emotion. As a result, many of the red flags discussed previously (e.g., low self-esteem, false self, perfectionism, fear of failure) will develop. These children also will never experience true happiness and will never learn the value and importance of happiness in their lives. Without the opportunity to receive or express emotions, these children cannot gain the experience necessary to develop emotional maturity.

Another painful byproduct of children who grow up in a "cold" family is that they develop beliefs that emotions are not acceptable or, even worse, that emotions are signs of weakness. These children build up internal walls that keep their emotions in check; they simply don't express strong emotions of any kind. Unfortunately, these children still feel emotions even though they might not express them, particularly negative emotions. Every time these children feel frustration, anger, or sadness, they must suppress it. The emotions continue to roil around inside of them unresolved and actually leak out in subtle and indirect ways (e.g., feelings of anxiety, passive-aggressive behavior). These "Inertials in the making" are often sullen, withdrawn, and depressed, though usually undiagnosed or untreated. They grow up to be emotionally detached adults who struggle in every facet of their lives because they lack the capacity to feel and experience their emotions in healthy ways.

I worked with a young professional athlete, Kyra, who grew up in such a family. Her parents showed no real love or affection for her. They obviously had some very serious emotional baggage from their own upbringings because they were incapable of having an emotional conversation with Kyra. Her parents provided her with every other kind of resource and often said to Kyra, "Isn't that enough?" Whenever Kyra reached out emotionally or tried to talk to them about what she was feeling, they would change the subject or end the conversation. As a result, Kyra learned to shut off all of her emotions. She learned never to express emotions in front of her parents or to ask for emotions from them. This emotional habit transferred into all of her relationships. Kyra grew up to become a very successful athlete, but she began to realize how truly unhappy she was as she entered her early twenties. While recovering from an injury that kept her away from her sport for an extended period, Kyra was finally ready to face her pain. During one of our first sessions, she described how she never felt loved by her parents, and I was struck by the absolute absence of emotional expression shown as these difficult words came out. The disconnect between the emotions of her words and the lack of emotions behind her words was unsettling. I asked her what she was feeling at the time, and she said matter-of-factly, "I don't feel anything."

After several months of hard work on Kyra's part, I began to see cracks in her armor: teary eyes, a sad face, and signs of emotions that were consistent with her painful words. Then one day Kyra's emotional floodgates opened. As she spoke about her parents, she cried. She described it like "releasing twenty years of pain." This experience was the turning point for Kyra, who has discovered her emotions and her happiness with increasing frequency.

> Sadly, no one in our family ever said, "I love you." Do you realize that? The truth is, I think we were all frightened of saying it, since the obvious reply would've been, "Well, if this is love, what is hate like?"
>
> —Louie Anderson, American stand-up comedian and actor[10]

## Emotional Maturity

All of the attitudes that Captains possess result in an emotional life that is mature, appropriate, and healthy. These emotional qualities enable Captains to experience the full range of emotions that constitutes a rich emotional life. This allows them to respond constructively to the inevitable emotional challenges they will face in their lives, to be capable of establishing and maintaining positive relationships, and to use these emotional attributes to find meaning, fulfillment, and joy in their lives.

### Mature Attitudes

The life of an adult is one of self-awareness, understanding, and sensitivity to others. As children mature emotionally, they come to understand that the world does not revolve around them and that their needs will not be met in the same way as when they were younger. Maturing children recognize that others have needs and that they have to be responsive to needs other than their own.

Emotionally mature children lose their egocentrism and understand that they will not always get what they want when they want it. They also come to recognize that other people have needs and feelings too. In a sense, these children develop a more realistic view of the world and how they fit into it. They come to see that they are no longer the center of the universe. For example, when emotionally mature children want something but can't have it, they don't throw a tantrum because they have developed attitudes such as "If I can't have it now, maybe I can get it later" or "I want it, but if I can't have it, I can accept that." These mature attitudes remove the inevitable frustration that children feel when they don't receive immediate gratification, allowing them to respond in a more reasonable and effective manner to the uncertainty of the adult world.

Emotionally mature children discover that they are not always in control. There will be times in which they can do nothing about their circumstances and that they must accept that. They learn that the only thing they can control is themselves—more specifically, their attitude toward what life gives them. Emotionally maturing children also learn that they will not always be able to count on their parents or others to meet their needs. Instead, they must take responsibility for their own needs. These children learn that they are no longer their parents' singular priority. They must strike a balance between their own needs and interests and those of others, including their parents, siblings, and peers.

Perhaps the most fundamental change that exemplifies emotional maturity is the ability to gain self-validation for their self-esteem instead of being dependent on others for how they feel about themselves. Of course, everyone receives some validation from others, but children making the healthy transition to emotional maturity don't need to gain love and affirmation from *everyone*. This realization enables emotionally maturing children to be more selective in whom they please and by whom they must be liked. They develop attitudes such as "I only need to please those people who are important to me" and "It's okay if not everyone likes me."

Emotionally mature children also have attitudes about achievement that are healthier and will serve them better in the adult world. They are able to place success and failure in a healthy perspective and at a proper distance from their self-esteem because they have the ability to validate their own self-esteem outside of their accomplishments. Attitudes such as "I want to do my best" and "It's okay for me to fail sometimes" allow these children to see their achievement efforts as an emotional challenge to embrace rather than an emotional threat to avoid.

Unlike the rigid absolutism that is characteristic of emotionally immature children, emotional maturity provides children with a world composed of many shades of gray. These children view the world in degrees: they can have some of their needs met, different people will like them to varying degrees, they will make some mistakes, and they will both succeed and fail. This "gray thinking" creates a fluid world that gives children many opportunities to learn and grow. This flexibility enables the emotionally mature child to adapt to the uncertain, ambiguous, and ever-changing nature of the adult world.

Emotionally mature children also lay the foundation for attitudes that will enable them to develop into Captains rather than Inertials. They establish realistic beliefs about themselves that allow them to take control over that which is within their control and accept that which is beyond their control. Because it's not "all about me," they are aware of and sensitive to the needs and feelings of other people, which results in the ability to connect in deep ways and create healthy relationships with others.

Attitudes are nothing more than habits of thought.

—John C. Maxwell, American author, speaker, and pastor[11]

## Mature Reactions to Disappointment

Disappointment is a normal, though difficult, part of life. You have experienced disappointment in school, sports, friendships, and your career. How you learn to respond to disappointment will determine its impact on your future success and happiness. Captains see stumbling blocks as opportunities to improve and grow. By gaining a different perspective on your disappointment, you develop tools that turn obstacles to your advantage: "I know it feels bad, but what can I learn from it?" This perspective allows you to avoid the intense disappointment—the devastation—that Inertials experience in the face of mistakes, setbacks, and failures.

After "falling off the horse," you naturally will feel a brief period of letdown. Unlike the devastation that Inertials feel, you will be able to pick yourself up and get back on the horse. By staying positive and enthusiastic, you can show yourself another, better way of feeling in response to failure. You can look for ways to overcome your setback and return to your life's path. Rather than the disappointment disheartening you and causing you to feel bad about yourself, you use the experience to affirm your capabilities by showing yourself that you can conquer your past difficulties. For example, if you aren't improving as fast as you want in some area, you can recognize that people often reach plateaus. You can acknowledge that these "flat spots" in your progress are necessary and usually a prelude to another period of improvement. You also can support yourself by continuing to work hard and express confidence that your progress will continue.

Your attitude toward your inevitable disappointments will influence how you respond to life's obstacles. You should view your disappointments as opportunities that will better prepare you for future difficulties. Failure and disappointment are part of life. What matters is how you react to them. Following disappointment, don't distort the situation to make yourself feel better. Allow yourself to express your feelings about the setback ("I feel really sad") and offer yourself a constructive perspective that may give you another, healthier way of looking at it ("If I keep trying, I'll get it sooner or later"). Be realistic about your goals and capabilities. Gain feedback from others to help put the disappointment in a realistic context that considers your true abilities. Look for ways to surmount the causes of your difficulties. Finally, realize that you will survive these disappointments and continue to make progress toward your goals if you keep trying hard.

> It was one of those times you feel a sense of loss, even though you didn't have something in the first place. I guess that's what disappointment is, a sense of loss for something you never had.
>
> —Deb Caletti, American writer and award-winning author[12]

## Mature Reactions to Frustration

Captains respond to frustration in ways that will most likely lead to getting some of their needs met at some point. Their maturity allows them to step back from the immediate frustration of not getting what they want and to think clearly about how they can best get their needs met moving forward.

This capacity starts with a healthy perspective about their unmet needs. Captains accept the situation for what it is, that they're not readily going to get what they want. They consider what they can have rather than dwelling on what they can't have. By doing so, they let go of those things over which they have no control and focus on that which they do.

Captains perceive the "failure" to get their needs met as a challenge that they can overcome with positive action, because not having their needs met immediately is not overly connected to their self-esteem. As a result, they are able to stay calm and avoid the strong upset that is associated with emotional threat. Captains feel encouraged to confront the situation, rather than actively avoiding a threat. They also realize that they will have to rely on themselves for finding a resolution to their needs if they are going to ultimately have their needs met.

Captains engage in a thoughtful and deliberate process in which their goal is to look for solutions to their present situation. If they do experience any negative emotions—and some disappointment and frustration are natural—Captains have the maturity to withstand their negative feelings and redirect their energy in a positive, constructive way. Their ability to engage in gray thinking also allows them to consider varying degrees of getting what they want instead of persisting futilely in trying to get all of their needs met. Captains realize that if they persevere in their efforts, then they will approach and perhaps surpass their goals and have their needs met in time.

> To conquer frustration, one must remain intensely focused on the outcome, not the obstacles.
>
> —T. F. Hodge, American writer[13]

## Mature Anger

Of course, even Captains get angry. It's a normal and healthy part of being human. What separates Captains from Inertials is not that they don't get angry, but rather how they react to their anger and how they express it. Inertials are consumed by and lose control of their anger. In contrast, Captains are able to maintain control of their anger and redirect the negative energy in a positive direction that provides a resolution to the problem. Research by Diana Tice and Roy Baumeister discovered that venting anger actually heightens and prolongs anger rather than dissipating it (1993). This is contrary to the belief most people have that expressing anger has a cathartic effect. They found that a much more effective approach was to calm down and then seek a solution with the person or situation that caused the anger.

> Anyone can become angry—that is easy. But to be angry with the right person, to the right degree, at the right time, for the right purpose, and in the right way—this is not easy.
>
> —Aristotle, Greek philosopher[14]

The fundamental, overriding goal for a Captain's reaction to anger is to resolve the situation that is causing the anger in the most beneficial way instead of just letting out their anger. Also, they're not compelled to try to "win" at all costs because they understand gray thinking. Rather, they appreciate the value of compromise; it is better to have some of their needs met than none at all. And they look for "win-win" results, whereby they get some of their needs met and resolution occurs to the satisfaction of everyone involved.

Unlike childish anger, emotionally mature anger is appropriate to the magnitude of the perceived offense. Thus, the situation that causes the anger is kept in perspective. Instead of reacting impulsively and often escalating the problem, Captains are able to examine its cause, consider their options of how to react, and choose the best course of action. Captains learn to express their emotions in ways that resolve their immediate emotional need to communicate and relieve their anger, which leads to a long-term solution to the cause of the anger.

Captains understand that the message they communicate in expressing their anger will determine the ultimate resolution of its cause. Because of this, they recognize that they need others to hear the substance of the message and not just the emotional content. In this way, other people will understand that the Captain is angry *and* why he or she is angry in a way that doesn't cause them to feel emotionally threatened and to react defensively themselves. With this information and the way it is conveyed, others will hear the message, be open to it, and want to respond positively. In turn, this response encourages Captains to express their anger in healthy and constructive ways. It also maintains the integrity of their relationships with others.

## Mature Language

Children whose parents encourage emotional maturity when they are young become fluent in an adult emotional language at an early age. The vocabulary, inflections, and tones of this language are grounded in constructive expression of their emotions and the resolution of the situation. This language enables Captains to respond positively to the frustration, anger, and sadness that is an inevitable part of the adult world.

Again, this mature language includes the emotional tone of the communications and the vocabulary that is used. Captains use mostly "we" statements that include and respect other people involved. They recognize and act on the needs of others as well as their own. Mature statements also tend to use questioning and collaborative language that draws others into the conversation. The vocabulary of Captains also tends to include words and phrases of possibility such as "may," "could," and "might." These words and phrases send the message of empathy, understanding, conciliation, and compromise.

This emotional language allows Captains to interpret others' words in a similar manner. Since this language is not filtered through emotional threat, Captains are able to respond in a healthy way to emotional messages from others, even when those messages are spoken in an emotionally immature language. Rather than adding "fuel to the fire," this openness often has the effect of encouraging the person who is using emotionally immature communication to change their vocabulary. This staves off escalating the conflict into a battle between two people who are speaking the same emotionally immature language.

A significant strength of using adult language is that the message is clear. The goal of emotionally mature language is to communicate concerns unambiguously and to encourage a similar response from others. With this language, others know where they stand and can act on the real issues rather than reacting to the strong negative emotions that are present with emotionally immature language. This allows others to respond in kind with the goal of creating a win-win outcome for everyone involved.

A part of the transition from Inertial to Captain is learning to speak emotionally mature language. This process can be difficult because emotionally immature language is deeply ingrained from years of use. Building awareness of when this unhelpful language is used enables Inertials to understand what triggers its use and allows for efforts to be made to speak a more mature language. With patience and perseverance, this will result in replacing emotionally immature language with emotionally mature language.

Adult language serves Captains well. Captains typically manage their emotions more effectively; respond more successfully to disappointment, frustration, and anger; and resolve conflict with others more easily. Additionally, they are respected and trusted more by other people because they can be counted on to stay cool in crisis. These advantages to emotionally mature language result in healthier and more meaningful relationships with others.

> Speak softly and carry a big stick, you will go far.
>
> —Theodore Roosevelt, twenty-sixth president of the
> United States of America[15]

### Mature Decision Making

Sound decision making is a hallmark of the emotionally mature adult and an absolute necessity for anyone to be Captain of Starship You. Mature decision making is a deliberate process that is grounded in reason, not emotion. It takes into account many variables before a decision is rendered that produces the best possible outcome for all of those involved. Mature decision making starts by resisting impulsive urges in the face of an emotional threat. The ability to withstand these forces alone is strong evidence of emotional maturity. This capacity enables Captains to make hard decisions—that is, to make a decision that may not suit them in the near future but will be in their best interests further down the road, not only for themselves but also for others.

Beyond the ability to avoid making rash decisions, mature decision making considers both the immediate and the future implications of the decision. Captains ask themselves, "What short-term needs must be taken into account and what long-term concerns must be addressed?" Captains also care about their "crew" (i.e., the people they impact), the needs of the crew, and how decisions will affect them. Ultimately, Captains attempt to make decisions that will stand the test of time, are in the best interests of all of those who will be influenced, and will result in a win-win outcome for everyone involved.

> Urgency and despair don't get along well.
>
> —N. K. Jemisin, American writer and psychologist[16]

## Transition from Inertial to Captain

Making the emotional transition from childhood to adulthood is a fundamental change that must occur for you to make the shift from Inertial hurtling uncontrollably through life to Captain of Starship You. This development requires that you let go of immature ways of thinking, feeling, and acting. In their place, you must adopt ways that facilitate your best interests based on who you are now and who you want to be in the future.

### Selfish to Selfist

The egocentrism that is common among children and Inertials causes them to behave in selfish ways. Children often lack awareness of other people's feelings and the empathy to be responsive to others' wants and needs. They are blind to the benefits of being concerned for others. Similarly, Inertials are focused on themselves. They must be the center of attention. Inertials must get their needs met before anyone else. They often show a fundamental disregard for other people in which they consistently act in ways that promote their own interests and discount those of others, no matter how unintentional or nonmalicious their intent.

In contrast, Captains have the capacity to behave in selfist ways. The term "selfist" refers to the ability to focus on themselves or others in ways that are reasonable and appropriate to the situation. Selfists can put their own needs first when it is required of them—for example, when their health or happiness is a concern. At the same time, they also have the ability to set aside their own needs and make the needs of other people a priority. Selfists are sensitive to and considerate of the feelings of others and appreciate the value of placing other people ahead of themselves. It feels good to care for others, and this consideration is reciprocated.

Whatever you choose, the idea is to give back selflessly.

—Madisyn Taylor, cofounder and content curator
of Daily OM[17]

## Validation from Others to Affirmation from Self

Because Inertials' self-esteem never developed fully or in a healthy way, they are insecure in how they feel about themselves. They may question whether they are truly loved and their level of competence. This uncertainty in their self-esteem causes them to be dependent on others for their sense of self-worth and to need validation from others to feel good about themselves. This reliance places them in the vulnerable position of having to actively seek out confirmation from people whom they value, such as parents, teachers, coaches, and friends. Moreover, they may be compelled to act in ways that ensure that they obtain the confirmation they need if they are not naturally receiving this validation (e.g., obedience, ingratiation, and pleasing). Gaining this validation meets their immediate self-esteem needs, but it can also create a dependence on others that that is unhealthy because it inhibits their growth into autonomous and mature adults.

Captains have the capacity to affirm their own self-esteem. They have a fundamental belief in their self-worth. Captains believe themselves to be capable of being loved. They view themselves as competent people who can be successful in their lives. Though Captains do receive support and affirmation from others, this feedback is not essential to how they feel about themselves. Rather than relying on others to confirm their self-esteem, they gain validation directly from the life experiences and relationships in which they engage. This self-confirmation allows Captains to have greater control over their self-esteem and frees them from having to act in ways that gain validation from others.

> What the superior man seeks is in himself; what the small man seeks is in others.
>
> —Confucius, Chinese philosopher[18]

## NEED! to Want

Inertials can be driven to act because they feel that they *NEED!* to (as described in chapter 1). This compulsion is often related to gaining validation from others, especially their parents. Inertials may believe that if they don't behave a certain way, they won't receive the love they need and their self-esteem will suffer. This *NEED!* stems from their false self, which drives them to satisfy its extreme demands. From these two sources, children often create a set of rules that allows them to survive psychologically and emotionally. Even when this set of rules propels them along an unhealthy life trajectory, Inertials feel that they have no choice but to act on them.

By contrast, Captains are not driven by such irrevocable *NEEDS!* Rather, their lives are guided by what they *want* to do and what they believe is in their best interests. This ability to act on what they want comes from self-esteem that is validated by themselves, not others. It is also directed by their true self, which does not place limiting rules on what they think, how they feel, and how they behave. Captains are not compelled by unhealthy *NEEDS!* to act in ways that are restrictive and destructive. Rather, they are free to choose the path they want to take and that brings them the most meaning, satisfaction, and happiness.

> A lot of people get so hung up on what they can't have that they don't think for a second about whether they really want it.
>
> —Lionel Shriver, American author and journalist[19]

## Outcome to Process

Inertials are focused primarily on the outcome of their efforts because their self-esteem is based on results. Instead of being focused on achieving success, they are more concerned with avoiding failure because it carries greater emotional weight. This preoccupation with outcomes keeps Inertials from connecting with more substantial aspects of their lives, such as the process of achieving the outcomes. This distancing helps Inertials to protect themselves from caring too much about activities in which they invest themselves. Unfortunately, this detachment precludes them from experiencing true success and any joy in the experience.

Captains, however, are most interested in the process that they believe will lead them to success. Captains are unthreatened by failure so they are able to focus on what they need to do their best and to be successful. They also have a healthy perspective on the inevitable failures they will experience as they progress. Rather than being a looming and potentially painful endpoint of their efforts, Captains see failure as only one step in a long journey. These attitudes enable them to be totally immersed in their efforts and experiences. This connectedness allows Captains to enjoy the process deeply and to gain lasting fulfillment in their efforts regardless of the outcome.

> How you climb a mountain is more important than reaching the top.
>
> —Yvon Chouinard, American rock climber and outdoor industry billionaire[20]

## Dichotomous Thinking to Continuous Thinking

As noted previously, Inertials tend to think dichotomously; life is "either-or" and black and white. This way of thinking has the benefit of simplifying life and making decisions easier; however, it is also limiting because Inertials have only two choices, which tend to be extreme. Dichotomous thinking is also a problem for Inertials because they are preoccupied with failure and have a very narrow view of success. They are faced with a reality that dictates only one possible opportunity for success while everything else is failure. This way of thinking leads them to believe that they have little chance of success and great likelihood of failure.

Captains engage in continuous thinking in which they see a spectrum of possible outcomes with varying degrees of success and failure. Continuous thinking allows them to look at all possible outcomes and decide on their own definition of success. Having a "zone" of success rather than one small point allows Captains to focus on what they can do to succeed without the specter of failure hanging over them. From this perspective, success is more likely and failure is less threatening, less extreme, and less likely.

## Short Term to Long Term

Inertials' vision extends only into the immediate future. They are concerned primarily with avoiding immediate threats and having their short-term needs met without consideration of the long-term consequences of their actions. This limited perspective causes them to rely on their most recent past experiences and the most immediate ensuing activities to determine what they think, how they feel, and the way in which they will behave. Inertials have difficulty planning for the future and may act in ways that are immediately beneficial but not in their best interests in the long run. They are also more powerfully affected by negative experiences because they are not able to place these events in a broader present perspective or a long-term context in the future. Their immediacy carries great emotional weight that hurts them in both the immediate and the distant future.

Captains have a long-term perspective that allows them to weigh immediate benefits with long-term ramifications. They are able to draw on past experiences and yet-to-come events when deciding what is best for them. This outlook enables Captains to recognize the inevitable ups and downs in life and accept them as natural occurrences. They will have bad days and they will have good days. When they are successful, Captains don't congratulate themselves too much. When they fail, they don't punish themselves excessively. This attitude enables Captains to stay focused on what they need to do to find success, connection, and happiness in their lives.

Always ask yourself what will make you happy over the long term.

—Steven Redhead, professor[21]

## Failure to Success

Inertials are absorbed with and terrified of failure. It is their focus and the guiding force that propels their life inertia. What they think, how they feel, and the way they behave is predominantly driven by their need to avoid failure and the emotional meaning they attach to it. Inertials view failure as an emotional threat that makes self-protection their foremost priority because failure is overly connected to their self-esteem.

Captains are focused on and pursue success with vigor and without reservation. They believe strongly that they are competent and capable of being successful. Captains also know that they will fail periodically and that these failures are normal and expected. This attitude enables them to recognize that failure does not make them failures. This understanding lifts the burden of failure off their shoulders and frees them to pursue success unencumbered by any threat to their self-esteem. With this perspective, Captains gain validation from their efforts and the process of the experience; they draw value from pursuing life itself, not just achieving success.

Failure is the condiment that gives success its flavor.

—Truman Capote, American novelist and actor[22]

## Keys to Emotional Maturity

1. *Confidence.* A sense of control and mastery of one's body, behavior, and world; the child's sense that he is more likely than not to succeed at what he undertakes and that adults will be helpful.

2. *Curiosity.* The sense that finding out about things is positive and leads to pleasure.

3. *Intentionality.* The wish and capacity to have an impact and to act upon that with persistence. This is related to a sense of competence, of being effective.

4. *Self-control.* The ability to modulate and control one's own actions in age-appropriate ways: a sense of inner control.

5. *Relatedness.* The ability to engage with others based on the sense of being understood by and understanding others.

6. *Capacity to communicate.* The wish and ability to verbally exchange ideas, feelings, and concepts with others. This is related to a sense of trust in others and of pleasure in engaging with others, including adults.

7. *Cooperativeness.* The ability to balance one's own needs with those of others in a group activity (Goleman, 1995).

## Part V

# HARNESSING THE FOUR LIFE FORCES: CHANGING YOUR LIFE INERTIA

C hanging your life inertia is essential for your health and happiness, as well as your growth and development as a person. Without change, you will continue just the way you are, doing things just the way you have always done them, and experiencing the same outcomes. For some people, that's a good thing; they're happy and fulfilled in their lives. For many others, their current life trajectory lacks meaning, satisfaction, and joy. They feel stuck on a life course that they didn't choose and that they don't want to be on. They want to change direction in their lives but can't seem to figure out how.

On the face of it, changing your life inertia doesn't seem like it should be that difficult. If there is something that you don't like about yourself, why can't you just change it? The reality is that profound change is often slow, frustrating, and painful. It's filled with struggles, setbacks, and disappointment. Whether you want to have a more positive view of yourself, to be a better spouse, to strive for professional goals, or to deal with stress more effectively, change may be the most difficult thing you will ever do. It's also one of the most rewarding.

Let us cultivate our garden.

—Voltaire, French Enlightenment writer[1]

The reality is that changing your life inertia is difficult. How difficult? Well, consider the failure rates for everything from New Year's resolutions, stopping smoking, and losing weight to improving self-esteem, feeling less stress, and having better relationships. The picture is not pretty. Examine your own life and how many times you've attempted to alter its course. Reflect on the four life forces I have shared with you up to this point and how much power they have over your life trajectory to date. Think about how long those forces have been guiding your life and the momentum that's been created. As Isaac Newton (1687) might tell you, the energy behind those forces is highly resistant to change.

Part of the problem is that many of us have unrealistic perceptions about what it takes to change direction in our lives. We have been told by the self-help industry that change should be easy, happen quickly, and require little effort. On the contrary, anyone who has ever tried to make a significant change in their life knows it is not easy at all.

*Change Your Life's Direction* is about gaining an understanding of what it really takes to shift your life inertia and produce meaningful, long-lasting change in your life. Up to this point, my focus has been on educating you about the different forces that have shaped your life as it is now. This plethora of information provides you with a deep understanding of who you were, who you are now, how you became who you are now, and who you want to be in the future. Part V utilizes all of the information and insights you've garnered so far to show you how to harness the four life forces, alter your life inertia, and produce meaningful change to shift the direction of your life.

He who conquers himself is the mightiest warrior.

—Confucius, ancient Chinese philosopher[2]

## "Know Thyself"

The first step in making meaningful changes in your life involves gaining a better understanding of yourself in essential areas that impact life inertia. This self-knowledge can provide you with the power to regain control of the four life forces and exert them on your current life inertia in a way that benefits you in the present. Self-knowledge also can help you to be more focused and more effective in altering your life inertia.

> We have all a better guide in ourselves, if we would attend to it, than any other person can be.
>
> —Jane Austen, English novelist[3]

## Now, Discover Your Weaknesses

In order to develop greater self-understanding, you must recognize both your strengths and your weaknesses. Most people love to talk about their strengths but don't like to admit their weaknesses. I disagree with Marcus Buckingham, the coauthor of *Now, Discover Your Strengths* (2005), who asserts that the way to achieve goals is to focus on your strengths. This approach may work for some parts of your life, such as a job that involves one or two highly specialized skill sets. The reality is that most aspects of life require a constellation of competencies, which means the focus-on-your-strengths model actually limits your ability to make substantial changes in your life.

Let me explain why: Most people think that the ability to achieve their goals depends on their greatest strengths. For example, a man may believe that his outgoing personality and social skills will enable him to develop a healthy romantic relationship. This is a misconception. The truth is that you are only as good as your greatest weakness. If that man lacks the empathy and emotional openness to build an intimate relationship, his other abilities may get him into a romantic alliance but will be inadequate to build the strong emotional bond required to maintain a healthy relationship. Additionally, focusing on your strengths doesn't address what is preventing you from channeling the four life forces, which will lead to shifting your life inertia. To overcome the real obstacles for change, you need to acknowledge and understand your weaknesses before you can remove them.

Let's think of your strengths and weaknesses for changing your life inertia in the same way you might look at them when pursuing a promotion at your job. Using a scale from 1 to 10 (in which 1 is very poor and 10 is the best), we will rank various skills and use math to show the importance of knowing and understanding our weaknesses. For this example, we will use task and relationship skills. If you have very good task-related skills (8/10), but you are quite poor at relationship building (2/10), then your overall performance would be moderate (8 + 2 = 10 out of a possible 20). Since you are working toward a promotion, you definitely want to improve your overall performance rating. If you focus on and improve your task-related capabilities (say, from 8 to 9), your overall performance wouldn't improve that much because you were already capable in that area of your work (9 + 2 = 11). However, if you improve your relationship skills (say, from 2 to 6), then your overall performance will rise significantly (8 + 6 = 14). Of course, you want to continue to refine your strengths, but improving your weaknesses gives you a better chance to make the overall changes you want.

Only courageous hearts can endure the bitterness of truth.

—Michael Bassey Johnson, Nigerian playwright and poet[4]

## Why Self-knowledge?

Nobody likes to admit—much less focus on—their weaknesses. Yet when you gain self-knowledge that both appreciates your strengths and confronts your weaknesses, you are opening up new possibilities for harnessing the four life forces and altering your life inertia.

So be receptive to self-knowledge rather than uncomfortable with facing your weaknesses. Consider the information in a positive and constructive way. Identifying your weaknesses doesn't mean that you're incapable of change; it actually allows more room for change. It may be that you haven't had to use these skills in your life yet, so they are underdeveloped, or you've been able to disguise them with the strengths you have. The great thing about self-knowledge is that it gives you the power to improve those weaknesses. The information you gain from actively seeking self-knowledge will enable you to really understand your weaknesses as well as your strengths, which allows you to plot a course that maximally leverages both to produce meaningful life change.

## Gaining Self-knowledge

There is no magic to gaining self-knowledge. You must actively seek self-knowledge both within and outside of yourself. You can sit down and simply ponder your existence. Examine your life up to this point, look at impactful experiences, identify seminal relationships, and characterize persistent patterns.

You can learn about yourself by asking others you trust for feedback about yourself. These may be people in your family, group of friends, or coworkers. Often, other people can provide us with a mirror that best reflects our strengths and weaknesses. Life has a way of communicating powerful messages about what works and what doesn't. Important lessons can be gained from simply reflecting on your life experiences, if you're open to them.

Valuable self-knowledge also can be garnered from outside resources. Books, articles, and workshops by experts and laypeople alike may stimulate self-knowledge by offering information, perspectives, and insights. Well-validated psychological assessments, either found online or administered by an expert, also can be illuminating by making the ethereal nature of the "self" more tangible.

Finally, one-on-one work with a qualified mental health professional can enable you to explore in greater depth the who, what, where, why, and how of your being. These trained professionals can help you clarify the specific changes that you would like to make in your life. They can act as detectives with you to help uncover the obstacles that may be preventing you from achieving your desired change. Finally, they can use proven strategies to help you make the changes you want.

> The things I carry are my thoughts. That's it. They are the only weight. My thoughts determine whether I am free and light or burdened.
>
> —Kamal Ravikant, author[5]

## CHAPTER NINE
# CLEARING THE PATH
## From Asteroid Field to Open Space

*Open space /ōpən spās/:* An expanse void of obstacles; an area offering unfettered freedom of movement.

An unfortunate aspect of life inertia is that it is often propelled by patterns of self-destructive thinking, emotions, behaviors, and interactions that arise from unhealthy early life experiences, most frequently from dysfunctional families. This is commonly referred to as "baggage." Baggage is expressed in self-doubt, self-criticism, self-defeating behavior, and strong negative emotions like anger or sadness. It is often driven by the lack of healthy fulfillment of basic needs in childhood, including feeling competent, valued, and in control. Regrettably, this baggage becomes intractable and ends up hijacking the four life forces, which sends our life inertia in an unhealthy direction.

The most common types of baggage include low self-esteem, fear, and shame, which result in perfectionism, the need for control, and the need to please. This baggage causes you to think, feel, and behave based on who you were and the circumstances you were in as a child rather than the very different person you are and circumstances you are in as an adult. Most of this baggage causes you to react to the world in an unproductive way that sabotages your efforts to guide your life along a healthy trajectory.

The unwanted path you have been on all of your life began with baggage. You were an innocent child who wanted nothing more than to be loved and supported by your parents. Unfortunately, your parents had baggage of their own, and, sadly, they passed it on to you. Even worse, there wasn't a darned thing you could do about it. The good news: now there is! Let's start with understanding your baggage and how you express it.

> The quickest and healthiest way to move on is to own it so you can disown it! Travel lightly!
>
> —Evinda Lepins, author[1]

## Understanding Your Baggage

The ironic thing about baggage is that it started out as being highly functional in childhood but has become quite dysfunctional in adulthood. What becomes baggage starts out as a way for you to manage otherwise untenable situations, usually involving protecting yourself from some perceived threat. For example, becoming a perfectionist may have ensured that you were successful enough to earn love from your overly demanding parents. Or having a negative outlook on life served to protect you from being disappointed when things didn't go the way you wanted. These early experiences and the thoughts, emotions, and behaviors associated with them become entrenched in your psyche, take control of your four life forces, and drive your life inertia in an unhealthy direction.

As you grow up, your baggage continues to propel you along a bad trajectory by causing you to think, feel, and behave in ways that are highly dysfunctional (e.g., it makes you unhappy and hurts your relationships). Your baggage is not only not helpful any longer but also usually unnecessary because you and your life are very different than you were when it first developed. As an adult, you have many tools (e.g., experience, perspective, emotional control, intentional thinking) that make your baggage obsolete; you don't need to protect yourself in that way anymore because those threats are no longer present in your life or you have better ways of dealing with them. The problem is that your baggage remains influential in your life because it has taken control of your four life forces. You still engage in these behaviors because they have been woven into the fabric of who you are. As an adult, that behavior becomes downright dysfunctional, as it no longer helps you in your life. On the contrary, it hurts you immensely. Returning to the previous examples, your perfectionism now prevents you from ever finishing projects at work because nothing is ever good enough. And that negative attitude now makes you a downer to be around, which hurts and limits your relationships.

This dysfunctional behavior is now officially labeled as baggage and interferes significantly with your ability to function in the world. Not only does it cause you to feel poorly about yourself, but it also wreaks havoc on your life. For example, your baggage makes you feel worthless and unloved, or it repeatedly sabotages your professional or personal life. What makes this baggage so frustrating is that it continues to manifest in your life despite the fact that it is no longer necessary or helpful.

> I've been alive a long time, long enough to know that the more baggage you carry in life, the more unstable you'll be, until eventually you get sick of carrying it, and then you just fall down.
>
> —Rebecca McNutt, author[2]

## Messages = You

Here is a simple, yet painful, reality: we become the messages we get the most when we are young. If the messages from our childhood were mostly healthy, we probably started out on a positive life course from an early age and have generally stayed on it throughout our life so far. If the messages were mostly unhealthy, we most likely were propelled down an unpleasant life path as a child, and here we are, still on that same trajectory.

We get these messages in several ways. Overt messages involve what our parents (and other influential people like teachers and coaches) said to us. These messages are powerful for young children. These messages also can be hurtful, because parents are supposed to know everything and always be right. I'm sure you're familiar with the old parenting adage, "Do as I say, not as I do," which suggests that what parents say is right. Unfortunately, what parents often say to their children is well intended but actually creates the baggage you are attempting to address—for example, comments like "You're too smart to be getting B's in school," "You're a bad boy for hitting your sister," and "If only you hadn't missed that shot, you would have won the game and been the team's hero." It's not difficult to imagine how children might feel when hearing these comments (i.e., that they are incompetent, angry, and ashamed, respectively).

That negates the value of the "Do as I say" part of the saying. That gets us to the "Not as I do" part, which couldn't be more true. Though what parents say is important, perhaps the most influential messages children receive from their parents are in what they do. You learn a great deal about the world by watching your parents and seeing how they behave. Simply watching them in your family's daily life is where these role-modeling messages come through loud and clear. Because your parents were the most powerful people in your life during childhood, you naturally assumed that if they acted a certain way, that must be the best way to act. Unfortunately, that may not have been the case. First and foremost, you need to remember that your parents are human beings with their own baggage from their own upbringing. Much of their unhealthy behavior toward you was driven by their baggage rather than by what was truly best for you. The way your parents treated each other, how they treated you and your siblings, and how they behaved on a daily basis conveyed potent messages. Not all of these messages were healthy, to be sure, but they have been driving your life inertia to this day.

Instruction is good for a child; but example is worth more.

—Alexandre Dumas, famous French writer[3]

Finally, the emotional messages we got from our parents were perhaps the most devastating. As children, we lacked the sophistication to decipher the content from the emotions of the messages we got from people whom we loved and admired. Instead, we were highly intuitive little beings who were wired to pick up on subtle emotional messages (often ones that our parents weren't even aware of themselves). Even more powerfully than their words and actions, we likely became the emotional messages we got from our parents. If our parents were angry, we grew up with anger. If our parents were unhappy, they conveyed that message to us and now we feel similarly. If there was a lot of conflict in their marriage, we learned that that was how relationships worked and have likely experienced this ourselves.

## Messages That Cause Baggage

Though there are as many messages as there are parents in the world, I have found that there are several that are almost universal in creating burdensome baggage.

### Inadequacy

Feelings of inadequacy are passed very easily from parent to child. Parents who feel ineffectual themselves convey these messages to their children in their words, emotions, and behavior. In attempts to create children who are the antithesis of inadequate by pushing them to achieve and be successful, parents often end up continuing their lineage of inadequacy because their children can't meet their impossibly high expectations.

In a short time, you internalize your parents' messages of inadequacy. You feel stupid, incapable, and worthless. In every situation, you see yourself as inept despite objective evidence to the contrary. Your mission in life is to prove that you are not inadequate; yet there never seems to be enough proof to the contrary. Messages that you were incompetent can have lifelong implications in school, career, and relationships.

## Perfectionism

Many children get the message "You will be loved only if you are perfect" from their parents these days, no matter how unintentionally that message is transmitted. Perfectionism causes you to connect your self-esteem with being perfect. Nothing less than perfection will make you worthy of being loved and valued. It causes you to strive for standards that are impossible to attain, and you berate and diminish yourself when you inevitably fail to meet these absurdly high demands. At a deep level, you know that you can never be perfect, which develops into a profound fear of failure. As a result, you are driven to avoid the failure of not being perfect, which prevents you from taking risks and handicaps you in all aspects of your life.

## Social Awkwardness

Parents who are shy or socially awkward can send messages that cause their children to feel uncomfortable, socially inept, or disconnected from others. Not only do children of socially awkward parents receive these messages from their parents, but they often don't have healthy role models to teach them socially appropriate ways of behaving with others. Subsequently, they think themselves socially inept, and they may actually become socially unskilled. This message can hurt your ability to connect deeply with others and the quality of later relationships. This social awkwardness likely kept you from connecting with others when you were younger and causes you to feel like an outsider looking in at groups to which you would like to belong. This outsider status causes you to feel isolated, disconnected, and lonely.

### Unhealthy Emotions

Your family's emotional life is communicated by your parents' messages and can create the heaviest and most painful baggage. As I've noted previously, the most common kinds of troubling emotions are fear and anger. Families governed by emotional intensity can overwhelm children, causing them to either engage in (anger) or retreat from (fear) the emotional chaos. Families in which emotional expression is discouraged send the message that emotions are signs of weakness or are unacceptable. In either case, children who grow up in families dominated by unhealthy emotions (or the lack thereof) carry a lifelong burden that can wreak havoc on their personal and professional lives.

### Victimization

Messages of victimization from parents are another cause of baggage. The previous messages can contribute to a sense of powerlessness because they put children in untenable situations from which they can't easily extricate themselves. This particular message of being a victim communicates that "I can't do anything about my lot in life." Simply put, children who perceive themselves as victims feel helpless to change their lives for the better. This belief is a barrier to change and happiness throughout their lives.

## Expressions of Baggage

You should now have a good sense of what messages you got from your parents and the way they were delivered (i.e., overt, role modeling, emotional). You can now explore how those messages translated into your baggage and how you express it. Namely, how you perceive yourself and your world, the emotions you experience as you engage in the world, and the way you act on your world.

## Perceptions

Your baggage impacts your internal life at the deepest level, through the perceptions you hold about yourself and your world. These old and weighted perceptions negatively impact your four life forces and the direction your life inertia takes you because they are often out of touch with who you are now and what you want to be in the future.

### *Insecurity*

Insecurity may be the most common form of baggage. It is experienced as an undefined sense of unease or angst, like something is wrong without the ability to identify the problem. Insecurity causes you to feel unsafe, as if you are under a constant state of threat, with danger lurking around every corner. If you are insecure, you feel inadequate, unloved, and undervalued. You have a fundamental lack of confidence in your value and capabilities; you worry and doubt yourself.

Insecurity impacts your life directly. You are uncomfortable with taking risks because you don't trust that any good will come of them. You may be unfulfilled and lonely in your social life because your fear of rejection renders you unwilling to be vulnerable enough to establish deep and meaningful relationships. You may be frustrated in your professional life because you are reluctant to take risks that lead to career advancement. If good things happen, fear often rises because you believe they can't possibly last. If bad things happen, it's just what you expect and it's likely to continue.

### *Negativity*

Insecurity creates a filter of negativity, a "glass-half-empty" attitude in which you see the world in terms of daily setbacks, failures (past, present, and future), and unfulfilled dreams. You have little faith that anything in your life can or will turn out well. Not only will life not work out the way you want, but any hopes you may harbor that good things can happen will be dashed. By maintaining such a negative outlook on life, you protect yourself from the frustration and pain of unrealized goals and unmet expectations. When you expect the worst, you minimize the intensity of your disappointment because you didn't expect it to work out in the first place. The irony is that in an attempt to avoid intense disappointment, you feel chronic disappointment.

This dark lens that you look through colors everything you think, feel, and do in your life. This pessimistic attitude generates a wide range of defeatist emotions including fear, anger, sadness, frustration, and despair. The negativity also becomes a self-fulfilling prophecy that sabotages your efforts and prevents you from fully achieving your goals.

> Discouragers are the folks who regularly see the glass as half-empty, and they do not want anyone else to get one that's half full.
>
> —Cathy Burnham Martin, American author[4]

### Self-blame

A sad and painful message that you may have gotten from your upbringing is that you and your family had problems and you were to blame for them. This attitude may have led you to believe that everything bad that happens to you in your life was your fault, regardless of how much of it may have been outside of your control. This burden of guilt and shame carries a heavy emotional toll. It keeps you paralyzed with inaction to avoid causing more bad things to happen to you, which are also your fault. This self-blame also creates a powerful belief that you are undeserving of good things to happen to you and that anything that befalls you is just deserved punishment for the transgressions, however illusory, for which you are to blame.

*Paranoia*

Because you are your own worst enemy, you can't imagine that others actually could be supportive of you. Therefore, you assume that everyone else is against you and that they want the worst for you. You just know other people are saying awful things about you: "He is such a loser!" or "Who would want to be friends with her?"

How do you know that people are thinking these things? Well, you're a mind reader, of course. You are able to hear the thoughts of people around you. What you don't realize is that you can't actually read the minds of others, and when you think you are, the only mind you are reading is your own. Your so-called mind reading is really the projection of your own thoughts and baggage onto others. God forbid that others actually might like you and want the best for you. That is an expectation that surely would be proven wrong.

*Paralysis by Analysis*

All of the previously mentioned perceptions cause your internal world to be so cluttered and chaotic that it preoccupies nearly every moment of your waking life. Your thoughts lead you to suffer from "paralysis by analysis." This means that you overthink everything, from your thoughts and emotions to your decisions and achievements. The apparent value of being stuck in your head is that you are hypervigilant to any threats to your well-being, no matter how unrealistic or unlikely. This gives you a greater sense of control because you fool yourself into believing that you have a chance of avoiding the inevitable disaster if you think through everything thoroughly. Getting stuck in your head also prevents you from acting, which protects you from having to face the consequences of your actions, which are usually bad, at least as you interpret them.

I understand that your brain is large and perpetually at war with itself.

—Chris Cleave, British writer and journalist[5]

*Powerlessness*

For all that happens to you, you feel out of control and unable to gain a semblance of power to affect your life for the better. You are at the mercy of the world and feel helpless to do anything about it. This perception of victimization can be expressed in two ways. First, you simply give up on yourself by surrendering to the inevitability of your unsatisfying and frustrating life. You accept your life inertia and the trajectory your life is on. Your perception of powerlessness becomes a self-fulfilling prophecy. Because you believe that you are powerless, you don't take action, and then you truly are at the mercy of the outside world.

The other way this is expressed is by reacting to your beliefs of powerlessness by vigorously and forcefully trying to reestablish control over your life. Unfortunately, these attempts are often misplaced. Your efforts to mitigate your sense of powerlessness are misdirected toward controlling others, when your energy should be directed at regaining power over yourself—your thoughts, emotions, and behavior. These attempts also may be superficial, as they often are aimed at controlling the easiest, most controllable targets, which usually are trivial things related to cleanliness, punctuality, and routines. To really regain power over yourself, you need to gain control of the deep stuff that causes you to feel powerless.

I have found that these perceptions are common forces that drive life inertia. At the same time, you may have unique perceptions that are not in your awareness. I recommend that you ask yourself what perceptions you hold that propel your life inertia along its unsatisfying course.

> I am so tired—so tired of being whirled on through all these phases of my life, in which nothing abides by me, no creature, no place; it is like the circle in which the victims of earthly passion eddy continually.
>
> —Elizabeth Gaskell, English novelist[6]

## Emotions

Changing the trajectory of your life is so difficult because your baggage also creates powerful negative emotions in you that can dominate your life inertia. Fear prevents you from taking action and appropriate risks. Anger clouds your judgment and causes destructive behavior. Despair leads you to feel hopeless and helpless in your life. Shame causes you to be your own worst enemy. And don't even think about experiencing positive emotions such as excitement, joy, or contentment; your baggage would never allow that. These emotions shackle you to the way you have always thought, felt, and acted, which prevents you from acting in a way that is true to who you are and who you want to be.

Paradoxically, the negative emotions that arise from your baggage to meet your most basic need of protecting yourself from harm end up causing you more harm. The goal of *Change Your Life's Direction* is to neutralize the power of the negative emotions and the momentum that those unpleasant emotions have generated in your life, which has fueled your unhealthy life inertia, and to replace those emotions with positive ones that provide you with an entirely different type of fuel to power your life in a healthier direction. The impact of specific emotions on your life trajectory is explored later in this chapter.

## Action

You also express your baggage-laden thoughts and emotions in your actions as you engage with the world. Whether in your personal or professional life, behavior that is driven by your baggage is usually self-sabotaging and ultimately not in your best interests.

### Control

Because you feel powerless and out of control, you attempt to establish some semblance of control—however illusory—by controlling the minutiae of your life. This control may be expressed through compulsive or repetitive behavior, an excessive need for neatness or order, a rigidity in how things are done (only the "right" way, meaning your way), and aggressive reactions when you perceive that others are trying to control you.

### Passive-aggressiveness

Your baggage may prevent you from communicating or confronting others directly. You are unable to express your thoughts and feelings in a direct and open way because your baggage makes you terrified of conflict, criticism, or rejection. As a result, you convey your uncertainty, fear, and anger in a passive-aggressive manner. This "safe" approach has the beneficial effect of not having to directly face discord and tension while avoiding culpability for your actions. The costs are significant and can include being misunderstood, not having your needs met, and getting an aggressive reaction from others.

### Workaholism

Excessive commitment to work provides several benefits that reinforce the value of this behavior while encouraging you to ignore its costs. Workaholism often results in financial rewards and respect and admiration from others. These successes give you a brief respite from your low opinion of yourself with a fleeting moment of good feelings. Overworking also distracts you from your baggage and helps you to avoid the people and situations that trigger your baggage. At the same time, workaholism can be truly destructive by creating excessive stress, sabotaging relationships, damaging physical health, and producing a profound life imbalance.

We're not in this life just to work, we're in it to live.

—Cecelia Ahern, Irish novelist[7]

*Chaotic Life*

Your life may be truly chaotic and seemingly out of control, but you may like it that way, whether you admit it or not. A chaotic life creates a feeling of urgency and excitement that gives you a sense of meaning and importance. Most basically, your chaotic life protects you from your baggage. Being overscheduled, unorganized, perpetually late, and stressed out in your external life acts as a distraction from your truly chaotic internal life.

*Self-sabotage*

You may be shooting yourself in the foot constantly. You are really good at convincing yourself that a particular course of action is best for you, but that's because your baggage is very good at presenting compelling arguments. The usual result is self-sabotage, in which your behavior actually hurts you. This may be in how you feel about yourself, how you behave in relationships, or what you do at work.

Despite your wish for good things (e.g., happiness, success, and love) to occur in your life, you continually engage in sabotaging behavior. Whenever something good starts to happen, you unconsciously do things that cause the good to turn bad. The reason for this self-defeating behavior is that you would rather ensure immediate failure and have some control over it than wait for the bad things that are sure to happen in the future.

> I've memorized the best angles in the bathroom from which to see how badly I've disintegrated. I truly do go from sixty to zero.
>
> —Kris Kidd, American poet and essayist[8]

## Habits

Your baggage causes you to think, feel, and act a certain way every time you're in a particular situation. When something happens that triggers your baggage, you respond the same way every time. The repetition of these patterns over the years ingrains these thoughts, emotions, and behaviors deeper and deeper into your psyche. With sufficient repetition, they become, as I described in chapter 7, entrenched habits in the form of unhealthy knee-jerk reactions. You respond this way anytime you perceive a situation as similar to one that originally triggered your baggage.

These baggage-driven habits are very resistant to change for three reasons. First, they fulfill whatever need your baggage originally required of them. Second, through sheer repetition, you become very skilled at the bad habit. Third, they become literally hard wired into your brain circuits. The goal is to retrain your bad habits into healthy ones.

> Bad habits are demons that often push us into isolation because they know that in our loneliness they stand little chance of being overcome.
>
> —Richelle E. Goodrich, author[9]

## Emotions

The emotions that became a dominant force in your early life inertia and have fueled your life trajectory are displayed in every aspect of your life, including school, work, and relationships. The baggage-driven emotions you experience are generally unpleasant and overwhelming. Unsurprisingly, they also tend to be excessive to the situation in which you find yourself. Due to their intensity, these emotions are difficult to control or resist. Importantly, these negative emotions play such an overriding role in your life that they stifle your attempts to experience the positive side of the emotional coin, including happiness, joy, excitement, love, pride, inspiration, and contentment.

### Fear

Your baggage causes you to live a life dominated by fear, a life in which you perceive most things as threats to your safety and well-being. In this state, your primary motivation is to protect yourself from these perceived threats. Avoidance, inaction, and unwillingness to take risks are used to minimize your fear, but they also keep you from life's most enriching experiences. You are unable to fully engage in your life because it is a scary place to live.

## Sadness

Your baggage causes you to feel an ongoing melancholy, as if a dark cloud hangs over your head every day. You often feel uninspired and listless. You may frequently feel despair and often cry. You might wear your sadness on your sleeve. Others can sense it and feel both sympathetic to your plight and uninterested in joining you under that dark cloud. Alternatively, you may redirect your sadness outward into more aggressive forms of negative emotions such as anger and resentment toward others. In either case, your sadness makes it difficult for you to feel much more than brief moments of pleasure or joy.

## Pain

You feel a deep and enduring sense of distress and hurt. Whether from neglect or anger due to your upbringing, this pain suffuses all aspects of your life and colors your experiences negatively. This hurt makes you hypersensitive to perceived slights and vulnerable to anyone or anything that might worsen your pain. In turn, this pain can cause you to be attracted to anyone or anything that can ease it. Much of your life is devoted to finding ways to assuage, distract, or relieve your pain or deep hurt, despite how temporary the respite might be.

> Imagine smiling after a slap in the face. Then think of doing it twenty-four hours a day.
>
> —Markus Zusak, author of *The Book Thief*[10]

## Frustration

Frustration at its most basic level involves having the path toward your goals blocked and feeling unable to clear it. In other words, you feel stuck in how you think, the emotions you feel, and the patterns of behavior that control your life. And you are loath to figure out how to get unstuck. Your inability to clear the hurdles that block your path to your goals causes you to feel great frustration. You want to get where you want to go, but you feel that the roadblocks are insurmountable.

## Anger

Anger is a defensive emotion that attempts to protect you from far more painful emotions, such as sadness and fear. Anger toward others distracts you from the pain or frustration you feel toward yourself. It deflects those emotions and places the blame for your plight on others. Anger can be focused on specific people whom you hold accountable for your life inertia or it can be directed toward the world at large. You feel a brief moment of relief, control, and self-righteous vindication when you let out your anger. Such "ventilation" never actually enables you to let go of the real feelings that provoke your anger. It is also counterproductive because it damages your relationships, makes you more unhappy, and ultimately hurts you, since you never confront the real sources of your anger.

## Despair

All of these emotions exact a profound toll that may result in a state of utter despair and surrender to being a victim of your current life trajectory. You accept your sad lot in life and simply give up because you feel totally incapable of changing your life inertia for the better. Gosh, what's the point of continuing to try when all of your previous efforts haven't allowed you to break free of the life course on which you have been trapped for so long? Well, the point is this: If you despair, you admit defeat. And if you admit defeat, you stop trying. By definition, you lose any chance you have of ever changing the direction of your life if you stop trying. Most painfully, you send yourself the message that there is no hope. Without hope, you are doomed to remain on your current path for the rest of your life.

## Bitterness/Resentment

Bitterness and resentment are very unpleasant and yet highly protective emotional "bedfellows." They distract the focus of your emotional life away from yourself and toward others. Bitterness involves blaming your life course on the universal unfairness of life. This rancor absolves you of responsibility for your life situation, which makes you feel better about yourself but prevents you from doing anything about your life trajectory.

Resentment involves feelings of indignation or ill will toward others (e.g., parents, coworkers) for the real or imagined grievance of not getting what you want out of life. By blaming others for your misfortune, you can feel a little bit better about yourself because your life's difficulties are not your fault. Of course, resentment also keeps you from changing your life for the better because you can't dictate change without taking ownership.

## Shame

What may lie at the heart of all of these emotions and reach to the core of your baggage may be a deep sense of shame. Like a white-hot laser beam, this painful emotion focuses all of your baggage and combines unworthiness, guilt, embarrassment, regret, self-loathing, and disgrace. What a burden shame places on you! And the really sad thing is that you don't deserve to feel such shame. Chances are you were a victim of your upbringing and little of what befell you when you were a child was actually your fault; yet you carry the shame.

Oddly, you can free yourself of the shame of believing that you were the cause of those problems by blaming others for your early difficulties. The trick is not to blame them for your *current* difficulties. Continuing to blame others serves no purpose. As an adult, you must take responsibility for your life if you want to change its direction. By removing the shackles of shame through recognizing it wasn't your fault, you can regain control of the four life forces and begin to alter your life inertia.

> We can endure all kinds of pain. It's shame that eats men whole.
>
> —Leigh Bardugo, American fantasy author[11]

## Environment

You developed your baggage, habits, and emotions in childhood to manage a threatening environment. In turn, as you evolved toward adulthood, you created an environment that helped you to best manage your baggage, habits, and emotions. You surround yourself with people who make you feel better about yourself. You engage in activities that distract you from your baggage, habits, and emotions. Your home and community increase your comfort and security. The work you do plays to your strengths while also limiting your possibilities. Your daily routines offer you a sense of familiarity, predictability, and control that mitigate the threat that you feel as you are propelled through life. The entire world you've created around yourself is devoted to mitigating the discomfort you experience on your current life trajectory. It helps you maintain a manageable level of equilibrium and functioning in your life.

At the very best, this environment won't support your attempts to alter your life inertia. Worst-case scenario, this environment actively resists your efforts. It's virtually impossible to change your life inertia when the world in which you live is holding you back. You remain in a sort of purgatory, somewhere between devastation and contentment. You may be managing, but you're not truly thriving or happy. And you realize that this is no way to go through life.

> Purgatory is hell with hope.
>
> —Philip José Farmer, American science fiction author[12]

# PLOTTING A NEW COURSE
## From Lost to Foundation

> *Foundation* /faùn-'dā-shən/: A basis (such as a tenet, principle, or axiom) upon which something stands or is supported; a body or ground upon which something is built.

I n chapter 9, I described the four obstacles that prevent you from gaining control of your four life forces, changing your life inertia, and shifting the trajectory of your life. In attempting to remove those obstacles, you are swimming against the tide of many years of baggage, habits, emotions, and environmental factors. These obstacles are so deeply ingrained and present in your current life that only a massive and persistent force on your part will enable you to break free from their "gravitational pull" to chart a new course for your life. I don't mean to discourage you so much as to prepare you for what it will take to change your life inertia and shift from being an Inertial to becoming a Captain. On a positive note, putting those obstacles in your past and altering the direction of your life is one of the most inspiring experiences you will ever have; there may be no greater fulfillment than changing yourself.

After being adrift in your life for so many years—not knowing or having control over where your life is going—it is important to understand five states of mind that will help lay the foundation for changing your life inertia. These states of mind are epiphany, emotions, courage, leap of faith, and commitment. They prepare you for the rigors of change and gird you for the challenges you will face. The goal is to develop and use these states of mind to clear the obstacles discussed in chapter 9 to propel you along a new life trajectory.

To shift your life in a desired direction, you must powerfully shift your subconscious.

—Kevin L. Michel, author[1]

## Epiphany

Altering your life inertia is very difficult and can't be catalyzed by an uncertain or superficial desire for change. Thinking "it would be nice to change my life" just won't cut it. It also cannot be triggered by forces outside of yourself, whether from family, friends, or others (though their support is essential, as I discuss in chapter 11). Rather, the impetus to change your life inertia must come from a very deep and personal place inside of you. Most often, the wish to move from being an Inertial to a Captain comes from a place of need, even of desperation.

Such a transition begins with a simple, yet powerful, epiphany: "I just can't continue down the path that my life has been on any longer." This realization can be caused by many life experiences that are immediate and significant, such as a health problem like a serious illness or injury. It may arise gradually from a long-standing life situation, such as an unhappy marriage or an unsatisfying career. It may burst through or percolate to the surface with the simple realization that your life isn't the one you want to be leading. When you experience this epiphany in the most visceral and overwhelming way, when you feel it in every cell of your body, when it isn't really a choice or even a decision, but rather an existential imperative, then you have taken the first step in preparing to change the trajectory of your life.

Only the brave wake up from a bad dream.

—Ljupka Cvetanova, author[2]

## Emotions

As I discussed in part IV, emotions play a central role in your life inertia by acting as the fuel that propels it. Negative emotions (e.g., fear, frustration, anger, and sadness) are potent fuels that generate tremendous speed and momentum in your current life inertia. They can be so powerful that producing forces that exceed them can feel like a truly futile endeavor.

At the same time, emotions are two sides of the same coin. There are many positive emotions that can be equally potent and forceful to fuel a change in your life inertia. Just as emotions can cause you to feel helpless as you hurtle uncontrollably through life, they can also be used as fuel to take control of your life inertia and change direction. Positive emotions that catalyze change can include hope, inspiration, curiosity, pride, love, gratitude, joy, and happiness.

Paradoxically, the so-called negative emotions that can propel you down a path not of your choosing also can be used as fuel to shift your life trajectory if they act to propel you away from your current life inertia. Fear of losing a job, frustration about feeling trapped in your present life, anger at being mistreated by your spouse, and sadness at being estranged from your family are all negative emotional fuels that can be repurposed. As a result, these emotions can exert force on your current trajectory and propel you in a new and more positive direction.

Because emotions play such a vital role in motivating behavior, emotions that provide the fuel for change should emerge like a wellspring out of your epiphany. When you feel these emotions deeply and powerfully, they can override the negative emotions that propagate your current life inertia and help shift the direction that your life is taking.

> Depression, anger, and sadness are states of mind, and so are happiness, peace, and contentment. You can choose to be in any of these states because it's your mind.
>
> —Maddy Malhotra, author[3]

## Courage

Regardless of how much you may want to alter your life trajectory, parts of you (i.e., your baggage, habits, emotions, and environment) are equally resistant to change. A shift in your life inertia involves letting go of old ways of living that may not be serving you well but are, in an odd sort of way, comfortable. Human beings are wired through evolution to seek out that which is familiar, predictable, controllable, and comfortable; feeling otherwise signals a threat to our survival. There is no certainty that you will be able to make changes or whether the changes will produce the results you want. Embarking on a new path in your life means, to paraphrase *Star Trek* creator Gene Roddenberry, "to boldly go where you have never gone before."[4] With a new path comes the unknown, uncertainty, doubt, and discomfort. With all of these forces driving your life inertia along its current trajectory, attempting change is downright scary. Courage provides you with the fortitude, determination, and resilience to resist the "gravitational pull" of your current life inertia, confront the uncertainty and challenges, and commit yourself to harnessing your four life forces to change the direction of your life.

Change also requires risk. Taking a risk is terrifying because you may fail to alter your life inertia. Alternatively, it is only by taking risks that you can have a chance of making meaningful changes to your life. Courage to change doesn't mean not being afraid of what might happen; fear is natural because change takes you out of your comfort zone. Change is about your ability to confront and push through your fear rather than being paralyzed by it.

Courage means having the willingness to acknowledge aspects of yourself that you may not like or that may be unfamiliar and to experience "bad" emotions you may feel. It enables you to accept that you might fail in your attempts at change at first while simultaneously knowing that not trying would be much worse. Courage enables you to reject your old inertia, take control of your life forces, chart a new course for your life, and then actively seek out the life you really want.

Courage enables you to resist the forces of your old life inertia and its unhealthy habits and patterns while being able to make difficult choices. Courage allows you to do what is in your best interests, no matter how uncomfortable it might make you feel. Courage allows you to let go of the familiarity and comfort of your past life inertia and experience the hope that a new life inertia provides. Courage also provides the motivation that you need to harness the four life forces, initiate a new life inertia, and have the conviction to maintain that new path, no matter how uncomfortable and scary it might get.

Courage emboldens you to embrace the values that are important to you now. It allows you to act in ways that strengthen your self-esteem, rather than undermine it. Courage encourages you to take ownership of your life and assume responsibility for everything you do. Finally, courage allows you to welcome and accept all of your emotions. It allows you to feel comfortable in experiencing negative emotions because it is only by experiencing the complete spectrum of emotions that you will ever be able to fully experience joy, excitement, fulfillment, and happiness.

Having the courage to take command of the four life forces that propel your life and change your life inertia is much like jumping into cold water. You know it will be a shock at first. It will be uncomfortable, and you may initially regret having taken the plunge. Then you begin to adapt after a short while. What was intimidating at first becomes approachable. What had been unknown becomes familiar. What was once painful is invigorating. Courage enables you to take that plunge.

> Happiness depends on being free, and freedom depends on being courageous.
>
> —Maire Rutkoski, professor and children's writer[5]

## Leap of Faith

A significant problem with attempting to change your life inertia is that there is no certainty. You never know for sure whether you can shift your life inertia in the direction in which you want to go. If you do succeed, you don't know whether that change will be what you really want. Does the following sound familiar? "Gosh, my current life isn't great, but at least I know it and have learned to deal with it." No one—not your family, your friends, your clergy, your spiritual advisor, or your psychotherapist—can foresee what will happen to your life if you change your life inertia. There is going to be that fear of the unknown: How will you change psychologically and emotionally and how will the world around you change?

Ultimately, if you really want to change your life inertia, you must take a "leap of faith." The leap of faith begins with the conviction that you do not want your life to continue on its current trajectory any longer, as it will bring you only more unhappiness and discontent. The leap of faith also involves having a basic belief in yourself and a fundamental trust in the vision of who, what, and where you want to be in the future. The leap of faith involves your commitment to creating a new and healthy life inertia. You must choose to believe that good things will happen when you do make that change.

I use an analogy from the film *Indiana Jones and the Last Crusade* (1989) to illustrate the leap of faith. In this film, Indiana Jones is searching for the Holy Grail (an appropriate metaphor here, wouldn't you say?) and is following a map that leads him along a treacherous path. Near the end of his journey, Jones comes to a bottomless chasm across from which is the doorway to the Holy Grail. Unfortunately, there is no apparent bridge across the abyss. Fittingly, the map indicates that taking a leap of faith will enable Jones to traverse the gap. He wrestles with his doubt and uncertainty before mustering the courage to take a leap of faith. He steps into the abyss. To his surprise and relief, he finds that there is an invisible bridge that he can walk across to seize the Holy Grail. Just as Jones believed that the path he had chosen was correct despite the direst of consequences if he was wrong, you also must have the strength of your conviction to take that initial leap into changing your life inertia. And don't forget that your worst-case scenario is nothing like that of Indiana Jones, who faced plummeting to his death (though that was just a film, of course).

The leap of faith begins with, well, faith that you can change your life inertia. It also means recognizing all the strengths and resources that you have to take the leap of faith. Remember, it's not blind faith, but a faith born of the many capabilities you possess that give you confidence that your leap of faith will be rewarded. That well-grounded faith gives you hope—a truly powerful force for change—which enables you to focus on the positive aspects of your new life direction. Hope will guide your thoughts and emotions toward the encouraging new course of your life inertia. It's important to recognize that some misgivings are a normal part of the process, as you can never be 100 percent sure that things will work out the way you want. If you didn't have doubts, it wouldn't require a leap of faith!

> Life is a gamble. There are no sureties. If you want something badly, you'd have to trust your heart and your instincts and then take a leap of faith.
>
> —Alyssa Urbano, writer and registered nurse[6]

## Commitment

These states of mind result in a wholehearted and steadfast commitment to changing your life inertia. This resolve expresses itself in an unwavering determination to harness your four life forces, resist the momentum that your current life inertia exerts on you, and take active steps to shift your life in a new and better direction. This resolve will motivate you to engage in the sometimes slow process of shifting your life inertia even when you are discouraged, frustrated, and uncertain about whether you can achieve the positive change in your life that you want.

## Three Ds

Commitment to changing the trajectory of your life means putting immense amounts of time, focus, and energy into all aspects of your efforts. It involves doing everything you can to gain control of your four life forces and leverage them to their fullest on your life's direction.

Developing and maintaining this resolute commitment begins with what I call the three Ds. The first D stands for *direction*. The initial step in harnessing your four life forces involves considering the different directions you want your life inertia to take you in the future. This step is more complicated than you might think. It's one thing to know that your current life path isn't the right one for you; it's another thing to know which path *is* best for you. Just like that asteroid hurtling through space with an infinite number of options for what direction it could go, your life has many directions toward which your life could be guided. A clear vision based on who you are and what you want for your future is necessary to determine the direction you want your life inertia to take you.

The second D represents *decision*. You must select one direction from all of the different directions in which you could propel your life. There is no "right" direction; they're simply your options. You must choose the direction that you deem right for you at this point in your life. Your choice will dictate how you channel your four life forces and the ultimate direction that your life takes.

The third D stands for *dedication*. Once you've made your decision, you must dedicate yourself to it. Your decision is to change your life inertia. Your level of dedication largely determines how successful you are in exerting force on your life and shifting it in your chosen direction. This dedication is so important because commitment starts out as a state of mind and is realized through the choices you make and the actions you take. Your choices include making the decision that changing your life inertia is a top priority in your life. And your actions include doing the hard work every day to shift your life inertia. Only through complete dedication to your direction and decision will you do what it takes to take control of your life inertia and shift the trajectory of your life.

> You've got to get up every morning with determination if you're going to go to bed with satisfaction.
>
> —George Lorimer, author and journalist[7]

## Effort = Goals?

When people tell me that they want to change their lives, they always have big goals. They may be hoping to embark on a new career, live a healthier lifestyle, or find a life partner. I ask them whether they are doing everything they can to achieve those goals. Rarely do I receive a confident "yes" in response. What this answer tells me is that there is often a disconnect between the goals people have to change their lives and the effort they put into those goals. Given the momentum of your current life inertia, anything less than complete alignment between your efforts and your goals likely will result in failure, and you will remain on your present life course.

It's easy to say that you want to take your life in a new direction (as they say, talk is cheap!); it is much more difficult to actually do what is necessary to make it happen. If you have this kind of disconnect and you are truly committed to altering your life inertia, you must "raise your game" to meet the challenge and ensure you're doing the work necessary to achieve your goals.

> We all have dreams. But in order to make dreams come into reality, it takes an awful lot of determination, self-discipline, and effort.
>
> —Jesse Owens, Olympic 100-meter sprint champion[8]

## Commitment Is a Moment-to-Moment and a Long-term Choice

It's one thing to say that you are committed to changing your life inertia. It's an entirely different thing to demonstrate that commitment every day, in every aspect of your life. In fact, commitment is a moment-to-moment choice that involves many situations that will determine whether you ever get on a life trajectory of your choosing.

As I discussed in chapter 9, there are many major obstacles to those moments of commitment including baggage, habits, emotions, and environment. There are also smaller obstacles that can arise every day, such as exhaustion, stress, monotony, frustration, impatience, and a multitude of distractions. In those moments, you must decide what is important to you. Whether you ultimately can establish a new life trajectory will be determined by aspects of your commitment. How determined are you to change your life inertia? How high a priority do you place on finding a new direction in your life? And are you able to resist the competing forces of your current life inertia acting as a Siren's call for your attention, time, and energy?

> Commitment means staying loyal to what you said you were going to do long after the mood you said it in has left you.
>
> —Jonathan Field, five-time martial arts world champion[9]

## Seven Ps

Once you've established the foundation of the mindset needed to change your life inertia with the three Ds, it's time to build on them. The seven Ps will prove useful as you tackle one of the biggest challenges of your life.

### Positivity

One of the most common barriers to achieving the life changes people want is negativity. As the challenges get greater, you may start to have doubt and your mindset may become negative. The high hopes and dreams of a better life that you held when you embarked on this journey can plummet as you focus on all of the complications and problems that can arise and your confidence falls. You may go from being your best ally to your worst enemy (for more on this concept, see chapter 6). What are the chances of changing your life inertia with this "dark" mindset? Let me answer that question for you: pretty darned low.

Your only chance to shift the direction of your course is to stay positive and remain your best ally. Make sure that you stay on your own side, particularly when you're faced with those inevitable down periods that are a normal part of life and an expected part of change.

> Remember an arrow can only be shot by pulling it backwards; so when you feel like life is dragging you down with difficulties, it simply means that it's going to launch you to something great. So just focus and keep aiming.
>
> —Megan Street, author[10]

### Process

One of the most common problems that occurs when people attempt to change their life inertia is that they continually focus on the ultimate trajectory rather than what they need to do to get there. They forget to focus on how to leverage their four life forces to achieve that life path. Let me explain: A process state of mind involves paying attention to the things that help you get your life on the course that you want. In contrast, an outcome state of mind involves focusing on getting where you want to go. Let me make this very clear: an outcome state of mind is the kiss of death in your efforts to change the direction of your life.

You might ask why focusing on the end result will sabotage your efforts. Here's why: Many people believe that focusing on the outcome increases the chances of that outcome occurring, but the opposite is actually true. The outcome of changing your life inertia happens at some point in the future. And if you're focusing on the future, what are you *not* focusing on? Well, the present and the process to get to that point in the future. Here's the irony: By focusing on the process rather than the outcome, you have a much better chance of doing what you need to do because you are paying attention to things that will help you harness your four life forces and exert them on your life inertia. If you do that, you're more likely to make the change you wanted in the first place.

Another reason that focusing on the outcome sabotages your efforts is fear. Why do you get fearful when you think about the life trajectory you want to be on? You're afraid that you won't be able to make the changes necessary to change course. By focusing on the outcome, you're more likely to feel anxious and less likely to stay focused on what you need to do to change your life inertia. A little anxiety can be helpful, but too much is distracting and disheartening, which feeds negativity. In contrast, staying focused on the process decreases your fear of failing and you'll be able to stay relaxed. Focusing on the process makes it more likely that you will continue to pursue the new direction in your life with vigor and without hesitation, the result of which is the outcome you desire.

If you quit on the process, you are quitting on the result.

—Idowu Koyenikan, author[11]

## Present

As you immerse yourself in the process of changing your life inertia, another shift can happen that will hurt you. You may lose focus on the present—what you need to do now—due to your focus on either the past or the future. Focusing on how your life has been or how it might be in the future distracts from the process.

Let's start with a past focus. There's a saying: "You can't change the past, but you can ruin a perfectly good future by worrying about it." The reality is that you can't change the past, so there's no point in thinking about it unless you are learning from mistakes so you don't repeat them. If something bad happened in the past, be disappointed and then let it go. If something good happened, revel in it and then let it go. Looking back only interferes with your present.

Now about the future: thinking about the future also has only limited value. On the plus side, reminding yourself of the life trajectory you want to be on when you change your life inertia can inspire and motivate you to maintain your efforts. On the minus side, it can cause doubt and worry because you fear that you won't be able to change the course of your life. A future focus can cause anxiety because it creates high expectations that you want so bad. In essence, if you're focusing on the future, you're not focusing on what you need to do now to get on the life path to the future you want.

If it's over, then don't let the past screw up the rest of your life.

—Nicholas Sparks, American novelist[12]

## Patience

Patience is a powerful tool that you will need as you strive toward changing your life inertia. The dictionary defines patience as "the capacity to accept or tolerate delay, trouble, or suffering without getting angry or upset" and being "even tempered" and "diligent." Sounds like an important attitude when you're trying to alter your life trajectory, doesn't it? Your life inertia isn't likely to shift due to one massive blow to it. Instead, the application of the four life forces in a steady and determined manner will get you the results you want. Therefore, patience is essential for long-term success. It allows you to stay positive and motivated during setbacks when you are struggling to gain control of or to apply those forces. You aren't looking for unrealistic progress or quick results, so patience keeps you focused on the small steps that are necessary to continue toward your change goals. It also allows you to recognize and accept that it might be a long road ahead. Patience allows you to continue to expend the effort and put in the time to get on the life path you want.

> Patience is not passive waiting. Patience is active acceptance of the process required to attain your goals and dreams.
>
> —Ray A. Davis, author[13]

## Persistence

One of the most important things you can do to make changing your life inertia a likelihood (there are no guarantees) is simply to keep exerting those four forces on your life. In other words, be persistent. Your best, and perhaps only, chance of getting your life on the course you want is to keep steadily plugging away at all of the things you need to do to shift your life inertia. Persistent people continue to do what it takes, day in and day out, week in and week out, month in and month out, and sometimes year in and year out, simply because they know they must. Moreover, they persist in the face of monotony, boredom, and the desire to do other things.

> Persistence is the key to solving most mysteries.
>
> —Christopher Pike, American author[14]

## Perseverance

Perseverance is a variation of persistence. It emphasizes continuing to pursue your goals in the face of all of the ups and downs that are an inevitable part of changing the trajectory of your life. Whether it's pain, fatigue, illness, injury, plateaus, lack of progress, or setbacks, perseverance allows you to keep taking steps forward every time you are forced to take steps back. Metaphorically speaking, as you hurtle through life, it's easy to get discouraged, lose confidence, and question whether you will ever get on the path you want to be on as you hit space debris. You may begin to wonder how you can handle the jostling without breaking up. Maintaining your perseverance in the face of this will determine the ultimate direction your life takes.

> The man who moves a mountain begins by carrying away small stones.
>
> —Confucius, ancient Chinese philosopher[15]

## Progress

As with most things of value in life, changing your life inertia is not likely going to be immediate or sudden. It will probably involve a steady accumulation of forces that you begin to exert, which results in incremental shifts in the direction of your life. This state of mind encourages you to focus on how far you have come, instead of how far you have to go in shifting your life trajectory. This glass-half-full attitude enables you to savor every step you take and allows you to stay focused on changing your life inertia in the direction of your choosing. You will always have setbacks and plateaus, but the key is to see that you are heading in the right direction.

# CHANGING TRAJECTORY
## From Reaction to Action

*Action /akSH(ə)n/*: the fact or process of doing something, typically to achieve an aim; the bringing about of an alteration by force; an act that one consciously wills and that may be characterized by physical or mental activity.

A rriving at the final chapter of this book, you are now ready to gain control of your four life forces, apply them to your life inertia, and produce a course correction that will put you on a new and desired trajectory. You now understand why you have been stuck on your current life path for so long. You have insights into the life forces that have propelled you to this point. You know the obstacles that have prevented you from altering your course until now. You appreciate the states of mind that lay the foundation for changing your life inertia.

Now the real work begins. It is at this point that you must confront and overcome Taylor's three laws of human motion (first presented in the introduction):

1. Law of life inertia: Every life persists on its established trajectory unless it is compelled to change course by internal or external forces.

2. Law of life momentum: The force that propels a life trajectory is determined by the individual's investment in and amount of time already spent on that course. The intensity and point in time when a force is applied determine the extent of the change in direction of the life path.

3. Law of life action-reaction: For every action taken by a person in their life, there is an equal and opposite reaction that maintains a life's current trajectory.

By following the prescriptions of chapters 9 and 10, you set the stage to exert sufficient forces that I describe in this chapter to resist the momentum of and alter the trajectory of your current life inertia. How difficult this process will be and how much time it will take depends on many factors:

- The strength of the four life forces that have driven your life so far.

- How long you've been on your current trajectory.

- The amount of momentum your present life path has.

- Your ability to remove the obstacles that influence your four life forces.

- Your willingness to fully embrace the states of mind that are necessary for gaining control of your four life forces.

- Your commitment to the moment-to-moment process of taking control of Starship You.

I have found that when someone makes a deep commitment to changing their life inertia, it is reasonable to expect to see early signs of changing direction within the first month and a lasting new trajectory in six to twelve months. If that seems like a long time to you, compare it to how many years you have been stuck on your current life path. It's also helpful to think about how many years you have ahead of you during which you can either remain on the same unfulfilling life course or find a new and meaningful trajectory for the rest of your life.

> They always say that time changes things, but you actually have to change them yourself.
>
> —Andy Warhol, American artist[1]

## Identify Obstacles

You may have all of the motivation in the world to change your life inertia, but that determination will be for naught if there are structural obstacles in the way of you taking the helm of Starship You. These obstacles will either soften or blunt whatever forces you must harness to knock your life off its current trajectory. So before you do anything else, you need to identify the obstacles that are keeping you on your present life path. In chapter 9, I described the four primary impediments to altering your life inertia: baggage, habits, emotions, and environment. If you haven't already done so, please return to that chapter and try to pinpoint what those barriers are for you. Ask yourself the following questions:

- What are the specific obstacles that are guiding my life inertia?

- In what ways do these obstacles keep me on my current life course?

- What do I need to do to neutralize the force of these obstacles?

When you understand these obstacles, you take the mystery out of what has been holding you back. This perspective also gives you clarity about what you need to change, which you can put to use later in this chapter when you set goals and specific action steps.

> It does not do to leave a live dragon out of your calculations, if you live near him.
>
> —J. R. R. Tolkien, author of *The Lord of the Rings* trilogy[2]

## Embrace the Positive States of Mind

Once the obstacles are removed, you must adopt the positive states of mind that I described in chapter 10: epiphany, emotions, courage, leap of faith, commitment, and the seven Ps (positivity, process, present, patience, persistence, perseverance, progress). These states of mind give you the confidence to believe you can change your life inertia and the determination to do what it takes. Each of us holds these states of mind in our own way based on our life trajectory. It's up to you to examine your relationship to them and decide how you can fully embrace them. In doing so, you ensure that these states of mind are capable of exerting maximum force on your life inertia. Ask yourself the following questions:

- To what degree have I embraced these states of mind?

- If not fully, what is preventing me from adopting them?

- What can I do to leverage these states of mind to my advantage in changing my life inertia?

## Discover Best Practices

There is no point in reinventing the wheel when it comes to changing your life inertia. No matter how unique you may believe your life challenges are, the reality is that many thousands (and probably millions) of other people have struggled in similar ways. So rather than figuring out what works through trial and error (rarely an efficient or effective means of change), why not explore what has worked and not worked for others? Then you can apply those ideas to the changes you want to make in your life.

Best practices can be garnered from many sources: family, friends, mental health professionals, books, articles, blogs, podcasts, webinars, and online courses. Thanks to the internet, you can gather relevant information from an untold number of people who share your challenges and offer insights and recommendations that can help you. Of course, there's no guarantee that what works for someone else will work for you, but an understanding of best practices will at least give you some direction for the best course to take for changing your life-inertia. Best-case scenario, best practices can show you the smoothest and most direct route to take. Be warned that you should pay careful attention to the credibility of whatever sources grab your attention. Remember, there are a lot of people out there trying to sell you a pig in a poke. At the same time, there are many intelligent and thoughtful people who have reasonable ideas worthy of consideration. Ask yourself the following questions:

- What best practices will help me remove the obstacles?

- What best practices will help me embrace the constructive states of mind?

- What best practices can I use to gain control of my four life forces?

- What best practices can I learn from to shift my life inertia?

Best practices are useful reference points, but they must come with a warning label: The more you rely on external intelligence, the less you will value an internal idea.

—Gyan Nagpal, award-winning talent strategist and author[3]

## Set Change Goals

You can't change the direction of your life if you don't know in what direction you want to go. Establishing clear goals and objectives for the changes you want to make to your life inertia enables you to identify in what direction you want your life inertia to take you, focus your efforts, and direct your energy toward producing a change in your life trajectory. You also are able to understand which of the four life forces need to be leveraged most and how best to harness them in pursuit of a new direction in your life. These goals should identify what areas you want to change and the ultimate outcome you want to achieve. Goals work because they are a constant reminder of where you want to go, and objectives tell you how to get there.

There is both a science and an art to goal setting. One of the most effective models is based on the acronym SMARTER, which represents seven criteria that enable you to get the most out of the goals you set by incorporating how to achieve them:

- *Specific:* Your goals should be specific instead of general. "I want a better job" is a goal that is too general. You want to be specific with your goals, such as "I want a job that is personally meaningful and rewarding and enables me to collaborate with others in pursuit of social change."

- *Measurable:* Your goals should be objective and measurable. For example, "I will explore my values, identify career paths that will express them, and search for five jobs per week that fit the criteria I identify."

- *Accepted:* You should set your own goals (with help from others, if necessary). For example, "Though I will seek advice from those I trust, I will establish goals that are consistent with my values and the new direction I want my life to go."

- *Realistic:* You want to set goals that are both realistic and challenging but not overwhelming. This means that you can achieve them through working hard without feeling defeated if you experience setbacks. For example, "I am going to seek out job positions that are the next step in my career path based on my current level of experience."

- *Time limited:* The best goals are ones in which there is a time limit for their achievement. For example, "I will identify three possible career paths that interest me and research four specific positions in the next two weeks."

- *Exciting:* You want to set goals that inspire and excite you. For example, "I will seek a position that inspires and motivates me to be successful."

- *Recorded:* You are more likely to stay committed to your goals when you write them down. For example, "I will keep track of my goals I set for myself."

A goal properly set is halfway reached.

—Zig Ziglar, American best-selling author, salesman, and
motivational speaker[4]

## Choose Your People Wisely

One thing is for sure: you won't be able to change your life inertia alone. The people in your life play an essential role in whether you remain stuck on your current trajectory or are able to break free and set a new course for your life. For better or for worse, as social beings, we are powerfully impacted by those around us.

People influence you in one of two ways. First, they can prevent you from harnessing your four life forces. As mentioned in chapter 9, we tend to build a world around us that supports our present life path and makes us feel safe and comfortable. Whom we marry, the friends we have, those with whom we work—they all generally provide momentum to our lives, whether or not it is going in the direction we want. Whatever baggage, habits, and emotions we experience are usually mirrored by those around us. If we smoke cigarettes, have certain eating habits, or engage in particular activities, it's likely that the people in our lives introduced us to these behaviors, or else we met them through those activities.

If you decide to change your life inertia away from those activities, it is likely that the people in your life will not be very supportive of your wish to change. Some will actively do what they can to prevent those changes from occurring. These reactions are not surprising for two reasons. First, making a change in your life that moves you away from your current trajectory can be seen as a judgment of "wrongness" on the lives led by those close to you. Trying to alter your life path communicates that there must be something wrong with your present path. This is threatening to those who have shared and are highly invested in your life. Second, people in your life may resist your efforts for fear that they will lose their relationship with you. This is particularly true if the change in your life direction is dramatic. If the change you are making moves you away from whatever it is that acts as the bond in some of your relationships, then those relationships will be at risk. For example, if you choose to give up drinking alcohol, you likely will lose touch with those with whom drinking is the bond that connects you. A sad fact of shifting the direction of your life is that you may very well have to replace some people in your life who may not be supportive of or who are actively sabotaging your efforts at changing your life inertia.

The simple reality is that your chances of changing the direction of your life are very low without strong support from important people in your life. In fact, just as easily as people in your life can undermine your efforts, they can also boost your efforts at creating a new life trajectory. You want to seek out people who will support the changes you want to make in your life. This backing can be demonstrated in various forms, whether through verbal encouragement of your efforts, being a role model, offering guidance, providing emotional and motivational support, or joining you in a shared journey of change.

You want to surround yourself with people who either already embrace the changes you want to make (e.g., to lead a healthier lifestyle, it will be essential to spend most of your time with others who value healthy eating and exercise) or are willing to support your efforts even if the direction you want to go isn't aligned with their own life path (e.g., to not tempt you to return to your old life path). It will be a useful exercise to identify the people in your life who will interfere with or support your efforts at changing your life inertia. It will also be helpful for you to identify the people in your life who hold you to your current life path and then look for others who can help you redirect your life inertia in a new, more positive direction. You can ask the following questions:

- Who are the most influential people in my life?

- Who are most likely to support my efforts at changing my life inertia and in what ways would I expect them to support me?

- Who are most likely to not support my efforts and in what ways?

- Who are most likely to actively undermine my efforts and in what ways?

- For those identified in the latter two questions, how could I either enlist their support or minimize their interference?

To throw away an honest friend is, as it were, to throw your life away.

—Sophocles, ancient Greek tragedian[5]

CHAPTER ELEVEN

# Change Your Environment

There is a well-known adage that goes something like "The trouble with running away from your problems is that you always take yourself with you." Though true to some degree because whatever challenges you have reside inside of you, there's no doubt that the environment in which you live can either exacerbate or help alleviate those problems. Admittedly, changing your environment—for example, moving to a new city or becoming involved in different activities—won't change your life inertia in and of itself; however, the chances of creating a new direction in your life are very low without modifying the world in which you live. At a minimum, your environment must not interfere with or prevent you from shifting your life inertia. At best, it should support that change.

As I noted previously, you make choices throughout your life driven by your baggage, habits, and emotions, with the intended goal of best managing those issues rather than guiding or supporting a life direction of your own choosing. These choices include where you live, where you work, the activities in which you participate, and even seemingly small decisions involving the route you take to work, the stores at which you shop, and your daily routines. What happens is that your environment ends up reinforcing the status quo and creating more momentum for your life inertia, which makes it more resistant to change. As a result, the environment that you have constructed ends up being the very obstacle that prevents you from changing your life path. For example, let's say that you have decided to shift your life inertia away from an unhealthy lifestyle of poor eating habits, excessive caffeine, and too much alcohol. Yet your morning route to work involves passing a coffee shop where you buy a cup of coffee and a scone every day. In addition, you pass a bar at the end of your workday, where you are invited in by friends. It's easy to see how maintaining this particular aspect of your environment will prevent you from making the life changes you want. As a result, to change your life inertia, you would need to change your route to and from work so as to avoid the gravitational pull of that old life pattern drawing you back to your old life course. Overall, if you can change your environment to one that supports and encourages the changes you want to make, even in simple ways such as I just described, then you have a better chance of mustering the forces necessary to alter your current life trajectory.

The goal of *Change Your Life's Direction* is to replace your current unhealthy environment with settings and activities that will reinforce the changes you want to make and propel your life in a new direction. Ask yourself the following questions:

- What aspects of my environment act as impetus for my current life inertia?

- How can I remove those influences from my life?

- What new facets of my environment can I replace the old ones with that will support my new life trajectory?

Life is like a dogsled team. If you ain't the lead dog, the scenery never changes.

—Lewis Gizzard, American writer and journalist[6]

## Create Action Steps

Anyone who wants to change can talk a heck of a game about all they're going to do differently, but, as I've said previously, talk is cheap; what matters is what you do. For you to change your life inertia, you must take action. Action steps describe the particular things you will do to achieve your change goals. They detail precisely what you need to do every day to harness your four life forces to redirect your life trajectory. Action steps may range from engaging in an exercise regimen to actively searching for a new career to showing daily gratitude for your family. In identifying specific action steps, you can also clarify the specific information, resources, and skills you will need to counter your old baggage, habits, emotions, and environment, such as more positive self-talk, building new and more supportive relationships, joining a health club, taking an evening class to further your career, or finding an attorney to discuss a divorce. Ask yourself the following questions:

- In what general areas must I make changes to alter my life trajectory?

- What specific steps must I take in these areas to exert sufficient force on my current life inertia?

- What information, resources, and skills must I avail myself of to increase my chances of changing my life inertia?

## Make Good Choices

In order for your efforts at changing your life inertia to bear fruit, you must recognize new possible directions that your life can take and start acknowledging there are choices that you didn't know you were making. These different life paths can be either bad or good, unhealthy or healthy. A bad trajectory is the one that you've been on for many years that can best be described as "feel bad, do bad," in which you are unhappy and your actions are not in your own best interests. The other life path that you may not have seen before is the good trajectory. This is the "feel good, do good" life course, which gives you meaning, satisfaction, and joy. On this life path, you can act in ways that are best for you. You have now arrived at the point where real change occurs.

> When you come to the fork in the road, take it.
>
> —Yogi Berra, Hall of Fame baseball player and noted misanthrope[7]

If you have made a true commitment to pursuing a new direction in your life and are willing to "put your money where your mouth is," then you can ask yourself one simple question when faced with difficult choices: *"Will it help me change my life inertia?"* This question takes all of the many competing forces you are confronted with every day and boils them down to one simple notion that lies at the heart of shifting your life inertia. This question also provides a clear distinction between what will keep you on your current life path and what will help you move your life in a new direction.

One of the most common responses I hear when people are faced with a choice that will either promulgate their current life path or propel them down a new course is "I don't feel like it today." I hear this frequently when the benefits of changing their life inertia are outweighed by the momentum and relative ease of their present trajectory; inaction is easier than action.

Once you've made a real commitment to your goals, the question "Will it help me change my life inertia?" makes your choice abundantly clear. The goal of *Change Your Life's Direction* involves seeing the choices you have available to you, having the determination to overcome resistance from your current life inertia, and choosing to apply your four life forces to a new and positive direction even when it's difficult. Ask yourself the following questions:

- What choices am I faced with that will impact the direction of my life trajectory?

- How will those choices influence my efforts to change my life inertia?

- Which choices will best support my goal of altering the path of my life?

But until a person can say deeply and honestly, "I am what I am today because of the choices I made yesterday," that person cannot say, "I choose otherwise."

—Stephen R. Covey, American educator and author[8]

## The Grind

It can be an inspiring experience to finally see and choose to take control of your four life forces and propel your life in a healthy direction the first few times it presents itself. Initially, it is exciting and motivating to see your life course begin to shift. The problem is that you will eventually experience "the grind" as you continue to redirect your life inertia. This is the point at which efforts to change the direction of your life lose their allure. The process is no longer exciting or motivating. The hope of "miraculous" change in the direction of your life that is immediate and requires little effort has been dashed. The grind is frustrating, exhausting, and boring. It can sap your confidence and commitment. It is also the point at which change meets its make-or-break point. Most people who thought they were truly committed to change until that point give up because the discomfort required to change outweighs the motivation to change.

> Doing great work is a struggle. It's draining, it's demoralizing, it's frightening—not always, but it can feel that way when we're deep in the middle of it.
>
> —Ryan Holiday, author of *Ego Is the Enemy*[9]

It is difficult to stay inspired and determined when you hit the grind because changing your life inertia is just plain hard. I have heard people say, "You must love it!" But let's be realistic: there's little to love about the process of changing your life inertia because it is so difficult. Unfortunately, hating the grind isn't an option because it will drive you to stop trying. I ask that you simply accept the grind as part of the deal. It's unpleasant, but it's not harmful, and it is essential. Even though the grind may be a real bummer, continuing along the trajectory that your life has been on for all of these years is even worse.

For you to create a significant course correction in your life, you must continue to do the work no matter how hard it gets. The grind means continuing to harness the four life forces in the face of internal resistance from your old life inertia and external resistance from people and your environment until your life is finally heading in the direction you want it to go. There is research that shows that it takes, on average, sixty-six days to change a habit (Lally, van Jaarsveld, Potts, and Wardle, 2009). You can be sure that long before you reach sixty-six days, you will reach the grind first. And it's your ability to push through the grind that will determine whether you reach the time required to change your life inertia.

You can either complain about it or grind, I choose to grind.

—Kyle Vidrine, author of *Wake up the Winner in You*[10]

# AFTERWORD
## Dancing with the Stars:
## From Unhappiness to Happiness

*Happiness /hapēnəs/:* A state of well-being characterized by emotions ranging from contentment to intense joy; the absence of angst.

C hanging the course of your life inertia means making a quantum shift in fundamental aspects of yourself: who you are, how you think, what you feel, the way you act, and how you interact with the people in your life. It means letting go of the past, living in the present, and looking to the future. Giving up the need to constantly *do* and finding peace in just being. Exorcising your false self and reconnecting with and embracing your true self. Relinquishing your dependence and need for validation from others and finding reliance and affirmation within yourself. No longer being your own worst enemy, in which you do things that are clearly not in your best interests, and becoming your best ally, always supporting yourself as you pursue your dreams. Instead of avoiding life as a threat that you thought it to be, starting to see life as the challenge that it is. Putting your childish ways behind you and responding to the world as the adult you have become. Ceasing to be a victim of whatever life presents to you and starting to be the master in a world of your own creation.

All of these changes result in the ultimate transformation from Inertial to Captain of Starship You. Taking the helm of your life means no longer hurtling uncontrollably throughout life. As Captain, you know what direction you want your life to go, you are in command of your four life forces, and you redirect your life toward a new trajectory that is consistent with who you are and what you want out of life.

> It isn't what you have or who you are or where you are or what you are doing that makes you happy or unhappy. It is what you think about it.
>
> —Dale Carnegie, American writer and lecturer[1]

So what has been the point of this journey of exploring ways to change your life inertia? As discussed in the introduction, one essential reason to take this journey has been to free yourself from living a life driven by negativity, whether that be fear, doubt, worry, anger, or despair. Another reason is to create a life course that allows you to feel all of your emotions deeply, take healthy risks, give and receive love freely, live a life consistent with your values, and realize your goals and dreams. Though this new life direction can mean different things for each of us, I suggest that the heart of this shift is the wish to move from unhappiness to happiness, for the opportunity for you to feel real, deep, enduring happiness for perhaps the first time in your life. I can't tell you what happiness means to you, how it translates into your life, or what it feels like; the definition of happiness is personal to each of us. At the same time, thanks to the burgeoning field of positive psychology, there is a growing body of research and practice that can help you understand what happiness means in your life based on who you are and what you want.

The happiness of your life depends upon the quality of your thoughts.

—Marcus Aurelius, Roman emperor and Stoic philosopher[2]

## The Unfulfilling Pursuit of Happiness

Is there anything more decidedly American than the pursuit of happiness? It is woven into the very fabric of the American ethos as "inalienable rights" bestowed on us in the Declaration of Independence ("Life, Liberty and the pursuit of Happiness"). Is there anything that we devote more time, effort, and money to than attempting to capture that elusive goal? And is there anything that we pursue with more vigor and yet with such poor results?

> But happiness cannot be pursued; it must ensue. One must have a reason to "be happy." Once the reason is found, however, one becomes happy automatically. As we see, a human being is not one in pursuit of happiness but rather in search of a reason to become happy.
>
> —Dr. Viktor Frankl, the author of *Man's Search for Meaning*[3]

## Happiness Is Like Sleep

Happiness is like sleep; the harder you try to fall asleep, the less likely it becomes. To fall asleep, you create external and internal states that allow sleep to come. The external states might include a cozy bed, a comfortable temperature, and a dark room. Internal states involve a relaxed body and a clear mind.

The same holds true for happiness. Rather than trying so hard to attain happiness, create the right internal and external states; then you are more likely to experience happiness (for example, feeling valued and more positive emotions, as well as engaging in fulfilling work and healthy relationships). This is where Inertials struggle.

They have been placed on a life course that prevents them from establishing those essential states that will lead to happiness. They may not enjoy their careers, their relationships often have little value, and their non-work life is void of meaning.

> The search for happiness is one of the chief sources of unhappiness.
>
> —Eric Hoffer, philosopher[4]

Unfortunately, at an unconscious level, Inertials often don't believe that they deserve to be happy; thus much of their lives is devoted to proving that they are worthy. They drive themselves unmercifully to succeed. They punish themselves when they fail. They don't have a moment's rest attempting to live up to the impossible standards they have set for themselves—all in the name of proving their worth as people and earning the right to be happy. Of course, as is plain to see, all of their efforts lead to the antithesis of happiness.

> It is bad enough that we are not taught how to find happiness, but for many people the situation is worse: They are actually taught how to be miserable.
>
> —Dr. Bernie Siegel, author of *Prescriptions for Living*[5]

Inertials are often afraid to experience happiness. In fact, they avoid happiness to protect themselves from even greater unhappiness. Opening your life to happiness would require that you open it to sadness and other uncomfortable emotions as well. Remember, emotions are two sides of the same coin; you can't just "cherry-pick" the experience of pleasant emotions and leave unpleasant emotions behind. You may have held yourself back because happiness seemed like such a distant and unreachable goal for many years, so it just wasn't worth the effort. Plus, you have much further to fall if you ever reach the summit of "Mount Happiness," which would mean more pain and unhappiness. If you allowed yourself to feel happiness, you never knew what can of worms that might open. So you decided that it was just safer to not feel happiness and you thought you had gotten used to your unhappiness. But you haven't and you never will.

You finally realized that being unhappy just plain sucks. After being stuck on a life trajectory that wasn't true to you, you have decided that enough is enough. You deserve happiness, you will find out how to experience happiness, and you will allow yourself to be happy.

## Pleasure vs. Happiness

The fact that we seek happiness with such fervor and so little success should cause us to reconsider what we believe happiness is and how we attain it. The first question to ask, then, is: What is happiness? Unfortunately, our superficial, immediate-gratification-driven popular culture has perverted our understanding of happiness. Many people mistake pleasure for happiness. They have come to believe that the sensations of pleasure that they experience periodically are actually happiness. They also look for happiness outside of themselves.

> [T]he problem might be that we are most of the time looking in the wrong places and, worse, seeking the wrong things. . . . The fundamental issue is the lack of clarity in our conceptions of happiness, combined with the fact that those notions of happiness we do have at our fingertips are created and molded by obscure social forces.
>
> —Mark Kingwell, author of *In Pursuit of Happiness*[6]

People seek happiness through pleasurable experiences like accumulating wealth, collecting material possessions, and accruing "friends" on social media. They also expose themselves to stimulating experiences such as drug and alcohol use, sex, and so-called extreme activities (e.g., marathon running, skydiving, and mountain biking). All of these things are attempts to make themselves feel good.

However, though these experiences may provide some transitory pleasure, feeling good is not the same as being happy. These attempts at happiness actually "medicate" you from the pain of unhappiness by temporarily assuaging, placating, and distracting you from your unhappiness rather than creating real, lasting happiness. Pleasure is a superficial and temporary sensation that makes you feel good for a short time, which means that it must continually be sought out. People who constantly look for pleasure are never satisfied and continue to look in other places for more pleasure, as they believe this will lead to happiness. In this fruitless pursuit of happiness, many people continue to search for things that will never give them the true happiness that they seek.

> My God, a moment of bliss. Why isn't that enough for a whole lifetime?
>
> —Fyodor Dostoevsky, Russian novelist and short story writer[7]

## Happiness Is a Process, Not an Outcome

Dr. Richard S. Lazarus, the noted University of California, Berkeley, researcher and coauthor of *Passion and Reason* (1995), suggests that, contrary to popular belief, happiness is not an outcome that can be pursued and achieved. Instead, happiness emerges when fully engaging in the process of life. Happiness is not a goal toward which we strive, but "a by-product of the continuing process of being personally involved and committed . . . in what we are doing."

Dr. Lazarus is saying that most people are going about experiencing happiness the wrong way. They believe that happiness will be there when they arrive at some destination and are so intent on achieving happiness that they pursue it relentlessly. Ironically, this prevents them from experiencing happiness in their daily lives. His understanding of happiness highlights two reasons why Inertials are unhappy. First, Inertials don't feel a strong sense of ownership, involvement, and commitment to their lives because they are living their lives based on values that are not their own. As a result, they are unable to find happiness in the process of their lives since they neither own nor fully engage in them. Second, when Inertials get "there" through accumulation of wealth, status, power, or celebrity, there is no happiness because, as Dr. Lazarus suggests, happiness is not a "there"; it is an "along the way."

## What Brings You Happiness?

An unfortunate result of having your life inertia established by your upbringing and popular culture is that you have been led to believe that certain things will bring you happiness. Most notable examples are money, material possessions, and fame. Yet every day we hear about the rich and famous who are lonely, depressed, drug addicted, violent, and suicidal. Recent research provides us with some insights into why people are unable to achieve the happiness they seek. Wealth and popularity are two of the most commonly cited and sought-after sources of happiness in our society but were found to be unrelated to happiness and actually were shown to have a negative effect on happiness (Kasser, 2000; D'Ambrosio, Jäntti, & Lepinteur, 2020). The reason why so many people are unhappy is that they don't know what brings them happiness.

The first step toward happiness is finding what brings you happiness. This same research found three factors to be most closely related to happiness: self-esteem, competence, and autonomy (Clark et al., 2018; Pink, 2011; Ryan & Deci, 2000). People who rated themselves as happiest were those who felt good about themselves, who felt capable in their activities, and who felt they had a choice in their activities. Further, one of the most robust findings indicates that happiness comes from loving and supportive relationships with family and friends (e.g., Cheng & Furhman, 2002). Additional predictors of happiness include being free of financial stress, being physically healthy, having a bright future, feeling safe in one's community, having deeply held goals to strive toward, and living in a culture in which people can live genuinely (e.g., Peterson, Park, & Seligman, 2005; Thaler & Sunstein, 2008). My own work with Inertials who make the transition to Captains shows that happiness comes from four primary sources: careers, personal time, relationships, and simply being.

## Career

Your professional life can have a substantial impact on your happiness because it is where you spend most of your time. Your career can be a meaningful foundation of your sense of competence, it is a source of income that supports your life inertia, and our culture holds a successful career in high esteem. One significant cause of unhappiness among Inertials is that they experience little fulfillment or joy in their accomplishments despite any success they may achieve because they don't feel a sense of ownership of their work. This disconnect occurs because the career path Inertials take is often dictated by outside forces, such as parents and popular culture. As a result, their careers are inconsistent with their values and true self. Importantly, *happiness comes from a passion for and deep engagement in a career that aligns with your values and offers intrinsic rewards in terms of meaning, satisfaction, and joy.*

Captains appreciate the minutiae of their work: the salesperson who loves the contact with prospective buyers, the teacher who loves to see the excitement when a student learns something new, the architect who loves to talk about home design and construction, or the researcher who loves inputting and analyzing raw data. All of these examples demonstrate that careers can be a great source of happiness and joy. Simply being involved in any way in their work makes Captains happy.

Having a career for which you feel great passion allows the experience of happiness at many levels. Sure, you love to be successful and gain all of the external benefits, including financial reward and high status, but that is not the overriding reason for why you do the work. Pursuing professional goals, being challenged, demonstrating competence, becoming more skilled, being productive, and being valued by coworkers can be tremendous sources of happiness. Professional happiness is not just about success. Working well with others, mentoring younger professionals, and caring about and contributing to the growth of your field can also make you happy. What I have learned from Captains is that they find meaning in all aspects and at all levels of their careers. It is this total absorption in their efforts that makes them both successful and happy.

Finding happiness in your career is important because you will spend most of your adult life working. At the same time, that is not always possible. As my friend Andy found out, you may have chosen a career path for its ability to support a certain lifestyle, to which you are now committed due to family or financial obligations (the proverbial "golden handcuffs"). Due to these realities, happiness must come from sources outside of your work, as Andy learned and has demonstrated.

> If you are going to devote your time to do something you claim you love, take this thought; "Do I love it? Can I have peace within if I refuse to have it done?" This is passion.
>
> —Israelmore Ayivor, author of *Dream Big!*[8]

## Personal Time

Captains derive happiness from personal time away from their work that is fulfilling and fun. For a police officer, it may be coaching her daughter's soccer team. For an accountant, perhaps it is his church involvement. For the hardware store owner, it could be his contributions to a homeless shelter. This personal time can include sports or fitness participation, involvement in cultural activities (e.g., attending the symphony or the opera), reading, cooking, watching movies, spending time with family and friends—the list is endless. These experiences balance the narrowness of your career and provide a healthy perspective on its importance in your life. Personal time is your opportunity to escape from the intensity of your career and to have fun and meaningful experiences. Many Captains comment that it is this personal time that "keeps them sane."

> Do anything, but let it produce joy.
>
> —Walt Whitman, American poet and essayist[9]

## Relationships

Captains come to learn that professional success can be a lonely and isolating pursuit. Imagine the computer programmer who must sit at his computer alone for hours on end. Or the stock analyst who gets up at 4:00 a.m. every day and arrives at the office before the sun is up. Or the author who spends her days writing. In these situations of solitude, Captains gain happiness from their relationships with others outside of work. The opportunity to give and receive love, friendship, and support from family and friends and to share experiences are essential to their happiness. Much like the famished person who celebrates his next meal, Captains can become hungry for meaningful relationships. They savor the simple joys of connecting and communicating with others and sharing ideas and experiences. The happiness research I described earlier also bears this view. Relatedness or feeling close to others was an essential need that was most associated with happiness; people who felt connected with others viewed themselves as happy.

There is something of a paradox regarding where you can find happiness. Earlier, I said happiness cannot be found outside of yourself. That is not completely accurate. What I meant was that happiness cannot be found in the form of superficial gratification outside of yourself. I have come to believe that finding happiness is a two-part process that requires you first to look inward and then outward. Introspection is the starting point because you must explore your inner world to understand your values, gain insight into your past "baggage," and identify what makes you happy. However, once this task is accomplished, I believe that you can find happiness outside of yourself.

A colleague of mine sent me the following note that I think describes eloquently what I am trying to say:

I had an epiphany yesterday when I was not even thinking about anything related to it (isn't that how most epiphanies emerge?). Remember how I told you that I love my life, but I am a bit tired of myself. And that I would like to get away, but the problem is that I can't get away from myself. I was wrong. My epiphany was that my work is my escape from myself. I live a very self-focused life; not narcissistic or self-absorbed, just that I am alone a lot and so I have nothing or no one else to focus on. And I am tired of being the object of my own focus.

My work allows me to shift my focus away from me. When I am with clients, they are my total focus and I get such satisfaction and joy out of sharing their struggles, helping them "get it," and seeing them change for the better. I suppose that a similar other-focus occurs when one is in a loving relationship. That, I would guess, is what makes a relationship so meaningful and rewarding.

I just realized that perhaps the happiness that my work brings me is that I am not focused on myself. Rather, I am invested in and connected with others, and I am giving of myself to them; yet I get so much from them as well. It is moving, rewarding, very fun, and there is a deep connectedness with people that brings me great happiness. The key to happiness, then, is that it comes when it is not about me.

## Simply Being

Captains are very task-oriented by nature. They like being in charge of Starship You because their work requires that they do a great deal to achieve their goals. Because so much of their lives is devoted to doing, it might be surprising to learn that Captains have a great appreciation for simply being. This means that they enjoy engaging in activities that serve no purpose beyond simple enjoyment: reading, watching movies, eating, walking, exercising, listening to music, the list goes on. The ability to just *be* grounds Captains in who they are instead of what they do. It gives them regular opportunities to be mindful and self-reflective, to enjoy the simple pleasures of life and rejuvenate. Slowing down and *simply being* creates moments for Captains to fully appreciate and be grateful for the life path that they have chosen. In other words, they can revel in the moment-to-moment happiness of a life that they have directed, steered, driven, and propelled.

## Your Choice

Based on this discussion and your own ideas about happiness, it's time for you to define it for yourself. What does happiness mean to you? How does it feel? What must you do to experience it?

I hope that *Change Your Life's Direction* has provided you with the insights and tools to help you gain control of your four life forces, use them to exert pressure on and shift your life inertia, and change course to a new trajectory that truly will make your dreams come true. The responsibility to use them is yours. You are now faced with a choice that will impact you for the rest of your life. You can continue as an Inertial, as the asteroid hurtling uncontrollably through life in a direction that you do not want to go. Or you can choose to take the helm of Starship You as its Captain and exert forces on your life that will propel your life inertia along a path you choose.

It's now time for you to set a new course for your life. To paraphrase the well-known introduction to the *Star Trek* television shows and movies, it's time for you "to boldly go where you have never gone before!"

Bon voyage . . .

Jim Taylor, PhD
August 2020

# NOTES

## Introduction

1. Sincero, J. (2017). *You're a badass at making money: Master the mindset of wealth.* New York: Viking.

2. Dyer, W. (2001). *Pulling your own strings: Dynamic techniques for dealing with other people and living life as you choose.* New York: William Morrow.

3. Shaw, G. B. (1903). *Man and superman.* Westminster: Archibald and Constable.

4. Breathnack, S. B. (2009). *Something more: Excavating your authentic self.* New York: Grand Central Publishing.

5. Kiley, D. (1989). *Living together, feeling alone: Healing your hidden loneliness.* New York: Fawcett.

6. Stephenson, S. (2009). *Get off your "but": How to end self-sabotage and stand up for yourself.* San Francisco: Jossey-Bass.

7. Wilde, O. (1890). *The picture of Dorian Gray. Lippincott's Monthly Magazine.*

8. Roosevelt, F. D. (1936, September 22). Greeting to the 74th anniversary of the Emancipation Proclamation.

9. Quote from Osbon, D. K. (1991). *Reflections on the art of living: A Joseph Campbell Companion.* New York: HarperCollins.

## Part I—Introduction

1. Rogers, C. R. (1942). *Counseling and psychotherapy.* Cambridge, MA: Riverside Press.

## Chapter One

1. Lee, B. (2015). *Bruce Lee Jeet Kune Do: Bruce Lee's commentaries on the martial way.* N.p.: Tuttle Publishing.

2. Baldwin, J. (1961). *Nobody knows my name: More notes of a native son.* New York: Dial Press.

3. Shakespeare, W. (1994). *The merchant of Venice.* London: Longman.

4. Forward, S. (2002). *Toxic parents: Overcoming their hurtful legacy and reclaiming your life.* New York: Bantam.

5. Wilde, O. (1890). *The picture of Dorian Gray. Lippincott's Monthly Magazine.*

6. Magee, S. (2014). *Toxic health* (3rd Ed.). N.p.: CreateSpace Independent Publishing Platform.

7. Coleman, T. K. (2015). *Freedom without permission.* Coldwater, MI: Remnant Publishing.

8. Hay, L. L. (1984). *You can heal your life.* Carlsbad, CA: Hay House.

9. Williamson, M. (1996). *A return to love: Reflections on the principles of "A course in miracles."* New York: HarperOne.

10. Jalāl al-Dīn Rūmī, M. (2004). *The essential Rumi.* New York: HarperOne.

11. Xenophon. (1848). *Xenophon's memorabilia of Socrates.* New York: Harper & Brothers.

12. Von Goethe, J. W. (1835). *Faustus: A dramatic mystery, part 1.* London: Longman.

## Chapter Two

1. Tony Robbins. (2018, January 12). Facebook. https://www.facebook.com/TonyRobbins/posts/the-only-impossible-journey-is-the-one-you-never-begin/10156207124529060.

2. Rand, A. (1963). *For the new intellectual.* New York: Signet.

3. Carlson, R. (2002). *Don't sweat the small stuff.* New York: Hachette.

4. Ramsey, D. (2007). *The total money makeover: A proven plan for financial fitness.* Nashville, TN: Nelson Books.

5. Franklin, B. (1773). From Benjamin Franklin to Thomas Cushing, 5 January 1773. *Founders Online.* National Archives. https://founders.archives.gov/documents/Franklin/01-20-02-0005.

6. Henley, W. E. (1888). *A book of verses.* Oxford: D. Nutt.

7. Duhigg, C. (2012). *The power of habit.* Toronto: Doubleday Canada.

8. Nideffer, R. (1992). *Psyched to win.* Champaign, IL: Human Kinetics.

9. Carnegie, D. (1936). *How to win friends and influence people.* New York: Simon & Schuster.

## Part II—Introduction

1. Bennett., R. T. (2016). *The light in the heart: Inspirational thoughts for living your best life.* N.p.: Roy Bennett.

2. Cohen, R. (2008). "Madonnarama!" *Vanity Fair.* www.vanityfair.com/news/2008/05/madonna200805.

3. Clarke, J. I. (1994). *Self-esteem: A family affair.* Center City, MN: Hazelden Publishing.

4. Eker, T. H. (2009). *Secrets of the millionaire mind: Mastering the inner game of wealth.* New York: HarperCollins.

## Chapter Three

1. Jung, C. (1969). *Archetypes and the collective unconscious: Collected works of C. G. Jung.* Volume 9 (Part 1). Trenton, NJ: Princeton University Press.

2. Laing, R. D. (1967). *The politics of experience and the bird of paradise.* Harmondsworth, Middlesex: Penguin.

3. De Angelis, B. (1994). *Real moments.* New York: Dell.

4. Buscaglia, L. F. (1985). *Living, loving, and learning.* New York: Ballantine Books.

5. Jourard, S. M. (1971). *The transparent self.* New York: Van Nostrand Reinhold.

6. Brown, R. M. (2009). *Venus envy.* New York: Random House.

7. Twain, M. (1884). *The adventures of Huckleberry Finn.* London: Chatto & Windus.

8. Maltz, M. (2001). *The new psycho-cybernetics*. Englewood Cliffs, NJ: Prentice-Hall.

9. Angelou, M. (1994). *The complete collected poems of Maya Angelou.* New York: Random House.

10. Peck, M. S. (1978). *The road less travelled: A new psychology of love, traditional values, and spiritual values.* New York: Simon & Schuster.

11. Goleman, D. (2009). *Emotional intelligence: Why it can matter more than IQ.* London: Bloomsbury.

12. de Montaigne, M. (1993). *The complete essays.* London: Penguin Classics.

13. Haskins, H. S. (1940). *Meditations in Wall Street.* New York: William Morrow.

14. Quoted in J. Clemmer. (2003). *The leader's digest: Timeless principles for team and organization.* Toronto: ECW Press.

15. Lao Tzu. (1972). *Tao te ching.* New York: Vintage Books.

16. Elliot, E. B. (1895). *An introduction to the algebra of quantics.* Oxford: Oxford.

17. Bolen, J. S. (2005). *The tao of psychology: synchronicity and the self.* San Francisco: HarperOne.

18. Brehony, K. A. (1996). *Awakening at midlife.* New York: Riverhead.

19. Pipher, M. (1994). *Reviving Ophelia: Saving the selves of adolescent girls.* New York: Random House.

20. Wilson, A. (1991). *Three plays by August Wilson.* Pittsburgh: University of Pittsburgh Press.

21. Brehony, K. A. (1996). *Awakening at midlife.* New York: Riverhead.

22. Hill, N. (1937). *Think and grow rich.* Meriden, CT: The Ralston Society.

23. Maxwell, J. C. (2011). *Beyond talent: Become someone who gets extraordinary results.* Nashville, TN: Thomas Nelson.

24. Castaneda, C. (1968). *Teachings of Don Juan: A Yaqui way of knowledge.* Berkeley: University of California Press.

25. Dyer, W. (2001). *Pulling your own strings: Dynamic techniques for dealing with other people and living your life as you choose.* New York: William Morrow.

26. Lao Tzu. (1972). *Tao te ching.* New York: Vintage Books.

27. Issacson, W. (2013). *Steve Jobs.* New York: Simon & Schuster.

28. Johnson, L. B. (1963). "Transcript of President Johnson's Thanksgiving Day Address to the Nation Urging 'New Dedication.'" *New York Times*.

## Chapter Four

1. Emerson, R. W. (1841). *Self-reliance*. Project Gutenberg.

2. Wilde, O. (1899). *An ideal husband*. London: Leonard Smithers.

3. Angelou, M. (1969). *I know why the caged bird sings*. New York: Random House.

4. Kabat-Zinn, M., & Kabit-Zinn, J. (1998). *Everyday blessings: The inner work of mindful parenting*. New York: Hachette Books.

5. Dyer, W. W. (2001). *What do you really want for your children?* New York: William Morrow.

6. Tugaleva, V. (2013). *The love mindset*. London: Soulux Press.

7. Nazarian, V. (2010). *The perpetual calendar of inspiration: Old wisdom for a new world*. Los Angeles: Spirit Norilana Books.

8. Shriver, M. (2000). *Ten things I wish I'd know before I went out into the real world*. New York: Grand Central Publishing.

9. Burns, D. D. (1980). "The perfectionist's script for self-defeat." *Psychology Today*, 34–57.

10. Gray, J. (2000). *Children are from heaven: Positive parenting skills for raising cooperative, confident, and compassionate children*. New York: HarperCollins.

11. Miller, A. (1996). *Prisoners of Childhood: The drama of the gifted child and the search for the true self*. New York: Basic Books.

12. Kabat-Zinn, M., & Kabit-Zinn, J. (1998). *Everyday blessings: The inner work of mindful parenting*. New York: Hachette Books.

13. Gould, S. (1978). *The challenge of achievement: Helping your child succeed*. New York: Hawthorne Books.

14. Dolbear, A. E. (1899). "An educational allegory." *Journal of Education* 50(14), 235–36.

15. Miller, A. (1990). *For your own good: Hidden cruelty in child-rearing and the roots of violence*. New York: Farrar, Straus, & Giroux.

16. Maxwell, J. C. (2005). *Today matters: 12 daily practices to guarantee tomorrow's success*. New York: Center Street.

17. Kalwar, S. (2010). *Quote me everyday*. Morrisville, NC: Lulu Press.

18. Clemens, C. (1931). *My father Mark Twain*. New York: Harper Brothers.

19. Goddard, D. (2018). *Circles of separation*. N.p.: CreateSpace Independent Publishing Platform.

20. Albom, M. (2003). *The five people you meet in heaven*. New York: Hyperion.

21. Todd, C. (2018). *Burn out of a fairy godmother*. Tree of keys: Book 1. Kindle.

22. Cline, F., & Fay, J. (2014). *Parenting with love and logic: Teaching children responsibility*. Colorado Springs, CO: NavPress.

23. Kabat-Zinn, M. (1998). *Everyday blessings: The inner work of mindful parenting*. New York: Hachette.

24. Ford, H., & Crowther, S. (1922). *My life and work: The autobiography of Henry Ford*. New York: Doubleday.

25. Branden, N. (1995). *Six pillars of self-esteem*. New York: Bantam.

## Part III—Introduction

1. Schuck, H. (2013). *The working mom manifesto*. N.p.: Voyager Media.

## Chapter Five

1. Forward, S. (2002). *Toxic parents: Overcoming their hurtful legacy and reclaiming your life*. New York: Bantam.

2. Tolstoy, L. (1869). *War and peace*. Moscow: The Russian Messenger.

3. Radiguet, R. (1923). *Le Diable au corps* (*The devil in the flesh*). Paris: Grasset.

4. Lee, J. (1981). "Looking for love." *Looking for love* (Vinyl). Asylum Records.

5. Marcus Aurelius. (1942). *The meditations of Marcus Aurelius*. White Plains, NY: Peter Pauper Press.

6. Herbert, F. (1977). *The dosadi experiment*. New York: Tor Books.

7. Heaney, S. (2005). *The burial at Thebes: A version of Sophocles' Antigone*. New York: Farrar, Straus, and Giroux.

8. Hazlitt, W. (1930). *Selected essays, 1778–1830*. London: Bodley Head.

9. Mead, M. (1928). *Coming of age in Samoa: A psychological study of primitive youth for Western civilization*. New York: William Morrow.

10. Jung, C. G. (1958). *Psychology and religion: West and East*. Vol. 11. Princeton, NJ: Princeton University Press.

11. Spock, B. (1946). *The common sense book of baby and child care*. New York: Duell, Sloan, & Pearce.

12. Perry, P. (2019). *The book you wish your parents had read*. London: Penguin UK.

## Chapter Six

1. Koontz, D. (2007). *Seize the night: A novel*. New York: Bantam.

2. Kiyosaki, R. (2014, May 28). (@theRealKiyosaki). "Get out of your own way. Often, we're our own worst enemy when working towards our goals." Twitter. https://twitter.com/theRealKiyosaki/status/471789316503797760.

3. Sophocles. (2004). *The Oedipus plays of Sophocles*. Trans. P. Roche. New York: Plume.

4. Allen, S. A. (2011). *The peach keeper*. New York: Bantam.

5. Coelho, P. (1988). *The alchemist*. New York: HarperTorch.

6. Quoted in Eisen, A. (1992). *Believing in ourselves: The wisdom of women*. Aukland, New Zealand: Ariel Books.

7. Heywood, J. (1562). *The proverbs and epigrams of John Heywood*. Cambridge: Spenser Society.

8. Burton, R. (1638). *The anatomy of melancholy*. Oxford: Oxford University Press.

9. Pipher, M. (1994). *Reviving Ophelia: Saving the selves of adolescent girls*. New York: Random House.

10. O'Mara, P. (2000). *Natural family living: The Mothering Magazine guide to parenting*. New York: Atria Books.

11. Ray, A. (2018). *Mantra design fundamentals*. Soquel, CA: Inner Light Publishers.

12. Brown, D. (2006). *The Da Vinci code*. New York: Anchor.

## Part IV—Introduction

1. Gilbert, E. (2006). *Eat, pray, love*. New York: Riverhead Books.

## Chapter Seven

1. Guest, J. (1982). *Ordinary people.* New York: Penguin Books.

2. Maraboli, S. (2009). *Life, the truth, and being free.* Port Washington, NY: Better Today Publishing.

3. Martin, T. (1999). *Under the circumstances: Ten sketches about the Christian life.* Kansas City, MO: Lillenas Publishing.

4. Sanders, B. (2014). *Martial arts wisdom: Quotes, maxims, and stories for martial artists and warriors.* Loveland, CO: Kaizen Quest.

5. Ellis, A. (2017, October 12). (@albertellis). "Strong feelings are fine; it's the overreactions that mess us up." Twitter. https://twitter.com/albertellis/status/918494983597957120.

6. Marcus Aurelius. (2002). *Meditations.* Trans. G. Hays. New York: Modern Library.

7. Carlson, R. (1997). *Don't sweat the small stuff.* New York: Hachette Books.

8. Epictetus. (1925–1928). *The Discourses as reported by Arrian, the Manual, and Fragments.* Trans. W. A. Oldfather. 2 vols. Cambridge, MA: Harvard University Press.

9. O'Mahony, C. (2017). *In quest of love.* St. Petersburg, FL: Starlite Publications.

10. Velandia, C. (2019). *Wake up! How to get out of your mind, stop living on autopilot, and start choosing your best life.* Vancouver, BC: Anvil Press.

11. Fine, A. H., & Sachs, M. L. (1997). *The total sports experience for kids: A parents' guide to success in youth sports.* Lanham, MD: Taylor Trade Publishing.

12. Giovanni, N. (1971). *Black feeling, black talk, black judgement.* New York: Harper Perennial.

13. Stoker, B. (1897). *Dracula.* Edinburgh: Archibald Constable.

14. Maraboli, S. (2013). *Unapologetically you: Reflections on life and the human experience.* Port Washington, NY: A Better Today.

15. Maas, S. J. (2015). *A court of thorns and roses.* New York: Bloomsbury.

16. Frank, A. (1947). *The diary of a young girl.* Paris: Contact Publishing.

17. Bennett, R. T. (2016). *The light in the heart.* New York: Roy Bennett.

18. Hodge, T. F. (2009). *From within I rise.* Bethesda, MD: America Star Books.

19. Albom, M. (2003). *The five people you meet in heaven*. New York: Hyperion.

20. Dark, D. (2018). *Blackout*. Miami, FL: Dannika Dark.

21. Murakami, H. (2000). *Norwegian wood*. London: Vintage Books.

22. Tolle, E. (2006). *A new earth: Awakening to your life's purpose*. New York: Plume.

23. Frost, R. (1916). "The road not taken." In *Mountain Interval*. New York: Henry Holt.

24. Machado, C. M. (2019). *In the dream house*. Minneapolis, MN: Graywolf Press.

## Chapter Eight

1. Miller, A. (1983). *The drama of the gifted child*. New York: Basic Books.

2. Halberstam, J. (1993). *Everyday ethics*. New York: Viking.

3. Lewis, C. S. (1942). *The screwtape letters*. London: Geoffrey Bles.

4. Angelou, M. (1969). *I know why the caged bird sings*. New York: Random House.

5. Krippner, S. (1967). "The ten commandments that block creativity." *Gifted Child Quarterly*, *11*(3), 144–56.

6. Garcia, K. (2009). *Beautiful creatures*. New York: Little, Brown.

7. Nkosazana, A. I. (2014). *Sweet destiny*. Roanoke, VA: Bernadette Watkins.

8. Panwar, N. (2014). *If money grew on trees, girls would date monkeys*. N.p.: CreateSpace Independent Publishing Platform.

9. Taleb, N. N. (2012). *Antifragile: Thing that gain from disorder*. New York: Random House.

10. Anderson, L. (1989). *Dear dad: Letters from an adult child*. New York: Penguin Books.

11. Maxwell, J. C. (2005). *Developing the leader within you*. N.p.: Thomas Nelson.

12. Caletti, D. (2007). *The nature of jade*. New York: Simon Pulse.

13. Hodge, T. F. (2009). *From within I rise: Spiritual triumph over death and conscious encounters with "the divine presence."* Bethesda, MD: America Star Books.

14. Socrates, Plato, Aristotle (1967). *Wit and wisdom of Socrates, Plato, Aristotle: Being a treasury of thousands of glorious inspiring and imperishable thoughts, vies and observations of the three great Greek philosophers.* Calcutta: Rare Book Society of India.

15. Roosevelt, T. (1902). *The strenuous life: Essays and addresses.* N.p.: Century.

16. Jemisin, N. K. (2016). *The obelisk gate.* London: Orbit.

17. Taylor, M. (2018). *Unmedicated: The four pillars of natural wellness.* New York: Atria Books.

18. Confucius. (1915). *The ethics of Confucius.* Ed. M. M. Dawson. New York: G. P. Putnam's Sons.

19. Shriver, L. (1989). *Checker and the derailleurs.* New York: Penguin Books.

20. Chouinard, Y. (2005). *Let my people go surfing: The education of a reluctant businessman.* New York: Penguin Books.

21. Redhead, S. (2016). *Life is simply a game.* Benicia, CA: Life Coaching Systems.

22. Capote, T. (1987). "Self-portrait." In T. Capote & M. T. Inge (Ed.). *Truman Capote: Conversations.* Jackson: University of Mississippi Press.

## Part V—Introduction

1. Voltaire. (1759). *Candide, ou l'Optimisme.* Paris, France: Cramer, Rey, Nourse, Lambert, & Others.

2. Confucius. (n.d.). Goodreads.com. www.goodreads.com/quotes/7308426-he-who-conquers-himself-is-the-mightiest-warrior.

3. Austen, J. (1814). *Mansfield park.* London: Thomas Edgerton.

4. Johnson, M. B. (2020). *The book of maxims, poems and anecdotes.* Morrisville, NC: Lulu.

5. Ravikant, K. (2013). *Live your truth.* Lisbon, Portugal: Founderzen.

## Chapter Nine

1. Lepins, E. (2012). *Back to single.* Mustang, OK: Tate Publishing.

2. McNutt, R. (2017). *Bittersweet symphony.* N.p.: CreateSpace Independent Publishing Platform.

3. Dumas, A. (1845). *Twenty years after.* New York: Little, Brown.

4. Martin, C. B. (2019). *Encouragement: How to be and find the best.* San Diego: Quiet Thunder Publishing.

5. Cleave, C. (2016). *Everyone brave is forgiven.* New York: Simon & Schuster.

6. Gaskell, E. (1854). *North and South.* London: Chapman & Hall.

7. Ahern, C. (2008). *The gift.* New York: HarperCollins.

8. Kidd, K. (2013). *I can't feel my face.* Scotts Valley, CA: CreateSpace Independent Publishing Platform.

9. Goodrich, R. E. (2017). *Slaying dragons.* Los Gatos, CA: Smashwords.

10. Zusak, M. (2006). *The book thief.* New York: Alfred A. Knopf.

11. Bardugo, L. (2016). *Crooked kingdom.* London: Orion Children's Books.

12. Farmer, P. J. (1979). *To your scattered bodies go.* Glasgow: Panther Books.

## Chapter Ten

1. Michel, K. L. (2013). *Moving through parallel worlds to achieve your dreams.* N.p.: Michel Leadership.

2. Cvetanova, L. (2013). *The new land.* Skopje, Macedonia: Machform.

3. Malhotra, M. (2013). *How to build self-esteem and be confident: Overcome fears, break habits, be successful and happy.* New York: For Betterment Publications.

4. Whitfield, S. E., & Roddenberry, G. (1968). *The making of Star Trek.* New York: Ballantine Books.

5. Rutkoski, M. (2014). *The winner's curse.* New York: Farrar Straus Giroux.

6. Urbano, A. M. R. (2015). *The billion-dollar marriage contract.* Mandaluyong, Philippines: Summit Books.

7. Lorimer, G. H. (1902). *Letter from a self-made merchant to his son.* Boston: Small, Maynard.

8. Owens, J. (1978). *Jesse: The man who outran Hitler.* Newberry, FL: Logos International.

9. Field, J. (2013). "Commitment means staying loyal." https://master jonathanfield.com/2013/09/04/commitment-means-staying-loyal/.

10. Street, M. (2017). *Well, this is growing up*. Glen Waverley, Victoria: Sid Harta Publishers.

11. Koyenikan, I. (2016). *Wealth for all: Living a life of success at the edge of your ability*. Fuquay-Varina, NC: Grandeur Touch.

12. Sparks, N. (2002). *A bend in the road*. New York: Grand Central Publishing.

13. Davis, R. A. (n.d.). Goodreads. www.goodreads.com/quotes/333889 -patience-is-not-passive-waiting-patience-is-active-acceptance-of. Accessed June 4, 2020.

14. Pike, C. (1994). *Black blood*. New York: Simon Pulse.

15. Confucius. (1938). *The analects of Confucius*. New York: Random House.

## Chapter Eleven

1. Warhol, A. (1977). *The philosophy of Andy Warhol (from A to B and back again)*. New York: Mariner Books.

2. Tolkien, J. R. R. (1937). *The hobbit, or there and back again*. United Kingdom: George Allen & Unwin.

3. Nagpal, G. (2013). *Talent economics: The fine line between winning and losing the global war for talent*. London: Kogan Page.

4. Ziglar, Z. (1974). *See you at the top*. Gretna, LA: Pelican Publishing.

5. Sophocles. (2004). *The Oedipus plays of Sophocles: Oedipus the king, Oedipus at Colonos, Antigone*. New York: Plume.

6. Gizzard, Lewis. (n.d.). Quotes.net. www.quotes.net/quote/13516. Retrieved June 4, 2020.

7. Berra, Y. (1998). *The Yogi book: I really didn't say anything I said*. New York: Workman Publishing.

8. Covey, S. R. (1989). *The 7 habits of highly effective people: Powerful lessons in personal change*. New York: Free Press.

9. Holiday, R. (2016). *Ego is the enemy*. London: Profile Books.

10. Vidrine, K. (2017). *Wake up the winner in you: Your time is now*. New York: Haon's House Publisher.

## Afterword

1. Carnegie, D. (1936). How to win friends and influence people. New York: Simon & Schuster.

2. Marcus Aurelius. (2006). *Meditations.* Trans. M. Hammond. London: Penguin Books.

3. Frankl, V. (1946). *Man's search for meaning.* Braunschweig, Germany: Verlag für Jugend und Volk.

4. Hoffer, E. (n.d.). Goodreads.com. www.goodreads.com/quotes/644309-the-search-for-happiness-is-one-of-the-chief-sources. Accessed June 6, 2020.

5. Siegel, B. (1998). *Prescriptions for living: Lessons for a joyful, loving life.* New York: HarperCollins.

6. Kingwell, M. (2000). *In pursuit of happiness: Better living from Plato to Prozac.* New York: Crown Publishers.

7. Dostoevsky, F. (1848). *White nights* (1st Ed.). New York: Macmillan.

8. Ayivor, I. (2014). *Dream big! See your bigger picture.* N.p: CreateSpace Independent Publishing Platform.

9. Whitman, W. (1891). *Leaves of grass.* London: Penguin Classics.

# REFERENCES

## Introduction

Newton, I. (1687). *Philosophiae naturalis principia mathematica.* London: Streater.

## Part II

Masten, A. S., & Coatsworth, J. D. (1998). "The development of competence in favorable and unfavorable environments: Lessons from research on successful children." *American Psychologist 53*(2), 205–20. doi: 10.1037/0003-066X.53.2.205.

## Chapter 4

Ablard, K. E., & Parker, W. D. (1997). "Parents' achievement goals and perfectionism in their academically talented children." *Journal of Youth and Adolescence 26*(6), 651–67.

Assor, A., & Tal, K. (2012). "When parents' affection depends on child's achievement: Parental conditional positive regard, self-aggrandizement, shame and coping in adolescents." *Journal of Adolescence 35*(2), 249–60.

Baiul, O. (1997). *Oksana: My own story.* New York: Random House.

Chamorro-Premuzic, T. (2013). *Confidence: Overcoming low self-esteem, insecurity, and self-doubt.* N.p.: Avery.

Ciciolla, L., Curlee, A. S., Karageorge, J., & Luthar, S. S. (2017). "When mothers and fathers are seen as disproportionately valuing achievements: Implications for adjustment among upper middle-class youth." *Journal of Youth and Adolescence 46*(5), 1057–75.

Frost, R., Marten, P., Lahart, C., & Ronsenblate, R. (1990). "The dimensions of perfectionism." *Cognitive Therapy and Research 14*(5), 449–68.

Harwood, C. G., Keegan, R. J., Smith, J. M. J., & Raine, A. S. (2015). "A systematic review of the intrapersonal correlates of motivational climate perceptions in sport and physical activity." *Psychology of Sport and Exercise 18*, 9–25.

Kamins, M. L., & Dweck, C. S. (1999). "Person versus process praise and criticism: Implications for continent self-worth and coping." *Developmental Psychology 35*(3), 833–47.

Love, D., III. (1997). *Every shot I take.* New York: Simon & Schuster.

Pearson, C. A., & Gleaves, D. H. (2006). "The multiple dimensions of perfectionism and their relation with eating disorders." *Personality and Individual Differences 41*(2), 225–35.

Shafran, R., & Mansell, W. (2001). "Perfectionism and psychopathology: A review of research and treatment." *Clinical Psychology Review 21*(6), 879–906.

## Chapter 5

Edelman, M. W. (1992). *The measure of our success.* Boston: Beacon Press.

## Chapter 6

Conroy, D. E. (2012). "Fear of failure: An exemplar for social development research in sport." *Quest 53*(2), 165–83.

Elliot, A. J., & Thrash, T. M. (2004). "The intergenerational transmission of fear of failure." *Personality and Social Psychology Bulletin 30*(8), 957–71.

Woodhouse, L. D. (1992). "Women with jagged edges: Voices from a cultural of substance abuse." *Qualitative Health Research 2*(3), 262–81.

## Chapter 8

Goleman, D. (1995). *Emotional intelligence*. New York: Bantam Books.
Tice, D. M., & Baumeister, R. F. (1993). "Controlling anger: Self-induced emotion change." In D. M. Wegner & J. W. Pennebaker (Eds.), Century psychology series. *Handbook of mental control* (p. 393–409). Englewood Cliffs, NJ: Prentice-Hall.

## Part V

Newton, I. (1687). *Philosophiae naturalis principia mathematica*. London: Streater.
Buckingham, M., & Clifton, D. O. (2005). *Now, discover your strengths: How to develop your talents and those of the people you manage*. New York: Simon & Schuster.

## Chapter 10

Spielberg, S. (Director). (1989). *Indiana Jones and the last crusade*. Hollywood, CA: Lucasfilm.

## Chapter 11

Lally, P., van Jaarsveld, C. H. M., Potts, H. W. W., & Wardle, J. (2009). "How are habits formed: Modelling habit formation in the real world." *European Journal of Social Psychology 40*(6), 998–1009.

## Afterword

Cheng, H., & Furhman, A. (2002). "Personality, peer relations, and self-confidence as predictors of happiness and loneliness." *Journal of Adolescence 25*(3), 327–39.
Clark, A. E., Flèche, S., Layard, R., Powdthavee, N., & Ward, G. (2018). *The origins of happiness: The science of well-being over the life course*. Princeton, NJ: Princeton University Press.

# REFERENCES

D'Ambrosio, C., Jäntti, M., & Lepinteur, A. (2020). "Money and happiness: Income, wealth and subjective well-being." *Social Indicators Research* *148*(1), 47–66.

Kasser, T. (2000). "Two versions of the American dream: Which goals and values make for a high quality of life?" In E. Diener & D. R. Rahtz (Eds.), Social Indicators Research series, vol 4. *Advances in Quality of Life Theory and Research.* Dordrecht: Springer.

Lazarus, R., & Lazarus, B. (1994). *Passion and reason: Making sense of our emotions.* Oxford: Oxford University Press.

Peterson, C., Park, N., & Seligman, M. E. P. (2005). "Orientations to happiness and life satisfaction: The full life versus the empty life." *Journal of Happiness Studies* *6*(1), 25–41.

Pink, D. (2011). *Drive: The surprising truth about what motivates us.* New York: Riverhead Books.

Ryan, R. M., & Deci, E. L. (2000). "Self-determination theory and the facilitation of intrinsic motivation, social development, and well-being." *American Psychologist* *55*(1), 68–78.

Thaler, R. H., & Sunstein, C. R. (2008). *Nudge: Improving decisions about health, wealth, and happiness.* New Haven, CT: Yale University Press.

# INDEX

# ABOUT THE AUTHOR

**Jim Taylor**, PhD, is internationally recognized for his work in the psychology of personal growth. He has been a consultant to numerous businesses, schools, and sports organizations and is a highly sought-after speaker who has given workshops through North and South America, Europe, the Middle East, and Asia.

He is a former associate professor in the School of Psychology at Nova University in Fort Lauderdale, a former clinical associate professor at the University of Denver, and a current adjunct faculty at the University of San Francisco.

Dr. Taylor is the author of seventeen books and the lead editor of four textbooks. His books have been translated into ten languages.

Dr. Taylor has blogged for psychologytoday.com, huffingtonpost. com, saturdayeveningpost.com, sfgate.com, seattlepi.com, and the Hearst Interactive Media group, as well as on his own website. His posts are picked up by dozens of websites worldwide and have been read by millions.

Dr. Taylor has appeared on NBC's *Today Show*, ABC's *World News This Weekend*, Fox News Channel, and major television network affiliates in the United States and Canada. He has been interviewed for articles that have appeared in *Time*, the *Los Angeles Times*, the *New York Daily News*, the *London Telegraph*, the *Chicago Tribune*, the

*Atlanta Journal-Constitution*, *Outside*, *Men's Health*, and many other newspapers, magazines, and websites.

A former internationally ranked alpine ski racer, Dr. Taylor is a certified tennis teaching professional, a second-degree black belt and certified instructor in karate, a marathon runner, and an Ironman triathlete.

Dr. Taylor lives north of San Francisco with his wife and two daughters.

To learn more, visit www.drjimtaylor.com.